Archival Theory and Practice in the United States:
A Historical Analysis

ARCHIVAL THEORY AND PRACTICE IN THE UNITED STATES:

A Historical Analysis

Richard C. Berner

UNIVERSITY OF WASHINGTON PRESS
SEATTLE AND LONDON

Library of Congress Cataloging in Publication Data

Berner, Richard C.
  Archival theory and practice in the United States.

  Bibliography: p.
  Includes index.
  1. Archives—United States—Management—History.
I. Title.
CD3021.B47   1983   025.3'414   82-48869
ISBN 0-295-95992-4

This book was published with the assistance of a grant from
the National Endowment for the Humanities.

Dedicated to the memory
of
Theodore R. Schellenberg
friend and teacher

Contents

Appendixes (continued)

Preface

Anyone who undertakes a work of synthesis is clearly in debt to all who have preceded. Obligations are due particularly to those who have themselves brought together segments of the history that this author has in turn attempted to convert into a more general contemporary statement.

The development of theory and practices is intertwined with the growth of archival institutions and the objectives of archival and manuscripts programs. Library and history organizations and some state archives had been the principal agencies concerned with archival development before 1936. In that year the Society of American Archivists was established. It began publishing the *American Archivist* in 1938. Since then an archival profession has interacted intermittently with the library and history fields. Intermittent interaction with records management practitioners has also occurred once records managers decided to spring loose from the archival profession and claim an independent identity. The lack of an effective institutional medium for continuous interaction of archivists with these other professions—each of which is vital to the operational effectiveness of archives—has hampered the intellectual development of the archival profession. Archival institutions similarly are less advanced than they might be in the absence of more effective relations with these other professions. One of the objectives of this book is to form a perspective that provides a broader approach to archival problems—one that is based on a shared concern about common problems and that will result in reciprocal benefits for all professions and the different publics that each serves.

Bibliographically, the touchstones for the present work are the writings of Theodore R. Schellenberg, Lucile M. Kane, Margaret Cross Norton, Lester J. Cappon, Waldo G. Leland, O. Lawrence Burnette, Ernst Posner, Frank G. Burke, Frank B. Evans, Oliver W. Holmes, and Philip C. Brooks. Two recent articles (1980) by Richard H. Lytle on the provenance method and content indexing method have crystallized my thinking and influenced the expression of certain concepts. Kenneth W. Duckett's *Modern Manuscripts* has also played a decisive role in my portrayal of the historical manuscripts tradition—although his book is more than that.

Special gratitude is owed to my earliest mentor, Robert E. Burke, professor of history at the University of Washington and former curator of manuscripts at the Bancroft Library. Out of friendship and a concern for the quality of the final product he volunteered to read the manuscript—as I hoped he would. That it has benefited immensely from his editorial skills and erudition is an understatement.

My long-standing admiration for Lucile M. Kane's many contributions to the literature—particularly her *Guide* and her splendid essay on the development of manuscript collecting—led me to ask her to read the manuscript. Her incisive critique improved it substantially. Her warm praise of the first draft was crucial to my own self-confidence in producing a monograph that we both know is apt to be controversial. But then, controversy in the field has been acutely needed for its development and internal health.

Richard H. Lytle, archivist of the Smithsonian Institution, who has a special background in current developments in the field and who understands my writings as they pertain to these developments, contributed significantly and earliest to improvement of the manuscript.

Lydia Lucas, head of Technical Services in the Division of Archives and Manuscripts of the Minnesota Historical Society, offered a fourth beneficial perspective, enhanced by her understanding of my earlier writings. She found many flaws of organization and awkwardness of style that others had not identified. Her suggestions and rephrasings were fully incorporated.

The chapter on automated systems was submitted by me to several readers, one for each system that was discussed. These are Frank G. Burke of the National Historical Publications and Records Commission (NHPRC), John Knowlton of the Manuscripts Division of the Library of Congress, William H. Maher of the University of Illinois, Charles H. Palm of the Hoover Institution, Trudy H. Peterson and Charles M. Dollar of the National Archives and Records Service, Nancy Sahli of the NHPRC, and Charles H. Lesser of the South Carolina State Archives. My colleague Edmond Mignon of the University of Washington School of Librarianship painstakingly read the entire chapter, and I have incorporated substantially all his recommendations. Frank Burke also subjected the entire chapter draft to a sharp critique, correcting several factual and judgmental errors. Thomas Hickerson of Cornell University kindly lent me a copy of parts of his draft manual on archival automation. John Burns, editor of SUN (SPINDEX Users Network), provided me with helpful unpublished material on SPINDEX.

Few archivists and manuscript librarians have dealt seriously with the *Anglo-American Cataloging Rules*, so I was particularly gratified for a stimulating criticism by Terry Eastwood, then of the Provincial Archives of British Columbia, now of the University of British Columbia School of Librarianship. Since 1980 (after my original manuscript was written), Steven Hensen of the Library of Congress's Manuscripts Division has headed a task force to revise chapter 4 of AACR2. Their draft recommendations are referred to in a footnote to chapter 8, but they are consistent with the thrust of my historical critique.

As a test of its readability and understandability to an uninitiated audience the manuscript was subjected to the keen editorial eye of a physiologist, Dr. Thelma K. Kennedy (my spouse), who contributed significantly to its improvement, and to my veteran friend and fellow librarian, Gerald J. Oppenheimer, director of the Health Sciences Library. Although it did not pass with flying colors, it did pass, and that was solace enough.

The readers mentioned above will recognize their own contributions to the final product, and while I assume responsibility for it, each of them will appreciate the differences between the original draft and the book, as well as their share in its improvement.

My indebtedness to many is acknowledged in the manuscript itself, but special thanks are due Harriet Ostroff, director of the National Union Catalog of Manuscript Collections (NUCMC), for providing copies of vital files essential for a study of the origins of the NUCMC rules. Philip P. Mason also contributed crucial information from his memory with respect to the cooperation of the Society of American Archivists in the possible publication of an archival manual in 1969–70.

During my sabbatical, Karyl Winn assumed responsibility for the University Archives and Manuscripts Division. It was her willingness to do so and her capacity for extra work that enabled me to devote undivided attention to the research and writing—an opportunity that I had looked forward to for many years. What made this book a reality, of course, was the willingness of the Director of Libraries, and of the university administration, to permit me one year of leave to do it. Without the leave the project would never have been completed. Also the book is a direct result of my teaching an archival management course since 1969 in the School of Librarianship.

The Interlibrary Loan Service staff of the University of Washington Libraries expedited the research by their efficient service.

The typing of the original manuscript was begun and largely completed by Francis Timlin until his doctoral dissertation diverted him. Camille Blanchette typed the second and final drafts. Both exercised considerable skill and judgment in translating my awkward handwriting into something more readable.

A glossary is included. The terms selected are from "A Basic Glossary for Archivists, Manuscript Curators, and Records Managers," compiled by Frank B. Evans, Donald F. Harrison, and Edwin A. Thompson, and edited by William L. Rofes (*American Archivist* 37 [July 1974]: 415–33). Some terms have been commented on, elaborated, or added by me and are so indicated by being placed in square brackets.

Appendixes 1–22 consist of examples. Hierarchical controls are illustrated in Appendixes 3–19, which should be consulted to clarify the hierarchical concept and any of the record levels in the hierarchy that are discussed. Appendixes 20 and 21 are devoted specifically to the illustrations of SPINDEX II and III. Appendix 22 illustrates the effectiveness of the provenance method as an inferential system.

Records management is vital to a successful institutional archival program, but because of the inappropriateness of including a section on it in the text, I have provided a summary of basic archival–records management relations in Appendix 23 for those who are not familiar with these relations or who might not be aware that records management was invented by the National Archives in the late 1930s.

Richard C. Berner

Abbreviations

AA	*American Archivist*
AHA	American Historical Association
ALA	American Library Association
AASLH	American Association for State and Local History
CRL	*College and Research Libraries*
HRS	Historical Records Survey of the Works Progress Administration, later the Work Projects Administration
LC	Library of Congress
LQ	*Library Quarterly*
LRTS	*Library Resources and Technical Services*
LT	*Library Trends*
NARS	National Archives and Records Service
NUCMC	National Union Catalog of Manuscript Collections
NHPC	National Historical Publications Commission (to 1975)
NHPRC	National Historical Publications and Records Commission (after 1975)
SAA	Society of American Archivists
WPA	Work Projects Administration

Archival Theory and Practice in the
United States:
A Historical Analysis

1

Overview

It seems timely for a historical analysis of archival theory and practice. The archival profession, as well as that of librarians, currently faces problems having extensive historical roots. If understood in historical context these problems could be dealt with more effectively than is indicated by contemporary developments. Recent writings and guidelines continue to lead in two directions, each stemming from a different tradition—the historical manuscripts tradition and the public archives tradition. Automation complicates decision-making, and is hurrying the pace, perhaps too rapidly. Since it is access to manual information systems that is to be automated, there ought to be general agreement about how to construct those manual systems; but there is not, and that is the main subject of the book. It is essentially a historical analysis, not a history of the field.

The historical manuscripts tradition, in relation to both collecting and intellectual control, was dominant from the eighteenth century until about 1960. In the twentieth century before 1960 practices were added from the public archives field from time to time. By 1960 the nature of collecting itself had changed from a concentration on papers of remote vintage to an emphasis on those of recent origin. The latter had many characteristics of public archives, because of their comparable extent, structure, and depth of documentation. As a result of this change in collecting emphasis, many major manuscript repositories borrowed practices and concepts from the public archives tradition, which originated institutionally in 1901 when the first state archives was established in Alabama. An amalgam of practices accumulated without a clear theoretical basis until Theodore R. Schellenberg began this effort in the late 1950s.

The historical manuscripts tradition is rooted in librarianship. Because manuscripts generally were brought under some form of library administration, it is understandable that library techniques would be applied to them. Indeed, the only theories and practices for bibliographical control that existed in the nineteenth century were those of librarianship. These practices were compatible with the kind of source materials that were being collected. Because of their rarity (unique handwritten items) and their separation from related papers, the collected materials were handled as discrete items. Each, in this historical setting, seemed to merit separate treatment. If they did not get it immediately, they would someday, sometime, it was hoped. Both public records and papers and records of private origin were collected, but they were only the fragmentary accidental documentary remains of what had originally been integral papers and records whose items were clearly related to one another. Divorced from their original file relationships, they represented artificial collections to which some conceptual unity was given by their collector. Preconceived classification schemes were employed to provide this kind of unity. The various practices that resulted represent the historical manuscripts tradition.

Periodically the tradition has been codified, if that term may be loosely construed in this context. Codification was first done in 1904 by Worthington C. Ford of the Library of Congress's Manuscripts Division for Charles A. Cutter's *Rules for a Dictionary Catalog*. The most recent codification is in the 1978 edition of the *Anglo-American Cataloguing Rules* (American Library Association).

The public archives tradition was affected by European archival developments in the nineteenth century. A body of European theory and practices for the administration of public archives was steadily drawn upon in the United States by state archivists and various other exponents of the European archival mode in the early twentieth century. Formation of the National Archives of the United States in 1934 gave impetus to the spread of these practices and the theory behind them. A review of this European legacy and of the focus given it by the National Archives will shed light on what follows.

With the French Revolution, a modern philosophy of archives began to take shape.[1] The French people were allowed freer access to public documents so that their legal rights, among others, could be officially determined. But it was not until 1839–41 that the modern system of arrangement by *fonds* was established in the Archives Nationale. Before that, arrangement was by subject matter as devised by two librarians, without regard to the record-creating source.* Records thus classified and arranged by them were subsequently rearranged after 1841 by bringing them together under their originating agency, the *fond* (see the Glossary). Bringing consistency to practice, the principle of *respect des fonds* was developed between 1839 and 1841, and was issued as a policy document of the Minister of Interior in 1841. Henceforth in the Archives Nationales and in many *départements* this principle would be followed. Records were to be kept together in the archives under the agency that

---

* An alternate term is "generating source." In the fullest sense though, original record items are created and associated items are accumulated, a twofold process. This meaning should be attached throughout whenever "creation" or "generation" is used.

originated them, and no longer scattered among preconceived subject classes. But within each such *fond* they were to be arranged according to their subject matter, and either chronologically, geographically, or alphabetically arranged within each subject class. This subject rearrangement within *fonds* was intended to serve scholarly research.

In the Prussian State Archives, beginning in the 1870s, the principle of *respect des fonds* was accepted as basic. But the Prussian State Archives interposed a registry office between the originating agency and the archives. The registry office arranged and serviced the records for the agency. This arrangement was retained when the records were transferred to archival custody. Unlike the French system, wherein the records were classified by subject within the records of a given agency, the Prussian system observed the original order imposed by the registry office, the *Registraturprinzip*. While the French rearranged the records to serve research needs, in Prussia the records were considered administrative records primarily, and reflected the agency's relative position in the overall government structure as well as its documentary connections with other agencies in the government.

The Prussian system was adopted by the Netherlands, where the first modern archival manual was produced, elucidating these principles. This manual on arrangement and description was first issued in 1898 as *Handleiding voor het ordenen en beschrijven van archieven*, by S. Muller, J. A. Feith, and R. Fruin. It was translated into several languages and finally into English in 1940, by Arthur H. Leavitt, as *Manual for the Arrangement and Description of Archives*.

In England, Hilary Jenkinson of the Public Records Office wrote a *Manual of Archive Administration* (1922, revised in 1937) in which the principles outlined above were also accepted, but with some additions.

Early archival activists in the United States, particularly Waldo G. Leland,* were greatly influenced by these European principles and practices and sought to propagate them through the Conference of Archivists of the American Historical Association from 1909 on. When the newly established National Archives began collecting federal records in the late 1930s, its staff quickly learned that no systematic records organization existed. Disorder was the rule. To deal with this situation, the staff, instead of using a registry system, invented records management to control the life cycle of records in the offices of origin. (See Appendix 23 on archival–records management relations.) Their

---

*Leland (1879–1966) trained as a historian at Harvard University. In 1903 he moved to Washington, D.C., where he joined the staff of the historical research department of the Carnegie Institution, under J. Franklin Jameson, and produced two major guides to American historical sources. He served as secretary of the American Historical Association, and while in this post joined Jameson in leading the movement to establish a federal archives. (Jameson was editor of the *American Historical Review*, and later became head of the Manuscripts Division of the Library of Congress.) Leland was a founder of the SAA and its second president. See the *American Archivist* 30 (January 1967): 125–28, for an obituary by Lester J. Cappon.

experience had shown that it is the degree to which archivists control records management that largely determines the quality of an institutional archive. In the mid-1940s the National Archives added the management technique of scheduling all record series that could be identified. The schedules established minimum retention periods and attempted to identify those series of potential archival value at their inception. The principle of provenance was accepted as basic to all these records management procedures. In addition, the record series concept, which is linked with the original order of records, was considered to be the chief means of dealing with the order of agency records. If at all possible, the agency's own filing order would be honored, assuming that if the arrangement was useful to the agency it would be useful to those who inherited the records in the archives. In the United States, practitioners tended to confuse the terms "provenance" and "original order." In applying the principle of provenance, papers or records that were generated by a person or organization are kept together under the name of the agency that created them, instead of being arranged according to a preconceived classification system, as in librarianship (see the Glossary). Papers and records are either received in some logical order or one is imposed on them by their processor in the archives. Either they were originally filed according to some common attribute or a filing system is devised by the repository's staff if no filing scheme is apparent. Series represent aggregates of related items, and provide a means of dealing effectively with items collectively instead of individually as is done in librarianship. Provenance, and the original order of record items that form series, relate to quite different aspects of what has become known as the "hierarchy of record levels." There are two broad categories within this hierarchy. Both provenance and *fond* relate to record generation, while original order relates to the filing system employed by the agency. The Archives Nationale makes this distinction clear with respect to original order when its staff rearranges files into subject categories within the *fond*, doing violence to the original file order but not to the *fond*. In chapter 4 this differentiation is made clear. The Glossary should also be consulted.

ARRANGEMENT AND DESCRIPTION OF ARCHIVES

This historical analysis of archival theory and practice in the United States is limited to arrangement* and description. Appraisal for documentary value is the only other phase of archival work that is unique to the field and susceptible to integration with arrangement and description as part of a general body of archival theory. Reasons for exclusion will be explained later in this overview.

---

*"Arrangement" is the archival substitute for "classification," which in library usage usually means grouping by subject. Before the twentieth century, public records and private papers typically were "classified," not "arranged" as by agency of origin—by provenance. See Frank B. Evans, "Modern Methods of Arrangement of Archives in the United States," *American Archivist* 29 (April 1966): 241–63, for this archival alteration of "classification."

The term "archival" is used generically to encompass manuscripts and manuscript collections as well as public and corporate records. Libraries and historical societies are the typical repositories for manuscript collections. Although public records are sometimes administered with manuscript collections, they are usually associated with the administrative governmental units in which they originated, if they have not been transferred to archival custody. Corporate records, too, are often administered by the organizations they document.

The focus of this book, as in most books and articles on archival theory, is arrangement and description, in inseparable combination. All else in the archival world, except appraisal, is a matter of philosophy and attitude, or is part of a body of theory from another field. Reference service, for example, is a matter of how an institution makes its sources available, or how a profession views its relations to the world it serves. Administrative practices in archival repositories, on the other hand, are part of the larger problem of administration in all sectors of human organization. Building construction, materials conservation, photoduplication, literary property, issues of privacy and freedom of information, and other special problem areas that impinge on the work of archivists and manuscript librarians lie outside the range of archival theory. They are suitable, however, for inclusion in an archival management manual along with treatment of other policies and procedures.

Arrangement and description, by contrast, are uniquely archival. They represent a body of practices that are coherent and are derived from a unique perspective in regard to material that is the subject of no other profession's attention. These practices are susceptible to an analysis that will reveal their underlying principles—among them, some principles of librarianship. The field of librarianship has been intertwined with that of archives, shaping the latter's early development. Both, being heavily practical in emphasis, have tended to be wary of theory, as though practices would only be confounded by interaction with theory.

Because the profession's approach has been preeminently practical, eclecticism has been rampant. There has been too little reflection on the broader basis of individual practices and techniques that have evolved in myriad institutional settings and subsequently are borrowed by others. Quasi principles have originated from commonsensical methods that have accumulated over time. As such, they have been time honored and resistant to objective examination. For example, many different kinds of finding aids—catalogs, registers, inventories, shelf lists, and calendars—are typically described side by side without ever becoming the object of analysis. Careful scrutiny would have revealed intrinsic relations between them, as well as the implications of these relations. Implications, in turn, would have indicated what these relations might have become if they had been more fully rationalized.

An example of the time lag in general acceptance of concepts that are now considered basic is the principle of provenance. It had been the object of nodding acquaintance among manuscript librarians and public records archivists before 1950, yet papers and records continued to be arranged according to some preconceived method that presumed to know how the materials were to be used. It was assumed that historians were the main users and that they were best served by chronological and subject arrangements. Historians themselves thought so. The descriptive practice of calendaring* responded to this felt need among historians and was a goal in most manuscript repositories before 1940. Like the principle of provenance, the record series concept as developed in the public archives field was available for application as early as 1940, when it was identified in some state archives, the National Archives, and the Historical Records Survey (HRS) as the "main catalogable unit." But not until after the mid-1950s did it become the generally accepted method for describing modern manuscripts. Instead, the catalogable unit continued to be the item and clusters of "important" items. In some major repositories of modern manuscripts the latter practice still persists, and it was the recommended mode in a major monograph as recently as 1975.[2]

Reinforcing the exclusively practical bent and the eclectic penchant in arrangement and description is the separation of description from arrangement. For example, the *Anglo-American Cataloging Rules* (AACR), issued in 1967 (AACR1) and 1978 (AACR2), reflect the view that intellectual control of manuscripts is only a descriptive process. These rules of librarianship stand in sharp contrast to Ford's 1904 contribution to Cutter's *Rules*, wherein Ford did not discuss cataloging except in relation to arrangement. The new rules also reflect what can happen in large administrative structures such as the Library of Congress, where increased specialization led to the transfer of responsibility for cataloging policy from its Manuscripts Division in the Reference Department to the Descriptive Cataloging Division in the Processing Department.† This is significant in view of the origin of the AACR. Represented here is a technocratic view of an organic problem, in which a mere technique—cataloging—absorbed exclusive attention. All other finding aids and the matter of arrangement itself lay outside the cataloger's perception.

Reference was made above to archival appraisal as lending itself to theoretical analysis within its archival setting for the same reasons that apply to arrangement and description. While this seems true, appraisal is not covered here, in what purports to be a general analysis of archival theory. The main reason for this omission is the primitive nature of its development. We have

---

*Calendaring is the practice of synthesizing the contents of individual items that have been arranged chronologically (see the Glossary). Morris L. Radoff defended this practice in "A Guide to Practical Calendaring," *American Archivist* 11 (April 1948): 123–40, (July 1948): 203–22.

†The Library of Congress's Manuscripts Division finds the AACR2 unacceptable and is now working on modification to serve as a standard for its cataloging. In the 1970s the Manuscripts Division was not consulted by the Cataloging Division when the latter published *Manuscripts: A MARC Format* (1973). The Manuscripts Division found this format unacceptable because of its item orientation, and later modified it for collective description. (Thomas Hickerson provided me with this information in a draft copy of a manual on archival automation.)

not yet moved significantly beyond the taxonomic stage in dealing with appraisal.* At present, common sense and good judgment of a very subjective, private nature prevail. A body of appraisal theory is perhaps the most pressing need in the archival field today.[3] If we delay much longer we will all be smothered by useless paper and all forms of machine-readable records, unable to distinguish those worth saving from all the rest. While appraisal theory is still in early gestation, arrangement and description have emerged from a protracted pregnancy, and have a coherence now that is lacking in appraisal practices. The latter will have to be the subject of deliberate collaboration, tightly rationalized within as brief a time span as possible. The collaboration must be interdisciplinary, the work of many professions, not only that of archivists and manuscript librarians.

ASCENDANCY OF THE ARCHIVAL MODE

The fateful separation of the historical manuscripts field from the public archives field began in 1910 at the AHA's Conference of Archivists, when the application of library principles was attacked as inapplicable to public archives. The differences that developed meant that the historical manuscripts tradition would remain linked to techniques of librarianship. Public archives, meanwhile, would develop along lines derived from European archival institutions where theory and practice had long been the object of scholarly discourse and refinement.

Not until the late 1950s would a serious attempt be made to rejoin these two traditions. Theodore R. Schellenberg was the leader in this effort.[4] Because modern manuscripts share "organic" or integral records characteristics with public archives, he considered them amenable to essentially the same kind of treatment. It is the record series, in records and papers of common origin, that is the basis of commonality.

The archival mode, at its core, recognizes the existence of a hierarchy of record levels. (See the Glossary; and see also Appendixes 3–19 for illustrations of control at different record levels.) In achieving intellectual control, one is advised to do so progressively, beginning at the record group or "collection" level and following this up successively by establishing controls at the subgroup, series, file unit, and item levels. In the librarianship mode, the item level has received the principal attention, but in isolation from its hierarchical relation to other levels. Item description, in turn, has determined the form and content of collection-level description, while other record levels are ignored. Individual repositories have tried to compensate for the deficiencies of the librarianship mode by cribbing from the archival mode. The end result has typically been a hodgepodge of finding aids having no unity. Even now the problems posed in these amalgamated systems remain unresolved.

---

*Taxonomy is concerned with classification and is one of the first stages of analysis in the descriptive sciences.

By consensus, record levels have become, since the early 1970s, a part of the conventional thinking of both modern archivists and manuscript librarians. With this conception has come recognition that the basic finding aid should be an inventory, and that cumulative indexes to the inventories should provide access to the repository's archival and manuscript collections.* Although automated programs are accelerating the pace of change, just as they are in the library field proper, in the archival field the tempo would have been faster if earlier attention had been given to theory and its role as both a guide to practice and a reflector of changes at the level of the workplace. Coupled with a better sense of our historical drift, this whole movement toward rationalization might have been considerably accelerated.

AUTHOR'S VANTAGE POINT

The manuscript collection and university archives at the University of Washington Libraries have served as a laboratory for the author. The historical manuscripts tradition, as described in this book, was inherited in 1958 and soon modified by use of elements in the public archives tradition before the author assisted Dr. Schellenberg in 1962 in the teaching of an archival management class. One result of that experience was a review of the relations between the elements of the finding aids system, in particular the relation of traditional cataloging† and the card catalog to the repository's inven-

---

*Society of American Archivists, Finding Aids Committee Annual Meeting, October 3, 1978, Nashville, summary of proceedings: The discussion following each of the reports on model finding aids systems and that of the Finding Aids Relationship Task Force indicates that (1) a consensus seems to have developed that "arrangement and description" of modern manuscript accessions and archives of corporate bodies (public and private) are, or should be, essentially the same: (a) intellectual access should be keyed to record levels in a fully conscious or rationalized manner, and (b) the inventory should be the basic finding aid, and (2) another area of consensus is that the main problem lies in providing access to the inventories. Indexing the inventories is the key to the finding aid system. To quote from Chairman Charles Palm's report: "The cumulative index is the only index to which other finding aids in a repository relate, is the key vehicle for providing subject access . . . , and is the weakest link in most finding aid systems."

†Traditional cataloging involves working with a published bibliographical item, a book specifically, and analyzing it to learn what is its main subject content, in conjunction with author and title information. These are registered in a catalog by main and added entries—historically in card format, according to standard rules. Orientation is to discrete bibliographical items that have been published. Publication itself is analogous to the archival practice of arrangement, wherein items must be arranged before they are described. This archival process represents the establishment of intellectual control and involves both arrangement and description. If viewed functionally, in this context the archival arranger acts like a publisher. Traditional cataloging, as applied to manuscripts, is done usually from the manuscripts themselves, not from secondary sources such as inventories and other finding aids. In the sections on the origins of the *National Union Catalog of Manuscript Collections* and the *Anglo-American Cataloging Rules* these points will be developed more fully.

tory/guides. Traditional cataloging was stopped and the card catalog was abandoned.

Over a period of years I published a number of articles, each one a step in the evolution of the University of Washington system.[5] The first article (1960) was written in the historical manuscripts tradition, as a variant or derivative of practices at many institutions. The method had been learned while working as a student processor at the Bancroft Library, under the aegis of Robert E. Burke, historian and curator of manuscripts, and Julia Macleod, a cataloger who had apprenticed at the Huntington Library.[6] The method of arrangement dealt with correspondence: outgoing letters should be arranged chronologically and incoming alphabetically by author (unless the author was acting as agent of another party). By this measure a two-way approach to the holdings could be made, serving a multiplicity of uses. The key feature proved to be the objective control of proper names, which could be acquired in the process of arrangement. This emphasis on proper-name control and its importance was consistent with the programs and experiences of the Clements, Baker, Newberry, and Houghton libraries. But I paid too little respect for original file order, and I also overgeneralized about the validity of the method. In subsequent writing, its application was limited to special cases.

Some background is relevant to an understanding of the articles that followed, but it is important to realize that the evolution of this system represents a microcosm of the larger historical changes in the field and is instructive as a case history. A number of internal changes in the program of the Libraries' Manuscripts Section resulted from working with Schellenberg in 1962, and in responding to his many positive criticisms and suggestions. Before that, I had mistakenly thought a bifurcated system* patterned on that of the Library of Congress had been established, since that had been my intention. Inventories and a catalog existed side by side, but with a difference; the catalog entries were derived from the inventory, and control of proper names aimed at comprehensiveness instead of selectiveness. In practice, this proved not to be a bifurcated system, but a single integrated one. This discovery was not made until 1962, when I recognized that the cards in the catalog were really indexes to the inventories. Functioning as indexes, the cards contained more information than needed. At this time, we learned that the Bancroft Library had developed a format as an alternative to the card catalog by using post binders with half sheets containing eighteen squares to allow for eighteen entries per page. (See Appendix 19 for an example.) This novel format, which eliminated narrative and minimized subjectivity, exactly suited our purpose,

---

*A bifurcated system as described in this book is one in which catalogs exist coequally with inventories, registers, shelf lists, and other finding aids. No attempt is made in such a system to use the catalog as an integrative tool by which the other finding aids would be cataloged, resulting in a single access point to the entire holdings. "Proliferated" might be a more accurate term, but "bifurcated" conveys better the sense of segregation or division which results. The Library of Congress still maintains its bifurcated system while moving into a fully automated on-line program.

and led to abolition of the card catalog entirely, while incorporating its indexing function into a series of three cumulative indexes: a name index, a topical subject index, and a chronological index. Use of the cumulative index concept was reinforced once its role in the volumes of the *National Union Catalog of Manuscript Collections* was demonstrated.

Another important variation that distinguished the system from the Library of Congress model was the practice of subgrouping during the arrangement process. At the Library of Congress subgroups are mixed with "subject files," are not sequentially arranged, and some record series of a subgroup are segregated under a general series, thereby impeding subgroup-level control. (These points are elaborated in chapter 4 and 6. See also Appendix 12.) At the University of Washington subgrouping was done from the start in 1958, by grouping together as subunits all record series that represented the separate corporate activities of the person or corporate body whose papers were being processed.

By 1962 we fully recognized the hierarchy of record levels and the need to key our controls to them. We realized also that proper-name control gave a high measure of control at least to the series level, and frequently to the file folder level, where that level of specificity in arrangement had been achieved. Having learned that users associate proper names with their subject and approach subject matter through proper names, we emphasized proper name control by posting them comprehensively to a cumulative name index, using forms adapted from the format devised at the Bancroft Library.

Once the conceptual framework was recognized to be hierarchical it became clear that progressively refined controls could be established objectively for topical subject matter by limiting the topical analysis to the primary subject matter acted on by the creator of the accession at hand. To minimize the randomness typical in topical content analysis it was decided to proceed no further than the subgroup level. Subject terms and scope notes were then established. To have proceeded to the series and lower levels would have required a more detailed list of subject terms and complex cross references because of the degree of specificity required. Coupled with this limitation was the comforting recognition that proper-name control, if keyed to the series and file unit levels, would provide a high degree of topical access at those levels as well, because of the inherent subject content that is derived from the proper name–subject matter association made by users in the course of their preliminary research.

It is from this vantage point, as a participant in the developments outlined below, that this book is written.

2

Public Archives and Historical Manuscripts, 1800–1936

PUBLIC ARCHIVES

Collections of both public records and private papers had been gathered together by famous collectors without distinction as to their origins—unless the papers were those of a "great American," to use a popular term.[1] Public records were embraced by the term "historical manuscripts." What was collected was largely the fragmentary documentary remains of the Colonial and Revolutionary past, the Confederation and Constitutional periods, and pioneer beginnings in the Trans-Allegheny West and Old Northwest. By the twentieth century lesser Americans also became targets of institutional collectors. Private collectors and their institutional legatees also typically published calendars, lists, indexes, and edited items.[2] Integral personal papers and records of a public office were rarely collected intact; instead, a few letters were acquired here, a diary there, a petition, a deed—the full range of textual documentation. Public records and private papers were not differentiated, and despite the striving of these collectors for integral or "organic" collections, such as those of colonial governors Jonathan Trumbull and Thomas Hutchinson, or the George Washington papers, what they collected was mainly random in character. One way the incoherence of their randomness could be overcome was by simply arranging the papers chronologically, usually under a mixture of classifications, under geographical subdivisions, and by form or topic. Chronological arrangement was one that most persons could readily comprehend, and it was particularly relevant if the intention of the collectors was to publish the material. In most of the original thirteen states and in some of the Old Northwest states, publication did occur. Jeremy Belknap, a founder of the Massachusetts Historical Society, spoke at the first meeting of the society in 1792 of his discouragement with the accidental, careless, and wanton destruction of manuscripts and public records. To safeguard the information contained in original sources he sought to "multiply" copies by means of publication. This motivated him to publish them soon after their receipt: "As these materials may come in at different times, and there may not be an opportunity to digest them in the best order previous to their publication; they will present them in such order, as may be convenient; and will arrange them, by an index, at the end of the year." [3]

The librarian of the society for the years 1836 to 1837 and 1842 to 1855 was Joseph B. Felt (1789–1875). At the society's meeting of December 31, 1835, he requested and was authorized "to make a catalogue, alphabetical and systematic, of all the books, pamphlets, and manuscripts in the Library." He announced that his plan was to segregate the manuscripts and arrange them chronologically. Governor Edward Everett, a trustee of the society, was present during this meeting, at which the trustees also voted to petition the legislature to arrange and bind the "public papers in the State House." Out of this concern for the public records Governor Everett appointed Felt to organize records which "were lying about in confusion in the Secretary's office." He completed this work in 1846, leaving behind 241 bound volumes chronologically arranged under seventy-six topical headings. A sampling of these headings will indicate his classification scheme: Agriculture, etc. (1 vol.), Colonial (5 vols.), Commercial (1 vol.), Domestic Relations (1 vol.), Ecclesiastical (5 vols.), Foreign Relations (3 vols.), Hutchinson's Correspondence (3 vols.), Indian Conferences (1 vol.), Journals (1 vol.), Judicial (7 vols.), Lands (2 vols.), Laws (1 vol.), Letters (6 vols.), Military (14 vols.), Minutes of Council (6 vols.), Muster Rolls (9 vols.), Speeches, Messages, etc. (3 vols.), Towns (1 vol.), Trade, etc. (2 vols.), Usurpation (4 vols.), Witchcraft (1 vol.), Revolution Reports (1 vol.), Revolution, Conventions, Indians, etc. (1 vol.).

Each volume had a chronological index. In 1885 an investigation of the public records led to the conclusion that Felt had made a mistake, because his divisions were arbitrary "and dependent upon form . . . instead of substance" and they led him to inconsistencies: "This confusion could have been avoided, and relations of time been better preserved in one chronological arrangement provided with a topical index." The investigating commission further recommended that the volumes be broken up and the materials rearranged in a "strict chronological order, as has been done . . . in the English State Paper Office." They recommended access by means of a single topical index. James Tracy, head of the archives division, referred to these volumes in 1900 as the "Felt Collection" and the "Massachusetts Archives." Felt's scheme was followed by New Hampshire and Connecticut. [4]

Jared Sparks, another avid collector, also was a publisher. In 1829 he undertook the publication of his *Diplomatic Correspondence of the American Revolution* from State Department records. To do this Sparks altered their arrangement by bringing "together those of each Commissioner, or Minister, in strict chronological order." He admitted that this rearrangement "was not easy to execute." But he commended the results: "The chain of events is thereby exhibited in a manner as much more connected and satisfactory." [5]

Peter Force, one of the preeminent collectors, had organized his own collection chronologically within geographical and topical groupings.[6] The Library of Congress purchased the Force Collection in 1867; it was to be the first Library of Congress collection processed by its Manuscripts Division beginning in 1897.[7] Force's own arrangement scheme would become the basis of the first American archival manual, as will be described below.

Variations on the chronological–topical/geographical classification system prevailed without serious challenge until the first decade of the twentieth century. Schellenberg credits Arnold J. Van Laer with being the first to challenge prevailing practice, at least within his individual repository. Van Laer had been trained as an archivist in the Netherlands before becoming head of the Manuscript Division of the New York State Library in 1898.[8] (In the Netherlands, papers of private origin were collected by the national archives.) Having learned the European practice of classifying records by the source of their creation, he changed the previous chronological arrangement and classified them according to record-creating agency. This innovation conformed with European practices that had evolved the principle of provenance.

A more general and systematic approach to these technical archival problems was provided by the American Historical Association in December 1899 when it established its Public Archives Commission. Issues of the kind noted above lay outside the scope of its Historical Manuscripts Commission, which had been formed in 1895. The purpose of the Public Archives Commission was to investigate and report on the character of the "historical public archives" in each state. This work was done by adjunct members residing in each state during the period from 1900 to 1917. Their reports were published by the AHA as part of its annual reports. Another important objective was to seek archival legislation in each state, using each status report as the basis of persuasion. Altogether forty-one reports were issued on the archives of thirty states and New York City and Philadelphia. The commission also sought legislation for a federal archives.

One of the first fruits of the formation of the Public Archives Commission was the establishment of a state Department of Archives and History, first in Alabama in 1901 and then in Mississippi in 1902. Thomas McAdory Owen, head of the Alabama department, reported that from the beginning all records were kept "as nearly as possible in the same order or classification as obtained in the offices of origin. We have carefully avoided any break-up of classes or groups and adoption of any arbitrary arrangement."[9]

In Mississippi, Dunbar Rowland followed the same plan, classifying records by their provenance. He would later be credited by commission chairman Victor H. Paltsits in 1912 for presenting the "first systematic suggestions for scientific archival practice" in the United States. In his first annual report Rowland advocated three broad classifications: provincial, territorial, and state. Under each period, records should be grouped by administration and department, and arranged chronologically within each class. During 1902–3 Rowland studied under Worthington C. Ford, head of the Manuscripts Division at the Library of Congress and became convinced that "loose files of manuscripts, even when arranged and indexed, are of little use to the investigator as compared to bound volumes." He thought that "every manuscript worth preserving should be placed in a substantially bound volume with a complete table of contents and an index." In 1905 he acknowledged his debt to Ford, especially, "along the lines of classification, binding, carding, and collecting." During 1905–6 Rowland went to Europe to arrange for transcriptions of documents relating to Mississippi, and was "gratified to find that the methods employed [in classification] were very similar to those which have been tentatively adopted by this Department." Rowland received favorable comment on his work from other Southern states and Maine. In 1912 he provided more details of his system while criticizing the application of library methods of classification and alphabetical arrangements. He arranged the Mississippi archives chronologically within series for each department. For a finding aid he used the page as format and included an agency history as well as series descriptions.[10] Other Southern states followed the pattern established by Alabama and Mississippi.

It was not until 1906, however, that a system of classification based on record provenance became readily available in published form. An Iowa historian, Benjamin F. Shambaugh, published his scheme in *Annals of Iowa* in 1907. John C. Parish fleshed out this system the following year, and Ethel B. Virtue presented the principles at the 1914 meeting of the Public Archives Commission. Later, in 1928, Cassius C. Stiles published the system as the *Public Archives: A Manual for Their Administration in Iowa*. Historian Theodore C. Blegen, writing in 1918 for the purpose of advising the State Historical Society of Wisconsin, reported that the Iowa system represented "the most successful archival practice in Europe and America."[11] Clearly, the Iowa system was considered a model.

The Iowa system was well known to the regular participants in the work of the Public Archives Commission. Records were classified by administrative agency within three chronological periods: the Territorial period and the first and second Constitutional periods. Records of any agency whose work continued without interruption through the chronological periods were kept together without regard to the period break. A classification outline was made, proceeding hierarchically from large administrative units through subordinate ones. The outline itself, Stiles would later report, served as an index to the material that followed "in exact conformity with the outlines [identifying] the records to the lowest subdivision and subject."[12]

Concurrent with these developments before 1909 was the archival experience that Waldo Gifford Leland was gaining in his work for the Carnegie Institution in Europe. In 1904 Leland and Claude H. Van Tyne had compiled the first federal archives guide, *Guide to the Archives of the Government of the United States*.[13] While collecting data for the Carnegie on a guide to holdings in Parisian archives and libraries, Leland attended the École des Chartres course, "Service des archives." This experience prepared him for the work ahead. When the Public Archives Commission decided to call the first Conference of Archivists in 1909, Leland presented a seminal paper that added to the ferment already in process. In his keynote paper, "American Archival Problems," Leland discussed the principle of provenance—for the "first time" according to Schellenberg. He advised that "archives should be classified according to their origin; they should reflect the processes by which they came into existence. . . . Nothing is more disastrous than the application of modern library methods of classification to a body of archives." He advocated development of progressively more refined controls, starting with a general guide and moving on to series descriptions, including "more detailed accounts of the more important series." [14]

The Conference of Archivists continued as a regular forum for those concerned with public archives until the Society of American Archivists was founded in 1936. Formation of the Conference of Archivists, however, tended to divert attention of state archivists from historical manuscripts, leaving the latter subject to administration and control by traditional methods, to be guided mainly by the precedents established by the Library of Congress in its 1913 manual. [15] Instead of a joint effort to address common problems, bifurcation occurred, with unfortunate long-term consequences. Evidence of this incipient separation could be seen in Gaillard Hunt's comment on Dunbar Rowland's paper at the 1910 Conference of Archivists. Hunt had succeeded Worthington Ford as head of the Library of Congress Manuscripts Division, and conceded the validity of Rowland's insistence that the administration of archives "should be based entirely upon the theory that their classification for public use is the main end" and only "secondarily with a view to the use by the scholar and the student." [16] At this same meeting, in the same vein, Arnold Van Laer complained about the American practice of combining public archives under such arbitrary series as "Colonial manuscripts," "Revolutionary Papers," "Military Papers," "Accounts," and so forth. These classifications were precisely the ones used at the Library of Congress.

Hunt, in making this concession, unintentionally diverted manuscript librarians to historical manuscripts—limiting their scope to documentation of private origin—and away from public archives. The main purpose of the Library of Congress and other manuscript collections was to serve scholarship, not administrators or the general public. Such collections focused usually on prestigious figures and pioneer beginnings, in which documentation was fragmentary, not consecutive or comprehensive in scope. Item description, mainly in calendar form, was the focus in this context. Scholars found such work helpful. With this diversion was conveyed the idea that historical manuscripts were not amenable to controls derived from the public archives field. Furthermore, because these manuscripts were mainly housed in libraries or under library administration, it was understandable that they would be dealt with by accepted library practices. As will be seen in the sections on the Library of Congress, this meant a preoccupation with calendaring, cataloging, the card catalog, and the formulation of a national cataloging code. [17] Because of this fixation there was no serious review and evaluation of the network of finding aids in a manuscript repository until 1962, when I did one at the University of Washington Libraries; publication of a general analysis was postponed until 1971.[18]

State archivists, in responding to their need for a common body of principles, agreed at the Conference of Archivists in 1912 that a manual on "archival economy" should be produced. It would follow the outline submitted by Victor Hugo Paltsits (1867–1952).* Production of the manual was never forthcoming, because the AHA, lacking money, never funded work on it. J. Franklin Jameson, editor of the *American Historical Review*, chilled any future substantive work of the commission by his comments on Paltsits's 1922 résumé of the commission's work. The AHA had not funded its operations since 1917. Jameson made it clear that he saw its goals as being substantially met and implied that funds could not be spared even for the valuable activities of the commission, mainly because of the expense of publishing the *American Historical Review*. A review of the AHA's annual reports from 1923 to 1936 shows little work by the commission and no reference to the archival manual. But the various papers presented at each of the annual AHA conferences were considered by Paltsits to constitute chapters in such a manual.[19] The papers dealt with a wide range of archival subjects: facilities, administration, conservation, classification, and other matters. If they had been cumulated, a superior manual would have been readily available, one that might also have influenced librarians in their historical manuscripts work. In the central matter of classification, arrangement, and description—the heart of theory—the manual would have led susceptible librarians away from the historical manuscripts tradition, because the principle of provenance became the *sine qua non* for public archivists. The principle was clearly stated by Leland in 1912 when he wrote that the "administrative entity should be the starting point," and the general guides and other finding aids should be published to make them generally accessible. "The general guide," he said, "should be an enumeration of the various groups or series of records, indicating for each series its title . . . grouped under the respective offices from which they emanate." [20] In this statement Leland outlined the essentials of the National Archives program as it would take shape during the reforms after 1941. His appears to be the first clear reference in the United States to "record series" as constituting an element in what has become recognized as a hierarchy or levels of control.

Margaret Cross Norton, state archivist of Illinois (1922–57), lent further strength to this drift at the meeting in 1930 of the National Association of State Libraries. Norton was to be a founder of the SAA, its fourth president,

---

*Paltsits was regarded by Margaret Cross Norton as a strong contender for the title of founder of the archival profession in the United States. He served as chairman of the Public Archives Commission from 1913 to 1922, and later became head of the American history section of the New York Public Library, where he gained a reputation as the foremost American bibliographer of his generation. See Norton, "Victor Hugo Paltsits, 1867–1952," *American Archivist* 16 (April 1953): 137–40.

and an influential writer on every aspect of archival administration. Reiterating the position of Rowland and Leland that archivists must serve their administrations first and scholars second, she urged that state archivists teach administrators the administrative value of archives—that archives are really an extension of the governments they serve. If this teaching was done successfully, improved state funding would follow.[21] Norton brought the Illinois State Archives to the forefront of public archives. Her extensive writing aimed in part at educating the administration that she served: the Illinois Archives were administered by the State Library under jurisdiction of the Secretary of State.[22]

State archival programs were generally weak, according to the survey conducted by Theodore C. Blegen in 1918.[23] The main goal had been, and continued to be, to bring archives of each state into a safe facility and under administration of a properly trained archivist. The Historical Records Survey of 1935–42 portrayed this sorry plight for which no general improvement would occur until after World War II.[24] Successful programs in Illinois, Iowa, Alabama, and Mississippi were the great exceptions, not the rule. Most archives remained with their administrative agency, not in archival custody, and they were usually stored in makeshift facilities that impeded ready access to them.

HISTORICAL MANUSCRIPTS

Upon its establishment by the American Historical Association in 1895, the Historical Manuscripts Commission conducted a mail survey of historical manuscripts in both private and public custody. The commission reported its frustrations at its fifth meeting in 1900. It complained about the lack of cooperation not only of private holders but also of public institutions, where few archives were systematically arranged and catalogued: "Their custodians are often . . . indifferent to the importance of making known their possessions . . . , while some of the societies evince a desire to keep their documents from public knowledge until they can themselves publish them."[25]

From the beginning of its work the commission encountered private and public collections with a mixture of both public archives and private papers, all of which the commission considered to be "historical manuscripts."[26] They were not to be differentiated conceptually by the AHA until it constituted the Public Archives Commission in 1899.

The Historical Manuscripts Commission quickly became preoccupied with publishing the correspondence of John C. Calhoun, beginning in 1897, and following that project with comparable publication of edited private papers. As a result of its surveying, the commission decided in 1898 to leave to the historical societies of the country "the tasks which more properly belong to them, and to confine its labors, as far as possible, to historical manuscripts of national importance."[27] Unlike the Public Archives Commission, the Historical Manuscripts Commission did not seek definition and reform of its field. Such work was to be undertaken, if at all, by the AHA's newly formed Conference of State and Local Historical Societies, beginning in 1904. (The conference was succeeded in 1940 by the American Association for State and Local History.) Partly in despair, a special AHA committee presented a status report in 1905: "Within the library [of the historical society] are properly deposited all manner of manuscripts." As for manuscripts, they should be, if possible, "calendared, or in any event indexed; the least that can be expected is, that manuscripts be properly listed on catalogue cards." [28] The annual meetings of the conference focused initially on problems associated with publication, cooperation, and organization. There is no evidence in the annual reports that they considered anything comparable to a "manual on archival economy." Their work seemed mainly to be a continuation of what such societies had been doing, only more of it by more of them through better organization and cooperation. [29]

Traditional initiative of the American Historical Association in public archives and historical society work flagged during World War I and never revived during the 1920s. Its lessened activity contributed to the separatism referred to above. But the commission leaders themselves must have rejected the idea of applying public archival principles to historical manuscripts. Many, like Norton, Paltsits, Rowland, Solon J. Buck, Leland, Owen, and Hunt, were members and active in the affairs of the Public Archives Commission, the Conference of State and Local Historical Societies, and the Historical Manuscripts Commission. Some cross membership and activity also existed with the National Association of State Libraries. Yet there was no recognition among them that principles upon which there was consensus in the public archives field were transferable, adaptable by the historical manuscripts field. This movement did not come until after World War II. By 1950 the nature of collecting had radically changed to an emphasis on papers of recent origin, thereby forming the basis for applying archival principles to modern manuscripts.

In the interim, the Library of Congress asserted its influence on those who dealt with manuscripts. When the Manuscripts Department, under Herbert Friedenwald, began organizing its collection in 1897, the first candidate for processing was an artificial one, the Peter Force Collection. Force had brought his collection together from diverse sources; these documents were but fragmentary remains, devoid of those intrinsic relationships that are part of record series emanating from a single source. Force imposed his own scheme by creating a classification system that reflected his collecting interests. His was a microcosm of historical manuscript collecting at large. What was collected was organized along lines of the collector's own interests. Fred Shelley, in his account of the early history of the Manuscripts Division, notes that Friedenwald intended to catalog and calendar "even individual pieces within larger collections," starting with the Force Collection. Influenced probably by Worthington C. Ford's section on manuscripts in Cutter's *Rules* (1904) and by Melvil Dewey's principles of classification for books, [30] but conforming also to Force's own organization scheme for his *American Archives*, Friedenwald devised a "chronologic-geographic" classification. His assistant, John C. Fitz-patrick, in 1913 produced from this experience the first archival manual in the United States, *Notes on the Care, Cataloguing, Calendaring and Arranging of Manuscripts*. By its publication it was intended "to make available in print a description of the procedure in the Library . . . with a view to its possible utility to other institutions having like problems." [31] Schellenberg has indicated the negative influence of Fitzpatrick's *Notes* on the manuscript work of the New York Public Library (1914), the State Historical Society of Wisconsin (1916), New York State Library (1916), Pennsylvania Public Records Department, and others. [32]

Fitzpatrick elaborated Force's own classification. [33] Because the Force Collection was made up of "miscellany," as distinguished from what Fitzpatrick termed "natural collections," most of Fitzpatrick's recommendations related to the handling of miscellany. For him, natural collections posed no special problems, since they were simply to be arranged in strict chronological order, but within "natural classes" if there were any.* By choosing to concentrate on the control of miscellany instead of organic papers he was diverted from attacking the central problem in the control of modern manuscripts collections—that is, the record series. Not until the Historical Records Survey of the late 1930s would the series concept receive systematic attention.[†] In the absence of a series concept, collections would have to be analyzed on an item-by-item basis while allowing the accumulation of unprocessed backlogs.[‡]

For the miscellany Fitzpatrick recommended a "chronologic-geographic" arrangement, and indicated the groupings he had established at the Library of Congress. The arrangement, he wrote, "follows the sequence of events from discovery of the Western Hemisphere," then proceeds by countries within these divisions and strict chronological order within the geographic subdivisions. "Other groups are those of Indians, Order Books, Journals, Diaries, Mercantile Accounts, the Army . . . , Federal Executive departments." Represented here are categories for topics, administrative departments, and document form which are invented for cataloging purposes without regard to the

---

* "Natural collections" are directly the product of their original record creator (see the Glossary under "Collection"). Fitzpatrick allowed for grouping by "natural class," a rough equivalent of the current term "series." "Natural collections" are roughly equivalent to "organic" or "integral" papers and records.

† Surveyors for the HRS were inexperienced, but they nevertheless recorded with considerable accuracy data about masses of county records (primarily) that were largely unorganized and unkempt. Recognizing the impossibility of doing this by traditional methods on an item-by-item or selective basis, the HRS directors devised forms to record data by record series. This was the first general effort in the archival field to develop means of collective description, the recording of aggregations of items having common filing characteristics.

‡ It was just this kind of situation that Solon J. Buck faced when he became chief of the Manuscripts Division in 1948. Buck brought with him his experience as a historian and as superintendent of a model state historical society, that of Minnesota, as well as his public archives exposure in the National Archives, where he had been the second archivist of the United States.

origination of the papers.[34] Even natural collections of public records, according to Fitzpatrick, should be rearranged chronologically, after first observing and analyzing their original order—the latter being "in no wise competent to answer the needs of the historical investigator." [35]

Because the Library of Congress manual was intended for a broad audience seeking proper instructions, its combination of ambiguity and the chronological absolute could well lead to a variety of adaptations. For example, while acknowledging the importance of observing and analyzing any existing orderly arrangement, Fitzpatrick advised against adherence to it, finding chronological rearrangement necessary. In his insistence on chronology he bypassed any discussion of "natural classes" and series in organized papers and records. Also ambiguous is his handling of the sequence of arrangement and cataloging. Although he advised cataloging before arranging the papers, he was willing to reverse this sequence if there was a demand for access, because "every separate paper" must be cataloged.[36] Cataloging was to be done from the actual manuscripts, not from a finding aid. This ambiguity was eventually carried over to the *Anglo-American Cataloging Rules* in 1967.

Fitzpatrick's various classifications also inspired other repositories to devise comparable preconceived schemes that would violate provenance despite his warning that classification by subject should be avoided. He did not recognize that his own scheme violated that admonition—that his own classification system was preconceived.

He adduced a host of reasons to justify strict chronological arrangement. Most important among them are promptness of access, presentation of a complete picture of the daily course of life, placement of the records before the investigator in an unbroken time sequence, reduction of the chances of misplacement, and the investigator's familiarity with chronological arrangement.[37] No less influential was an institutional aspect of manuscript collecting up to that time. Relatively few historical manuscripts having integral record characteristics had been collected, and public archives had hardly begun to take shape. Repositories were still oriented to the "great Americans," [38] pioneer origins, and the Revolutionary and Colonial periods. The collections of Jared Sparks, Force, Lyman Draper, and other famous collectors certainly bore this character. The resulting documentation was inevitably fragmentary, having been brought together from chance remains. Under these conditions it made sense to interrelate the collected items by arranging them chronologically just to ascertain completeness of chronological coverage. Concentration was on consecutiveness of documentation, not its comprehensive coverage.

Little if any attention was paid to the origins of the papers, to their "provenance" (see the Glossary). It is understandable that if provenance was ignored, record series determined by provenance also would receive no attention.

By closely examining some of the elements in this first practical manual it is easier to see how theory and practice took the form they did before 1950. That the manual was influential is attested by the three editions issued, the last in 1928 (reprinted in 1934). Many important twentieth-century manuscript collections were started in the 1930s, and undoubtedly it was used for guidance in organizing them.[39] Once committed to the system by both resources and habit it was difficult to change. The Library of Congress itself did not begin to break away until the late 1940s under the leadership of Solon J. Buck.

Having discussed the contribution of the Library of Congress to practices in the historical manuscripts field it remains to survey briefly some practices that were publicized but not structured into a manual.

Practices of the State Historical Society of Wisconsin were sketched in its *Proceedings* and in its *Descriptive List of Manuscript Collections*.[40] Just as Peter Force's classification became the basis for the Library of Congress system, Lyman C. Draper's classification of his own collection was the basis of the society's. As the society's first director (1854–86) he brought with him his own private collection of source materials, mainly dealing with the Trans-Allegheny West. Draper began by classifying "chiefly under the names of important border heroes or pioneers." He had collected generally "with a view to using the material for a series of biographies." The Draper Collection was assembled in 486 volumes that were subdivided into fifty "subcollections." Expanding on this classification, the Manuscripts Department developed "an alphabetical one based on geographical considerations" grouping collections of manuscripts "according to the state" and using a letter to designate the group.[41] Manuscripts were bound into volumes according to their classification, such as "Wisconsin Fur Trade Accounts" or "Papers of George Boyd, Indian Agent." The Manuscripts Department saw as its earliest need a "complete calendar of these documents."[42]

The Huntington Library developed its variant in the 1920s, one that was adapted by Duke University in the later 1930s. Huntington's curator of manuscripts, H. C. Schulz, outlined the system as one in which arrangement is by form (maps, plans), subject (drama, religion, English and European history), and "archives," such as those of Hastings and Ellesmere. The nature of the manuscripts determined their arrangement. Thus, "literary manuscripts are arranged alphabetically, historical manuscripts chronologically, and *horae* by their particular uses." He regretted that no "universally applicable" method had been developed for handling "loose" papers, stating that "it may be necessary to bind them." Paying his disrespect to provenance, he advocated interfiling future additions to any group regardless of its source,[43] apparently with priority given to the author, not the recipient, of a letter if it was the autograph that was valued by the Huntington. Other institutions seeking autographs instead of items and collections of substance might well have been inspired by this example.

Although a good sense of general practices can be gleaned from examining those of the Massachusetts Historical Society in the nineteenth century and those in this century at the State Historical Society of Wisconsin and the Huntington, these do not represent systematic expositions. This was left to the Minnesota Historical Society. Its practices and the theory behind them were articulated by Grace Lee Nute* in the society's *Service Bulletin*, number 4 (1936), supplemented by her later in a presentation at an annual meeting of the American Library Association in 1939.[44] In scale this manual was the only one comparable to the Library of Congress manual written by Fitzpatrick, and like the latter it was intended to affect practices elsewhere. It is unlikely that the practices of other institutions outlined above were similarly intended to be models, whatever their actual effect was.

Nute divided manuscript materials into nine main groups: personal papers, archives of organizations, miscellaneous source materials, transcripts and photocopies, calendars and field reports of MHS staff, secondary material, broadsides, autographs, and manuscript maps. This classification was always in the process of revision, and changes had to be inserted in the manual by hand, by the process known as "tipping in." The purpose of classification was to facilitate cataloging and filing in the public catalog. The manual sought "to parallel the Library of Congress system as nearly as possible so that duplicate copies of the cards" could be filed in the society's public catalog.[45] The cataloging unit was the box; items in the box were to be filed chronologically: "My rule for cataloging manuscripts is: use the box as the unit and within the unit arrange the pieces by date."[46] The manual does provide other options: "Occasionally it becomes necessary either to arrange an entire collection topically or to segregate into topics portions of a collection the remainder of which is filed chronologically."[47] An inventory sheet, which was a copy of the shelf-list card, was then prepared, giving contents and added entries. Finally, the cataloger "selects the names and subjects that occur most frequently and those that are of greatest local or national significance." Name entries usually were derived from the actual manuscripts, not from the inventory.[48] The subject list of the Library of Congress was used as its authority.[49]

Nute's suggestions could lead to confusion if one were to follow her lead. The place of arrangement in the work sequence is undefined: the chapter on arrangement follows the one on cataloging, and there is no other indication of sequence. Topical arrangements are encouraged without reference to the

---

*Nute's predecessor, Ethel B. Virtue, was the society's first in a succession of distinguished manuscript curators. She had been recruited by Solon J. Buck when he became superintendent of the society (1914–31). Buck had undoubtedly been impressed with her work in the state archives of Iowa, and by her paper on classification principles presented at the meeting of the Conference of Archivists in 1914. Virtue accepted provenance as the basis of classification, and saw special indexes serving as the means of access instead of rearrangement of manuscripts by preconceived subject classes. She brought these concepts to the society; Nute carried on Virtue's classification system after she became curator in 1921. Virtue had begun by separating the manuscript collection from the library holdings. See Lucile M. Kane, "Collecting Policies at the Minnesota Historical Society, 1849–1952," *American Archivist* 16 (April 1953): 127–36; information supplied by her as a reader of this manuscript; Theodore C. Blegen, "Solon Justice Buck—Scholar-Administrator," *American Archivist* 23 (July 1960): 259–62; and Ethel B. Virtue, "Principles of Classification for Archives," AHA, *Annual Report, 1914*, pp. 374–76.

provenance of the papers or records; record series as a cataloging unit is not recognized, although Nute allows room for series by her acceptance of some series based on physical type, such as account books, diaries, and letter-books. Her method gives no hint of a hierarchy of controls within a given collection. Like Fitzpatrick's system, Nute's encourages randomness. On chronological arrangement Fitzpatrick was rigid, Nute more permissive. But their respective classification systems are basically different. While Fitzpatrick classified by topic and physical type and arranged items chronologically within these classes, Nute only segregated personal papers from organizational records. She implied an adherence to provenance, and we know that Virtue followed that principle, but unfortunately Nute did not elucidate the concept. A place for it in her discussion would have reduced ambiguity.

On the eve of the birth of the Society of American Archivists and the beginnings of the Historical Records Survey, and one year after the National Archives had embarked on its career, there was a wide range of archival practices, and only one clear line of theory to serve as a guide for the future. Only in the public archives field had a solid foundation in theory been laid to prepare for the future of a new profession. In the historical manuscripts area there were simply practices, executed without recognition of their theoretical implications. In the public archives field, the principle of provenance had become generally accepted as the basis of accessioning, arrangement, and description. Those in charge of manuscript collections gave evidence of only a nodding acquaintance with provenance, believing it applied only to public archives. But in the 1930s modern manuscript collecting as a national phenomenon, in the sense of collecting organic papers, had hardly begun. The state historical societies in the sister states of Minnesota and Wisconsin were leading the way. Accelerating in the 1930s, this kind of collecting would become more typical after World War II, and would be predominant by the 1970s. Such collecting would only then inspire among manuscript administrators a respect for provenance—keeping papers and records together according to the source of their creation.[50]

Let us turn to the period after 1936, when papers and organizational records of more recent origin began to challenge traditional methods of handling both categories of source materials—historical manuscripts and public archives.

3

Public Archives and Historical Manuscripts, 1936–55

A flood of literature on archival theory and practice began to flow after the National Archives initiated its program in 1935. Its establishment led directly to the founding of the Society of American Archivists in 1936. And the Historical Records Survey (HRS) of the Work Projects Administration (WPA) provided the impetus nationwide for applying practices that were being developed in the National Archives. Margaret Cross Norton could write in 1946 that "most archivists of today were recruited from the ranks of the National Archives, the executive staff of the late Historical Records Survey, from historical libraries or from among history teachers." The National Archives also had special help in starting its work with a WPA-funded survey of federal records outside of Washington.[1] The HRS was the early catalyst for much that emerged in the literature. But so immersed were the workers in recording the huge masses of unorganized papers and records that they and their directors never seriously examined their practices; they simply followed instructions provided in their manual for filling out survey forms and compiling other related information.

At the beginning of this period the American Library Association was more actively involved in archival matters than at any time before or since through its Archives and Libraries Committee, chaired by Augustus F. Kuhlman. Papers were given at its annual meetings by recognized leaders from both the public archives field and the historical manuscripts field. They were published under Kuhlman's editorship as *Archives and Libraries*. Contributors constituted a who's who of the field: Margaret C. Norton, Grace Lee Nute, Solon J. Buck, Victor H. Paltsits, Theodore Blegen as superintendent of the Minnesota Historical Society, Luther Evans as director of the HRS, and various National Archives staff members.

Potentially these ALA meetings might have rejoined the separate traditions for historical manuscripts and public archives, beneficially stimulating each, with their practitioners working together on common problems. Unfortunately this was not to be. Kuhlman's chairmanship ended in 1940, and with it came the practical cessation of the ALA's interest. What interest remained for the ALA was sustained by its surrogate, the Library of Congress, through its work in developing a national cataloging code.[2] Librarians contributed to the literature because of their responsibilities for manuscript collections and their institutions' own archives, but they were ineffective in sustaining interest in archives and manuscripts within the library profession. Instead, many librarians joined the Society of American Archivists and contributed "how we do it" articles to the *American Archivist* and other journals. Rarely did the writers rise above their own practices to helpful generalization, but two who did were Ellen Jackson, writing for *Library Quarterly* in 1942, and Lester J. Cappon from his position at the University of Virginia and as secretary of the SAA.[3]

Given the centrality of the National Archives, let us turn first to a careful examination of its structure and its relation to the development of archival theory and practices. Its staff members were prolific contributors to the literature.

PUBLIC ARCHIVES

The National Archives, 1935–55

Originally the National Archives, like the Library of Congress, was organized along functional lines, with divisions of accessions, reference, classification, cataloging, and so forth. In 1938 the reference function and accessioning and disposal were transferred to each division that had actual archival custody. In 1941 the functional organization was substantially terminated by establishing new custodial divisions and giving each of them responsibility for arrangement and description as well. In Wayne C. Grover's * words, functional organization was supplanted by one that was "predominantly by record aggregates." All functions were brought under each custodial division, except for part of the reference service, that part "serving mainly persons interested in genealogy." It followed that "wide latitude was left to the divisions . . . to suit the different kinds of records."[4]

This functional form of library organization also carried with it the outlook of librarianship originally. Concepts and terminology derived from the library field were tested. "Classification" was such a term; in an archival context it would take on a different meaning. Within the National Archives Paul Lewinson was particularly critical of the early attempts to extend library usage to archives. The Classification Division came to accept provenance instead of subject matter as the basis of classification. This differed sharply from library classification principles. For the archivist the procedure is to group records by

---

*Wayne C. Grover was the third archivist of the United States (1948–65).

the name of the record-creating agency, and to identify series within that agency's records, retaining their orignal order insofar as possible—in the accepted European tradition. Roscoe R. Hill, who had transferred from the Manuscripts Division of the Library of Congress in 1935 to direct work of the Classification Division of the National Archives, indicated that the United States was probably the first national archives with such a division. Its purpose as he saw it was to identify the appropriate archival unit to serve "as the basis of classification . . . to give an orderly arrangement to the archivalia." *[5]

Once an accession was classified, and after an accession card had been prepared, the Catalog Division would begin preparing card catalog entries from information supplied in "identification inventories" provided by the Division of Department Archives. If necessary, catalogers would check the records themselves. Cataloging as such was by levels, beginning with a preliminary effort called "division cataloging" directed at recording general information down to the subagency or subgroup level. A main entry would be made along with whatever added entries could be preliminarily derived by the cataloger. "Series cataloging" would follow as soon as priorities allowed.[6] Commenting on this procedure, John R. Russell, head of the Catalog Division, indicated that "division cataloging is chosen if no great loss in subject or name approach to the material is caused by grouping series together in one entry. If the series in the collection are on a variety of subjects, or include the names of important people and organizations that warrant entries in the catalog, series cataloging is chosen." Russell saw special problems in dealing with records of an active agency, because the addition of entries for material received later was "impractical."[7] Continuing series posed a special problem, as he indicated. But Russell made two observations that the 1941 reforms should have taken into account when the divisions of cataloging and classification were abolished. For one, he claimed that in cataloging archives it is necessary to determine which of the different kinds of finding aids are to be prepared, and "how they will be related to each other."[8]

Russell's second crucial observation was that the added entries in the catalog were of the "greatest value," because they provided access to all the archives that had been inventoried.[9] When the 1941 reforms took place, cataloging ceased, leaving to provenance and staff mediation the task of revealing somehow the information that a central catalog or a cumulative index could have deliberately provided: a single point from which the entire holdings could be approached.[10]

Russell also acutely sensed the critical problem regarding topical subject access, an issue that did not surface for general attention until the late 1970s. As he saw it, subject references were complicated not only by having to use both broad and narrow headings, requiring cross references, but by having to key the headings to "different-sized units and different types of material,"

---

* "Archivalia" is a term that Hill tried to propagate. Although "classification" was debated within the National Archives, its library usage seems not to have been applied.

and by having to communicate this information in a single catalog. He added that this runs "contrary to the practice of cataloging books." [11]

Let us turn to the reforms of 1941 as they affected arrangement and description in the National Archives.[12] In the 1941 *Annual Report*, the archivist announced (pp. 65–68):

1. All finding mediums . . . shall be drafted by the personnel of the custodial division to which the records have been allocated. . . .

2. [dealing with recommendations on transfer and identification inventories]

3. The preparation of preliminary reports, identification of series reports, historical summaries, and classification schemes shall be discontinued.

4. Cataloging by accessions shall be discontinued and there shall be substituted therefor cataloging by record groups. The term "record group" is defined as a major archival unit established somewhat arbitrarily with due regard to the principle of provenance and to the desirability of making the unit of convenient size and character for the work of arrangement and description and for the publication of inventories.

5. The chief of each custodial division shall have made as promptly as possible a tentative identification and registration of each of the record groups in his custody in the form of a separate document for each record group, to be entitled "Registration of Record Group" . . .

6. The chief of each custodial division shall proceed as promptly as possible to have compiled "Preliminary Checklists" of all the material in his custody. . . .

7. Whenever the body of material belonging to a given record group in the custody of the Archivist is sufficiently extensive or complete to justify such work, and all of it has been covered by preliminary checklists or similar documents, the chief of the division having custody of the material shall proceed with the compilation of a "Preliminary Inventory" of such material. . . .

8. . . . When new accessions are received consisting of material belonging to any record group that has already been registered and for which a preliminary inventory has been compiled, the registration for that group shall be revised by the incorporation therein of data concerning the newly accessioned material, and the revised version shall be processed and substituted for the old version in all sets of such registrations maintained in The National Archives; separate checklists of the new material shall be prepared; and the previously prepared preliminary inventory shall either be revised or provided with a supplement, as the case may demand.

9. [dealing with preparation of a priority list]

10. As soon as a project for the final arrangement and inventorying of a record group shall have been included on an approved priority list, the

chief of the custodial division concerned shall have a plan for the project prepared and shall transmit it through the Director of Archival Service to the Advisory Committee on Finding Mediums, which shall return it with its recommendations to the Director of Archival Service, who, upon approval by the Archivist, shall authorize and direct the chief of the custodial division to proceed with the project. Such projects will involve the identification of series, the determination of the official title for each series, the evolution of logical groupings of the series, the compilaton of an inventory, the assignment of simple symbols, and finally the arrangement of the material itself in the order of the inventory, insofar as that is feasible. . . .

The units of description in the inventories shall, as a rule, be series, but may at times be smaller units such as subseries, volumes, or dossiers, or larger units such as groups of series. . . . When an inventory is completed, revised, and approved it shall be indexed. . . .

11. Cataloging, other than by record groups, except in special cases, specifically authorized, shall be deferred until after final inventories have been completed. . . . Such projects, which shall indicate the type of unit proposed to be used for cataloging purposes, shall be handled in the same manner as that proposed for the projects referred to in section 10. . . .

12. No change shall be made in the present procedure with reference to the compilation of guides.

13. Finding mediums of other types . . . may be planned as projects by the custodial division concerned as the need arises. . . .

14. Special reports . . . may be planned. . . .

15. All plans and procedures covered by this memorandum . . . shall be considered as experimental for the time being.

Partly to convey to a broad public its own experiences with these experimental programs, the National Archives published manuals and other helpful literature. These were in the form of circulars, bulletins, staff information papers, and its own annual reports (the last in 1949). Together they can be considered a public archives manual. Their wide dissemination influenced practices at the Library of Congress, state archives, and manuscript collections having holdings of integral papers and records—"historical manuscripts" of the twentieth century.

These publications grew out of the need to implement the internal reforms of 1941, and they represent first and foremost detailed instructions to the staff members. Before judging their outside impact, let us examine them as internal policy and procedures documents of the National Archives.

Basic to our examination is *Staff Information Circular* no. 15 (July 1950), "Control of Records at the Record Group Level." [13] Wayne C. Grover, archivist, reported in the introduction that this level of minimum control had been established by 1944 for all accessioned records. *Staff Information Circular* no. 15 recommended that, upon receipt, all accessioned records should be assigned to a record group. Additions to any records in archival custody are provided for. This principle largely conforms to the one devised by Iowa in 1907 and adopted by Illinois in the 1920s. Record groups in the National Archives were established down to the bureau level, and for independent agencies, executive departments, predecessor agencies, liquidating agencies, and "collective" groups for small agencies with some common characteristics.

Within each record group are "subgroups, series, and individual items." *Staff Information Paper* no. 18 (June 1951), "Principles of Arrangement," by T. R. Schellenberg, indicated how these are established. He began by quoting Waldo G. Leland: "[The record group] falls naturally into sub-groups, and the sub-groups into series following the organization and functions of the office." Schellenberg explained why the principle of provenance is the basis of arrangement. Subgroups are established according to some "logical relation," such as "hierarchy, chronology, function, geographical location, or subject." "Normally," he continued, subgroups "should reflect the hierarchical structure of the creating agency," and subgroupings can be done "in the degree to which organizational units . . . created and maintained their own filing systems." "Central files" are not a subgroup and "should be placed before all other records of the organization; those that are clearly identifiable as records of other single administrative units and not incorporated in a systematic filing system should be reunited with the records of the units to which they belong." This point is crucial in understanding the ways this principle can be adapted to arrangement of integral historical manuscripts, as will be demonstrated in chapter 4. Parentage of the records is here recognized by Schellenberg as the basis of subgrouping public archives.

Subgroups established on the basis of geography are for field agencies of larger administrative units. Those based on chronology are for units that have "passed through successive organizational changes" and whose records are coextensive with the period covered. If so many organizational changes have occurred that chronology is impractical as a basis for arrangement, then function should be considered as an alternative. When all options are exhausted, Schellenberg recommended subgrouping by record type (minutes, reports, account books, general correspondence, etc.). He seems not to have recognized that subgrouping on the basis of record type, function, and subject is inconsistent with all other alternatives, since subgroups formed on this basis are not established by the record-creating source. By employing these alternatives as a basis of subgrouping, Schellenberg confused series with subgroups.

Series is the next level in the arrangement hierarchy. Series "should be arranged [within the subgroups] according to some logical pattern that reflects the interrelationships among series, and where appropriate the relationships of series to organization, functions, chronological periods, places and subjects." Arrangement on the basis of any of these relationships depends on the character of the series.

File units represent the next level in the arrangement hierarchy. It is the "most detailed step in arranging records." Schellenberg recommended retaining file units as they are in an orderly series. But rearrangement is necessary "when this order has been disturbed or lost, or when, in exceptional circumstances, it is unintelligible." Restoration of an original order should be done if possible. If this cannot be done, then the archivist must devise his own, but one that "respects the integrity of the records by reflecting their functional or administrative origins and must be designed to facilitate the uses that can be anticipated for the records." Series of miscellany "should be arranged in whatever order is best suited to make known their character and significance." But Schellenberg urged "simplicity as the shortest road to accessibility."

In his treatment of the "file unit" level, Schellenberg introduced an important ambiguity that he also carried over into his later nonofficial writings. For example, *Staff Information Paper* no. 17 is entitled "The Preparation of Lists of Record Items." But "items" are defined to include "a number of documents that have been brought together in such a way that they must be treated as a unit. . . . All record materials, then, that are handled physically as a unit should be regarded as single record items." In other words, items, for him, embraced both discrete, individual units and their multiples if they were covered by a common file unit designation. The file unit level, as such, loses any distinction as an intermediate level between series and discrete item levels.

To make records accessible after they had been accessioned and arranged, guides, inventories, lists, and other finding aids had to be prepared. *Staff Information Circular* no. 14 gave instruction on "The Preparation of Preliminary Inventories" (May 1950). By 1962 only about 135 preliminary inventories had been published and "many record groups were without even unpublished preliminary inventories."[14] Nevertheless, the preliminary inventory was intended to be the key finding aid, to be supplemented by special lists, calendars, indexes and even "final" inventories. Only the latter were to be cataloged, since the preliminary ones were only "provisional and for internal use primarily." But final arrangement has never occurred; hence no catalog or comparable approach (such as cumulative indexes) has been provided by the National Archives to its general holdings. No serious role for a catalog seems to have been envisaged once cataloging itself had been terminated. (The published guides to The National Archives provide the only overall access to its holdings.) The absence of a catalog as the connective link in the finding aids network would affect the reforms in the Library of Congress, 1949–55, when it adapted both the record group concept and the preliminary inventory. The Library of Congress also neglected to relate its own catalog and cataloging to its register system, although it performed cataloging and maintained a union catalog, indicating familiarity with the latter, conceptually.

The heart of the preliminary inventory is in the series titles and descriptions. *Staff Information Circular* no. 14 describes in detail a variety of series arrangements, both within a series and in relationships between them. Instructions are provided for making titles and descriptions. It is implied that the inventory follows the order of arrangement. Preceding the section devoted to series is an introduction that describes the origins of the records. A third section includes any supplemental documents and relevant information.

In these manuals, record levels are discussed in detail and in relation to one another for the first time. Although Leland, in particular, had referred to levels, his were only passing remarks. But record series as a concept was first given concentrated attention in 1937 by Margaret Cross Norton and her Cataloging and Classification Committee of the SAA. The task remained to get practitioners in the historical manuscripts field to recognize the applicability of these principles to integral papers/records under their custody. Schellenberg himself would lead the effort.

Toward a National Cataloging Code for Archives: The Illinois Code as Model

Margaret C. Norton's influence was considerable during the 1930s and 1940s. As state archivist of Illinois she had established a model public archives. She contributed articles regularly to *Illinois Libraries* and the *American Archivist*; she interacted with members of the National Archives staff; she was a leader in founding the Society of American Archivists, becoming head of its Cataloging and Classification Committee; she was a popular speaker at professional meetings, and she was a successor for one year to A. F. Kuhlman in 1941 when he retired as chairman of the ALA's Archives and Libraries Committee.[15]

As head of the SAA's Cataloging and Classification Committee she led its members in revising a cataloging code that had been issued in 1936 by the Illinois State Library. It quickly became obsolete in its application to archives as a result of the experiences of the National Archives and the Historical Records Survey. The committee, whose other members were Reginald B. Haselden of the Huntington Library and Roscoe R. Hill and John R. Russell of the National Archives, had decided to begin with a revision of the Illinois Cataloging Code, because they believed it premature to attempt a more definitive code. They concentrated on rules for the cataloging of archival series. During this process they discussed the matter with leaders of the Historical Records Survey in order to address typical problems met in the survey.[16]

The archival card catalog was defined as "primarily an inventory list to which analyticals, subject headings, and cross references are added." "Archives are classified by provenance." The unit of cataloging is the series, usually a collective entity. "Individual documents or allied groups of records in a general series are cataloged as analyticals." Within departments "classification is by function . . . and the assignment of the series to its place in the classification scheme must precede cataloging" (see Appendix 1 for a sample page of the code).

Series is defined as "a grouping of allied material filed as a physical entity by the department of origin. . . . The classifier keeps each series, no matter how illogical its origin, inviolate as a series." The archivist should restore disarranged series. "The classification scheme attempts an arrangement reflecting functional relationships within the groups of series." If calendar or index cards exist, they should be referred to in the archival catalog but should not be filed in it. From this conceptual design the rules are stated in detail, dealing with the whole array of classification problems and showing how catalogers should handle them. Entries for functions are particularly important in the catalog, because "calls are from a functional angle primarily." Subject entries as well as function cards should be made. And because some users need access by date, date cards should be made.[17]

What was produced in this tentative code was the first substantial archival cataloging code in the United States. In contrast to the NUCMC rules for descriptive cataloging of historical manuscripts, which will be discussed later in this chapter, this code was designed to deal with almost any conceivable archival cataloging problem at the repository level.* The most serious shortcoming of the Illinois code lay not in its limitation to series cataloging but in neglecting to relate cataloging to other finding aids. If substantive work had been continued, that problem might have been dealt with, along with other record levels in the hierarchy. The series absorbed the committee's attention because of its centrality in achieving control.

While these important developments were occurring in the public archives field, there were also significant changes in the handling of historical manuscripts. Provenance, as the basis of classification and arrangement, was beginning to emerge as a consensus principle. Its general acceptance, combined with a greater willingness to adhere to an original filing order, would condition manuscript practitioners to begin seeking levels of control hierarchically as twentieth-century papers became the largest component in major manuscript collections throughout the country. Such acceptance carried with it the recognition of record series and of the need to provide access to them.

HISTORICAL MANUSCRIPTS, 1936–55

General

A number of articles and other writings appeared describing practices at individual manuscript repositories, beginning in the late 1930s. By presenting a cross section of them it will be possible to capture the ferment and even some of the tensions of the period before 1955.

---

*The NUCMC rules were devised for collection-level description for publication in a national union catalog and were mistakenly believed to be fully adaptable at the repository level. But they are useful for no other record levels in the repository than the collection level, and therefore they are not adapted to hierarchical control and searching. (Items are not treated hierarchically by the NUCMC rules.) A fuller discussion follows in chapter 5.

Herbert A. Keller,* curator of the McCormick Library, protested in 1938 against applying the principle of provenance to manuscript collections, doubting its advantage "particularly if availability for use is an important consideration." He said: "In dealing with personal papers and also moderate sized groups of institutional and business papers where the original filing system has been lost or destroyed, the chronological-alphabetical system of arrangement is best," that is, chronological within each alphabetical grouping. ("Alphabetical" was not defined but was probably meant to be by name of writer.) For larger collections he recommended subdividing geographically and then applying the alphabetical-chronological arrangement to each division.[18]

The Newberry Library of Chicago shared with the McCormick and the Huntington an indifference to provenance. At the Newberry a fivefold division was employed for North America, Spanish America, Philippine Islands, Hawaiian Islands, and Linguistics. "Bound volumes and bundles of manuscripts relating to the same subject are treated as single items." In an examination of entries in the Newberry's Checklist it seems that provenance was often ignored; for example, under "William Blount Papers" are five original letters to D. Henley and to others. Other entries also indicate this method of classifying by author, not the recipient who retained and accumulated the papers—at least for letters.[19]

Howard Peckham, also in 1938, reported that at the Clements Library, of the University of Michigan, arranging and cataloging manuscripts "has been determined by certain conditions peculiar to rare-book libraries as a class and to this library in particular." The basic system of arrangement was chronological within each accession—respecting provenance, in contrast to the Newberry and the Huntington. In cataloging, at least three cards were made for "every group of letters"—one to be filed by writer, one by recipient, and one by date. In addition, subject cards were made. He observed further that the users "will know the *dramatis personae* of their subject. This . . . has a most important bearing on cataloguing, as almost all entries are under names of persons." [20] Peckham's observation is important because it recognized for the first time in the literature that subject matter is implied by the instruments of action (people and their organizations), and that name control provides a means of subject access that is not dependent on content analysis. (Apart from my own articles I have found no systematic discussion of this proper name–subject association. Peckham's brief remark hardly ranks as an exposition, but it comes nearest.) Philip C. Brooks, director of the Truman Presidential Library (1957–71), would later underscore the need for researchers to read extensively about their subject before using archives, particularly making notes about persons and organizations linked with their topic. He advised the

* Keller was past president of the Mississippi Valley Historical Association, advisor to the HRS, and chairman of the AHA's Committee on Historical Source Materials. The McCormick Collection includes family papers and the McCormick Reaper Company records and non-McCormick papers. Originally administered in Chicago, they are now in the collection of the State Historical Society of Wisconsin.

researcher to do so in order to specify to the archivist more precisely what he wants.[21]

The system employed at Duke University was described in two articles, by Ruth K. Nuermberger (1940) and by Mattie Russell and Edward G. Roberts (1949). Nuermberger had visited the Huntington and used many of its practices in the course of setting up a system at Duke. She paid respect to provenance, however, refusing to raid collections for famous autographs. Within each collection a strict chronological arrangement was followed, echoing Fitzpatrick of the Library of Congress. For its "most important collections," following the Huntington practice, each letter would be placed in a separate folder and the folder would then be labeled in abundant detail. Descriptive sketches of each item would be made for incorporation on cards. The sketch cards were designed by Nuermberger "to be an acceptable substitute for a detailed subject catalogue." To prepare them she estimated that about 50 percent of a collection had to be read "in order to have a working knowledge of its contents." Russell and Roberts emphasized that before cataloging could be done "careful reading of all letters and other items of consequence and making careful notes on their contents" were necessary. When cards were prepared and ready for filing, the main entry card was followed by the sketch cards. Other cards were filed separately in geographic, subject, and autograph files. There was no single file to be used for access to the collection as a whole.[22]

At Harvard University two quite different kinds of manuscript collections were developed during the period. One was a literary manuscript collection at the Houghton Library, and the other a business records collection at the Baker Library. At the Houghton before 1948, "former catalogers had classified manuscripts by linguistic and geographic areas, generally numbering them seriatum under each category." Several new categories were established. "For convenience in shelving, the collections are divided into boxed and unboxed material, and within the latter group are divided by size." Curator William H. Bond retained the old classification system and expanded it. He considered the new manuscript catalog to be a "finding index," one that referred the user to the index where each piece is "described as an autograph." The indexes in the Reading Room were regarded as "far handier guides to the individual collections than a detailed and cumbersome card catalogue." In collections of private papers correspondence was normally arranged alphabetically by correspondent. Sometimes a chronological arrangement was used "when occasion demands."[23]

Two features, in particular, merit comment. One is the deliberate integration of the catalog with the "indexes" (really, inventories); the catalog entries act as indexes to their inventories. The result is a single integrated finding aid system instead of an array of unintegrated finding aids that existed elsewhere. A second departure from the traditional rigid chronological arrangement is the use of an alphabetical one by name of correspondent. Worthington C.

Ford, writing in 1904, had allowed for such an arrangement for a literary manuscript collection because of the "personal" emphasis in such collections.[24] Schellenberg would later be similarly permissive in urging construction of special aids to accommodate genealogists, antiquarians, and users of literary manuscripts, but he believed the personal element was relatively unimportant except in family and personal papers, and in literary collections.[25] In making this allowance, Ford, Schellenberg, and most of those writing between 1904 and 1962 failed to recognize that proper names were inherently associated with subject matter by reason of their association with activity, and propername control provides a high degree of specific subject access almost automatically, and with a high degree of objectivity. Such control contributes to the fuller exploitation of the provenance method in arrangement and description. It is a by-product of folder-heading lists in inventories.

A second collection at Harvard, the Baker Library, adopted in 1938 W. P. Cutter's *Industries List* as the basis of its classification system.[26] Because the Baker Library is a business records collection, and because business functions are inherently narrowly constituted as to primary subject matter, it was reasonable to employ such a classification system. In the work flow, arrangement precedes the cataloging process. Records of a given firm are arranged by series, although curator Arthur Cole, in 1938, did not use that term. "Descriptive inventories" list the contents by series. Robert W. Lovett, who succeeded Cole, reports that special lists and indexes are also prepared.[27] In addition, a catalog card "is prepared for each volume or group of volumes" (Cole). This descriptive system represents a bifurcated one, employing descriptive lists (inventories) on the one hand and the card catalog on the other. Indexes to the published guides, as well as the catalog, provide single points of access in their respective ways, to the collection as a whole. But neither is integrated with the inventories as a single system.[28]

At the State Historical Society of Wisconsin, the inventory system of the National Archives was adopted during this period. Inventories supplemented the card catalog. Each catalog card referred the user from entries for subjects and "major author" to the "proper inventory sheet." By this measure the size of the card catalog was contained within reasonable limits and the user had more information to read in a more comfortable format; the card catalog was considered too cumbersome a format for this information.[29] Like the Houghton Library, the State Historical Society had developed a single integrated system, but it was one with a limited role for the card catalog. The latter did not provide as optimally high a proportion of access points to its holdings as it might, because it chose to limit the size of the catalog. If the catalogers had made all the added entries required, the size of the catalog would have been excessive, however desirable the entries.

Lester J. Cappon, in his role as consultant in history and archives at the University of Virginia Library, wrote extensive introductions on various themes in the *Annual Report on Historical Collections*. The report for 1942–

43 was on "the accession and arrangement of manuscripts in the Alderman Library." Cappon urged adherence to provenance: "A *corpus* of manuscript papers, being something more than the sum of its parts, is not susceptible to regimented arrangement without loss of character. It should be preserved as an entity." Within any collection he preferred a chronological arrangement, "modified sometimes, however, by certain predetermining factors in relation to the original scheme of arrangement or to the evolution of an organic body of papers." Absent in Cappon's discussion is any specific reference to series. He appeared to recommend a simple chronological arrangement without respect to record type (letters, reports, minutes, etc.) or some other grouping, although in accepting an original order he would presumably accept series. Access to the entire collection should be by the provision of a "guide-index as a sort of master key . . . supplemented perhaps by other keys for more specific purposes." [30] Cappon had written about these procedures because of the need of practitioners in this relatively new field to learn from one another. Although there is missing any discussion of series, he viewed provenance as basic to arrangement and conceived the "guide-index" as the means for approaching the collection as a whole—that is, the rudiments of a single, integrated system.

Early in this period, Ellen Jackson also advised librarians to respect provenance, and to avoid subject classification. She also recommended that any original filing order be retained if usable. Jackson suggested making a unit card in the card catalog for each series, added entries for "important correspondents" (in the letters series), subjects, and so forth, and a shelf-list card. For "single items of importance" analytic cards should be made. [31] This was advice with which few public archivists would have disagreed, and Schellenberg cited it favorably in the syllabus used in his teaching at American University, 1956–61.

Despite Jackson's advice to her library kin, there was not yet agreement on the issue of provenance in the library world. Randolph W. Church of the Virginia State Library, which was responsible for the state's archives, spoke at the 1942 meeting of the Society of American Archivists against adherence to it. He argued that since most inquiries at an archive are "for specific subject information," subject classification should be used. Furthermore, since published and archival sources supplement one another "the approach to both classes . . . should have a similarity," which means that their arrangement "should be as nearly alike as possible," although they need not overlap each other. Church perceptively drew an analogy between archivists' use of the term "series" and that used by librarians in dealing with serial publications, but this was only a passing comment that was not developed. [32] Former SAA Secretary Philip C. Brooks of the National Archives had been troubled by Church's questioning of the validity of provenance. Reviewing in 1947 the effect of the war on archives, he cited Church's attitude toward provenance as one that would continue to be debated among archivists and librarians. [33] The drift of history, however, would prove that Jackson's voice was the weightier: by the mid-1950s the principle of provenance had gained general acceptance in substantially all major manuscript repositories.

A single integrated system of finding aids that should have provided a point of departure in handling both historical manuscripts and public archives was the one developed by Sherrod East.* That neither the National Archives nor the Library of Congress in their reforms paid it heed and moved forward from his lead is one of those mysteries of cultural lag, narrow fixation on technique, or both. His system of "describable item cataloging" was developed in the Army Department's Adjutant General's Office (AGO) beginning in 1947. It must have caught the eye of his archival colleagues, because it appeared in the *American Archivist* in 1953,[34] at the very time rules of descriptive cataloging for the NUCMC were being hammered out. A summary follows.

Describable item cataloging, East explained, "is to facilitate reference exploitation of large accumulations of records of diverse origin organized by record groups . . . comprising series." Before the system was developed in 1947, the AGO branch filed their "series identification sheets" by record group (standard National Archives practice) and assembled them periodically in a mimeographed guide. This guide was indexed alphabetically by name of organizational unit and by subject matter. Describable item cataloging displaced the guide. The card catalog became the keystone of the system, "the medium through which our depository attempts to synthesize its intellectual controls." It was considered the key to the record series, and to all finding aids, "and in many cases to file items of exceptional significance." What made the catalog so central as the point from which all of the branch's holdings could be approached was the fact that there were six or seven cross references made of three types: by agency, by functional headings, and special headings such as "key individuals, geographic, political, and administrative designations, code names." Functional headings were to be "at once both general and specific enough; as mutually exclusive as possible; historically authentic . . . ; and concise and easily understood." A functional heading list had been compiled for use within the branch. Adequate titles for individual series had to be made to bring out its "purpose, character, subject content, and form." As of 1953 all general series descriptions were represented in the catalog, and also "an undetermined number of file items or components of series . . . that are considered worthy of cataloging separately from the series of which they are a part."

Ken Munden of the Adjutant General's Office expanded on East's article in 1956. He explained that there are "three units of descriptive entry—the series, the individual document, and the dossier." Description of the series is

---

*Sherrod East became assistant archivist for military archives at the National Archives when that office was established in 1963. See McCoy, *National Archives*, p. 325.

the only cataloging required. This is to insure that all records in custody are represented in the catalog. Beyond what information is implied or even made explicit in a series description, some items need to be selected for "discretionary cataloging." Criteria are established for this selection, to eliminate the kind of randomness that is characteristic of item cataloging. The cataloged item also is tied by entries to the series of which it is a part. East concluded that the system is "the most comprehensive attempt yet made to bridge the gap between the traditional calendar and ideal inventory of the archivist and the general catalog of the librarian." Unfortunately for librarians and archivists, there were few if any among them who recognized the significance of East's appraisal. As a general system his went beyond those of the Houghton and the Clements libraries, with their special clienteles. His system was capable of general application, for it dealt with almost the entire range of elements in information control.

Toward the end of this period, Evelyn Hensel of the Pennsylvania State College Library, and formerly with the Historical Records Survey, summarized archival principles and practices as of 1953. For both private papers and public records an accession is kept together as a group, and the "integrity of the original order is [maintained] whenever possible." This view contrasted sharply with that of Randolph Church ten years earlier, when he objected to adherence to provenance.[35]

Neal Harlow, writing later (1955) in *Library Trends*, reinforced Hensel in observing that the trend was to treat manuscripts "as collections or groups centering about a person, family, institution, or subject. . . . The subject classification of manuscript collections is hardly typical or practicable. . . . Within large collections there may be sub-groupings by form, such as personal correspondence, business papers, diaries, speeches, etc., by subject or organizational divisions, or by period or place. Within groups of historical material a chronological arrangement is preferred, since this is the order in which they were produced; they may be sub-arranged alphabetically. For literary manuscripts, and even for some historical material, an alphabetical arrangement by name of writer may be desired; in one instance incoming letters have been so arranged, outgoing letters by date, as a useful compromise between the two possibilities." If there is an existing order, this "might be preserved." No arrangement should be disturbed without "due process of examination."[36]

Harlow observed the relation between the card catalog and other finding aids: "The card catalog . . . selects from the register or inventory only those leads which seem of sufficient importance to justify inclusion by name in a general alphabetical list, [but] most libraries which collect in the recent period find extravagant the making of card entries for any but the most important names. The relationship that Harlow notes is essentially an integrated one, but the catalog is not as fully enriched by added entries as it should or might be because of a fear of overloading the catalog. Also he provided no rational basis for subgrouping.

Library of Congress and the Origins of the NUCMC

Before we turn to Solon J. Buck's reforms, it is worth noting another development in the Library of Congress that was to have far-reaching consequences in
the development of a cataloging code. In 1940 the Library of Congress was
reorganized. The cataloging function remained in the Manuscripts Division,
but responsibility for cataloging policy and rules formulation was transferred
to the Descriptive Cataloging Division of the Processing Department. One
effect of this separation of responsibility was to set in motion a movement
toward establishing a cataloging code. In this work it was assumed that cataloging of manuscripts is usefully separable from their arrangement and the
production of other finding aids. Such a code emerged in 1954 as the rules for
making entries in the *National Union Catalog of Manuscript Collections*
(NUCMC), and as the basis of the *Anglo-American Cataloging Rules* in 1967.
The code represents a technocratic approach to an organic problem, ignoring
the total process whereby intellectual control begins with accessioning, extends through processing, and ends in description.

The Catalog Section of the American Library Association was eager to
work with the Library of Congress on this code. Augustus F. Kuhlman, chair
of the ALA's Archives and Libraries Committee, wrote in his introduction to
Archives and Libraries (1939): "One of the chief obstacles that has prevented
an effective organization of archival and historical manuscript materials has
been the lack of a simple guide or code for cataloging." In Illinois and the
National Archives, he said, "substantial progress has been made in determining what are the essentials in cataloging public archives," and Grace Lee Nute
of the Minnesota Historical Society had "laid the foundation for issuing a
code for cataloging historical manuscript collections." Kuhlman indicated
that the ALA Catalog Section would work jointly with the "archives group"
in developing a code.[37]

Substantial work did not occur until Luther H. Evans succeeded Archibald
MacLeish as librarian of Congress in 1945. Evans had been the first and
highly successful director of the Historical Records Survey before joining the
Library of Congress in 1939. In his work he had learned a great deal about
both historical manuscripts and public archives, having worked with many
key persons in the National Archives particularly. One of these was Solon J.
Buck, who resigned in 1948 from the position of archivist of the United
States. Before joining the National Archives in 1935 as director of publications Buck had been superintendent of the Minnesota Historical Society. He
was a unique person who brought a wide and deep experience with both historical manuscripts and public records archives to his new position as chief of
the Manuscripts Division of the Library of Congress. He was the first person
of such background to have headed the division. All of his predecessors had
been historians, first and foremost. The division had suffered as a result.
Evans had selected Buck for good reason, because he knew of the general
chaos in the division's processing and descriptive program. He asked Buck in

1949 to develop an internal cataloging code that might become the basis for a national one, once accepted by the ALA. Buck replied that developing such a code would require considerable time, because current procedures were outmoded "for controlling the great bulk of modern manuscript material in the custody of this division and of other repositories in the United States." [38]

The first product to emerge was the Library of Congress's *Manual 17* in 1950. The *Manual* commented thus on the current situation in the Library of Congress: "No adequate guide to or inventory of the holdings of the Division exists either in print or in manuscript, and much study, organization, grouping, identification, and description of them . . . will be necessary before an adequate guide can be prepared. . . . The most difficult problem is the identification of the manuscript unit to be described." In the absence of definite rules, "there has developed various Division 'catalogs,' or 'indexes.' . . . The so-called 'general catalog' contains cards for collections, groups, lots, series, and individual documents. . . . [The] 'shelf list' will continue to be the most reliable general guide to the holdings." [39]

As to a new direction, *Manual 17* provided impetus for the establishment of the "manuscript group system." This was analogous to the record group system of the National Archives. A manuscript group could be either "a comprehensive body of personal or institutional papers, [or] a collective group of several distinct bodies of papers pertaining to a given person, family, or institution." Provenance is one factor, and "convenience of their organization for processing, description, and reference activity" is another factor to be considered in establishing the group. Once arranged by manuscript group or subgroup,* a "preliminary inventory" would be prepared for each group or subgroup "supplementing the information on the 'registration sheet.'" Appended to each inventory would be "detailed listings" as necessary. Chronological lists and other finding aids would also be appended to the inventories. This pattern of arrangement and of finding aids was essentially the same as that developed in the National Archives during Buck's tenure as archivist of the United States. [40]

In this context it is worth quoting Walter Rundell, writing in 1970: "Unfortunately, too little relation exists between various types of National Archives finding aids. Each finding aid should explain how it fits into the over-all scheme of Archives guides." [41] This same weakness was carried over into the Library of Congress finding aid system, resulting in its bifurcation during this period of reform, as will be illustrated shortly.

By 1952 another milestone had been reached. Luther Evans announced the completion of the Library of Congress rules for cataloging manuscript materials, making "it possible for the Library to proceed with the development of another cooperative bibliographic project: The National Register of Manu-

---

* *Manual 17* did not define subgroup, but gave only a vague example: "For example, the Abraham Lincoln Collection may be subdivided into (1) The Lincoln Papers, (2) The Herndon-Weik Collection, [etc.]."

script Collections." He reported that work had been in progress since 1946, when the American Historical Association recommended creation of such a register. A Joint Committee on Historical Manuscripts, including representatives from the Society of American Archivists, the American Association for State and Local History, and the Library of Congress had been formed to prepare a proposal for a national register. With completion of the Library of Congress manuscript cataloging rules the committee reported that the Union Catalog Division was already planning for the development and maintenance of such a register for "historical manuscripts." [42] Public archives were not initially included; but they would later be added by the committee, only to be dropped by it finally, thereby eliminating the potential influence of the public records archivist in any future rules modification.

Katharine Brand of the Manuscripts Division reported in two influential articles on the direction of these recent developments in the Library of Congress. Because "recent materials comprise about 90% of L.C.'s manuscript holdings it had been necessary to develop a system of preliminary processing so that researchers could be more readily accommodated." If an existing order is usable and series are discernible, the arrangement is retained. Unorganized papers are usually arranged chronologically, but "sometimes, if the group is substantial enough, an alphabetical arrangement within years or group of years is set up." The processor establishes series, making work cards from which the processor drafts a register. [43]

The register, adapted from the preliminary inventory format of the National Archives, is in either a short or a full-length form. The short register is made for smaller accessions and single items. The full-length register is in five parts: part 1 gives the cataloger information for a main entry and title, physical description, and reference to published descriptions and to indexes or other unpublished guides in the repository; parts 2 to 5 give added entry information and information for scope and contents notes for the catalog card. [44]

The Manuscripts Division stopped short of developing a fully integrated system of finding aids by not pursuing an analysis of the relations between the card catalog, the registers, and other finding aids. In the register only the scope and contents note is used for cataloging, and it is composed in that conceptual framework. Neither the series descriptions nor the frequently more detailed and analytical container lists are systematically mined for cataloging data. Nor are container lists constructed to provide catalog terms or items. If container lists were to be compiled to serve as the cataloging source, the relationship would be an integrated instead of a bifurcated one. The end result for those who modeled their own systems on that of the Library of Congress was the perpetuation and strengthening of a bifurcated finding aid system in other repositories: the card catalog remained independent of the other finding aids, not deliberately integrated with them. Since the Library of Congress's own system was to become the national model, let us turn to another line of development which led to the *National Union Catalog of Manuscript Collections* (NUCMC).

The Historical Records Survey (HRS) had been a center of attention in the minds of archivists and manuscript librarians during its short life. Attesting to its significance was the special attention devoted to it at the annual meetings of the ALA's Archives and Libraries Committee, 1937–40.[45] As noted above, A. F. Kuhlman drew together for each of these meetings leaders from the public archives and historical manuscripts fields. The work of this committee probably represents the closest collaboration that has ever existed between the ALA and archivists. That it was not sustained has been attributed to its being the serious interest of only one ALA leader, Kuhlman himself.[46]

The state surveys conducted by the HRS were undoubtedly the inspiration for the NUCMC. Leaders of the HRS also became actively involved in promoting a national register, seeing the register as a logical culmination to the HRS surveys.[47] The surveys and publication program of the HRS were terminated once the unemployment problem was solved by the nation's entry into World War II.

As acting librarian of Congress, Verner Clapp in October 1948 recommended formation of a Joint Committee on Historical Manuscripts.[48] This joint committee, composed of Buck, Lester J. Cappon as secretary of the Society of American Archivists, Edith Fox of Cornell University, and Howard Peckham and Colton Storm of the Clements Library, organized and formulated a plan "for compiling and publishing a union list of manuscript collections and devising means for putting the plan into effect." Chairman Peckham reported that a union catalog was possible only if the catalog treated manuscripts by collections, not items.[49] Subsequently the committee gained assurance that there would be general library cooperation in submitting reports on collections.[50] In 1949 the librarian of Congress reported that "the Union Catalog Division is now making plans for the development and maintenance of a National Register of Manuscript Collections."[51] The "Register" would emerge as the *National Union Catalog of Manuscript Collections*.

During 1951–52 the National Historical Publications Commission (NHPC), a division of the National Archives and Records Service, indicated its support, although public archives were still excluded from the scope of the register.[52] Then two major events took place at a critical meeting of the Joint Committee at the Library of Congress on June 19, 1952. First, the Manuscripts Division and Descriptive Cataloging Division submitted "Rules for Descriptive Cataloging in the Library of Congress: Manuscripts." The rules were for guidance in preparing printed cards for manuscripts, representing an adaptation of that for books. It was claimed that the "essential information" on the cards was like that prepared by the HRS for its *Guides*. Second, the Joint Committee decided at this meeting that the "Union Catalog should include governmental archival materials on the national and state level as well as historical manuscripts." Philip C. Brooks of the National Archives was accordingly added to the committee's membership.[53]

Katharine Brand volunteered that "these rules will help all participating repositories in the difficult business of cataloging their own holdings."[54] In reviewing the draft rules within the Library of Congress itself, representatives of the Manuscripts Division "were there to say what we thought the rules should provide and the others were there to discover the means for effecting our purposes in accordance with the *A.L.A. Cataloging Rules* and the *Rules for Descriptive Cataloging in the Library of Congress.*" The entries that result "should be capable of incorporation into a general library catalog."[55] Howard Peckham, former head of the committee, frankly conceded that librarians would cooperate only if the card catalog format was retained. He looked for "widespread imitation of the proposed register entry [i.e., collection-level description] in local cataloging because the form will not challenge the capacity or the time of harried curators."[56] David C. Mearns, Buck's successor as chief of the Manuscripts Division, added that "the rules will be capable of adoption by repositories generally" and "procedures for descriptive cataloging will be standardized throughout the United States" once they are finally accepted by the American Library Association.[57]

In all of this work the Library of Congress was acting as the surrogate of the American Library Association. As viewed by the Joint Committee and by the Library of Congress's own Committee on Manuscripts, the need to catalog entries and to incorporate them in the general public catalog required the ALA's approval. Without its imprimatur, cooperation from the general library community would not be forthcoming. Yet this fixation on developing a cataloging code had had a relatively long history within both the Library of Congress and the American Library Association, dating back to the late 1930s. What resulted was a general acceptance of the card catalog and of traditional cataloging as the necessary operational base, without first examining the relation between that process and other internal finding aids. By giving ultimate authority to the ALA, cataloging policy was even further removed from the workplace, where policy had to be applied.

The nearest the Library of Congress came to examining its finding aid system was a pilot project set up in February 1955 to test the data sheet preparation for NUCMC entries. It needed testing. Using "The MSS. Division's registers, press releases, the *Information Bulletin* and the old handbooks," an attempt at cataloging was made. Information from these sources proved insufficient; consequently the "question was raised, whether the scope note could not be prepared by the MSS. Division as part of the register. . . . It was also suggested that the data sheet . . . might be prepared by the MSS. Division at the time a new collection is being organized, and cards edited for printing by the Descriptive Cataloging Division." In assigning subject headings, it was decided to have the same person do the descriptive and subject cataloging instead of relying on the scope note or going over the same material as the descriptive cataloger: "The problems of the descriptive and subject catalogers *would be solved to a large extent if the register, prepared by specialists in the

---

*Descriptive cataloging is oriented to developing a main entry. Subject cataloging is for the purpose of developing subject added entries.

MSS. Division, contained the data for the scope note and for the subject entries." [58] This was an emphatic example of the organic character establishing control. Policy formulation, in being isolated from the workplace, had institutionalized a mere technique—cataloging—that acted as the central control of the system.

The Committee on Manuscripts Cataloging, at its May 24 and May 26, 1955, meetings, addressed another highly significant issue raised by the Manuscripts Division that again underscores the integral feature of intellectual controls. This issue concerned an index. The inclusion of subject headings in the NUCMC had not yet been determined; however, both a card and book format had been tentatively agreed to. Members of the Manuscripts Division "felt that a name and subject index to a book catalog" would be better than filing subject cards in the Library of Congress's public catalog, because entries would not have to conform to cataloging rules and more entries could be included. Implicit in this preference by the Manuscripts Division is the possible development of the index for the Manuscripts Division itself as an alternative to the card catalog.

This experience could have inspired the Library of Congress to examine its own finding aid system—the relationships of its parts and the administrative organization that dealt with it. There is no apparent evidence that such self-examination ever occurred, despite this exposure to developing NUCMC rules and to the well-known reforms that had occurred in the National Archives in the early 1940s, leading that institution to abolish its divisions of cataloging and classification. [59]

In summary, there was lacking at the Library of Congress a clear recognition that in gaining control of manuscript collections one must start with the first step, accessioning, and conclude with describing—that is, developing finding aids. In other words, cataloging is only one step in a larger process, and the catalog product might be only one finding aid among many or it might be made to serve as the means of integrating all such aids: registers, calendars, shelf lists, special lists, and guides. If the latter choice is made, then cataloging policy must integrate cataloging with all other finding aids. The main task, as Walter Rundell indicated in his analysis of finding aids in the National Archives, is to provide some one point of access to the network of finding aids. [60]

In retrospect, it appears that the card catalog and traditional cataloging should have been challenged in the course of Buck's reforms, but vested interest in the cataloging process was so entrenched that it was like a conditioned reflex. This mental set was so unaccommodating that it led directly to the formulation of international standards a decade later in the form of the AACR. While praiseworthy for cataloging publications, these standards have not been realistically adapted to manuscript cataloging.

Be that as it may, the decision of the Joint Committee at its June 19, 1952, meeting to include public records in the NUCMC inspired the first strong dissent to the draft rules. Dissenting was Joint Committee member Philip C.

Brooks of the National Archives and Records Service (NARS). Brooks had been joined in dissent from within the NARS by Herman F. Kahn, director of the Franklin D. Roosevelt Presidential Library.

Brooks wrote to Lucile M. Morsch, chair of Library of Congress's Committee on Manuscripts Cataloging and head of its Descriptive Cataloging Division, expressing concern that the rules would be applied "as a guide to internal cataloging procedures in some depositories," and these depositories will need special instructions in cataloging government archives.[61] Kahn, however, more forcefully expressed the general fear that the rules would be applied to all archival/manuscript materials as internal guidelines within each repository.[62] From an examination of the minutes of the Committee on Manuscripts Cataloging, there is no evidence that Kahn's reservations were ever communicated, although Brooks's were handled as a mere technicality that could be covered by the rules. In this debate about NUCMC rules, consideration of the user was never a serious factor. Convenience to catalogers seems to have been foremost in the minds of the propagators of the NUCMC.

Further discussion of the NUCMC will follow in a separate section covering the period of its implementation, 1959 to the present. Changes within the Library of Congress will be described in chapter 6 on automated systems.

In the historical manuscripts field, there was not only the development of the NUCMC rules during this period but also a summation of the library orientation, by Dorothy V. Martin. She had apprenticed at the Minnesota Historical Society, joined the National Archives Cataloging Division in the late 1930s, and transferred later to the Detroit Public Library, where she worked on cataloging the Burton Collection. She also lectured at American University in the courses conducted by Ernst Posner. Writing in 1948 about books for use in cataloging manuscripts she recommended Grace Lee Nute's most highly, and commented that John C. Fitzpatrick's adherence to strict chronology is "still worthy of careful consideration."[63]

Martin, in 1955, saw a key role for the catalog "as a key to the collections as a whole, and to the description of the items composing it . . . , to the more important names, and subjects covered." The first step in the course of preliminary sorting was to define the "catalogable unit." She shared with Nute an ambivalence toward what constituted a unit, but she defined it more precisely than Nute, for whom the "box" was the unit. For Martin it was a "collection of mutually related items," a good rule of thumb for identifying series. But her precision slipped when she said that the unit "is not necessarily identical with the accession . . . ; in fact, an accession had better, for cataloging purposes, be broken up," because the order of private papers is "often more likely to be accidental than designed." Because of their variety, private papers and "the interests represented [in the accession] will be better described as several smaller collections." In her discussion she followed the standard practice in the arrangement of private papers and confused series with subgroups, a failure also of Schellenberg and others, as we shall see. Cataloging concludes the process of establishing controls, and is done from "copious notes" taken during the processing stage. In addition to making entries for "significant correspondents" and "particular subjects," attention should be called "to a single important item, group or type of manuscript included." Analytical entries are made for selected items or clusters. Because she did not use series in a precise way, she introduced a randomness into the cataloging process. Reinforcing this random tendency was the dependence on copious content notes instead of the actual arrangement of the papers in their "unit" sequence.[64] In other words, she did not think yet in terms of record levels, keying of controls to specific levels, and relying on arrangement by provenance to record basic information for cataloging. Although exposed to this method through her experience with the National Archives, where the record levels concept was being developed, she clearly believed it to be not applicable to private papers.

In the following chapter, we will see that this attitude toward the applicability of public archives principles to manuscript collections changed radically. The period is marked by the convergence of practices at major manuscript repositories with those of public records archives. Running counter to this tendency, but declining in influence, is the historical manuscripts tradition. With the ongoing publication of the NUCMC volumes and the formalization of international cataloging rules in the form of the *Anglo-American Cataloguing Rules*, this tradition is strengthened among its adherents, although the shunning of these rules by the SAA leadership indicates that these adherents are not part of the archival mainstream.* To reflect the more systematic writing of the period and the concurrent convergence and polarization of the two traditions, considerably more detailed analysis is required. It is a watershed period.

---

*An SAA president in the mid-1970s declined an invitation to join in the revision of the first edition of *The Anglo-American Cataloging Rules*. The author was a member of the SAA Council at that time and knows of no discussion about the invitation; he would have srongly supported its acceptance.

4

Schellenberg and the Merging of the Public Archives and Historical Manuscripts Traditions, 1956–79

TWILIGHT OF THE HISTORICAL MANUSCRIPTS TRADITION

During this period, Lester J. Cappon redefined the term "historical manuscripts." Cumulative changes in collecting policies forced this redefinition. Cappon began the process of revision in an illuminating article in 1956.[1] T. R. Schellenberg responded dramatically to Cappon's lead, as witness the different treatment given by him to "historical manuscripts" in *Modern Archives* (1956) and *The Management of Archives* (1965).[2] Because he became the most influential writer on archival management during the period, his metamorphosis will be examined in detail, for it reflects changes that occurred in the field generally. Before examining his writings, however, it is well to outline those of others early in the period.

Marking the progress then being made is the January 1957 issue of *Library Trends* devoted to "Manuscripts and Archives." On the topic of arrangement and description is a summary by Paul S. Dunkin of the Folger Shakespeare Library. He said that cataloging of manuscripts had moved "steadily toward standardization and simplification with accent on the catalog as a finding list." The items described "have meaning as a group" rather than as individual items. This marks a clearer recognition of the record series as the main catalogable unit, and the relevance of collective description to the cataloging of aggregates of items and file units. Dunkin also praised Howard Peckham's association of people with subjects and events and the Clements Library's generous provision of "entries for people."[3]

In the same issue of *Library Trends* Robert W. Lovett, curator of the Baker Library's business manuscripts collection, distinguished nongovernmental archives from historical manuscripts on the basis of their "bulk," "the importance of series," weeding as a major requirement, recent nature of much of the materials, and their more varied forms. Lovett recommended that provenance be the basis of classification, that original order be accepted if at all possible, but that in arranging disorderly files a chronological order should be only one of a range of options. The latter approach represented a clean break with tradition. Like Dunkin, he recognized series as the basic element for arrangement within any collection. For a large collection "the inventory or descriptive list in sheet form, such as is used in the National Archives and similar large institutions, become invaluable." The curator also should "prepare an index listing" of the most important names and places for the time when a general guide is published.[4] Such an index could have displaced the card catalog if it had been kept current and had been publicly accessible; however, neither Lovett nor anyone else made this observation in the 1950s.

A consensus seemed to be jelling. Cappon, in the same issue of *Library Trends*, said that procedures used eighteen years earlier in the Historical Records Survey to format and collate entries "became uniform throughout the H.R.S. and *subsequently have been generally adopted*" (italics mine).[5]

Cappon, in 1956, had written the article critiquing the concept of historical manuscripts.[6] It represents one of those significant reflective pauses that rarely are taken by those in a field that has concentrated on day-to-day practice, and in which practitioners have ignored the theoretical implications of practices and a perception of their historical drift. Cappon, one of the most widely experienced archivists, observed that manuscript collecting had taken the form of acquiring private papers and records that were no longer to be usefully differentiated from public archives. In sharing with public archives the feature of having integral records with series characteristics, private papers and records were also amenable to archival treatment. Continual use of the term "historical manuscripts" he believed to be misleading. In citing Cappon's article, Philip C. Brooks commented in 1969 that the term "has resulted in much confusion."[7] Brooks traced its probable origin to the attempt to distinguish historical manuscripts from "literary" manuscripts. In his book he substituted the term "private papers." I would add that the term is traceable also to the period when item collecting and collecting of prestigious papers were more typical; such papers usually lacked organic characteristics and were typically cataloged, indexed, and calendared as items, not submerged in a collective description entry. Ernst Posner, writing in 1964, remarked that the term "historical manuscripts" was being superseded by the term "private papers."[8]

CATALYST FOR CHANGE: T. R. SCHELLENBERG

Let us turn to the metamorphosis of Theodore R. Schellenberg.* In 1954 Schellenberg went to Australia and New Zealand as a Fulbright lecturer. His

*Born and educated in Kansas, Schellenberg had earned a Ph.D. in history at the University of Pennsylvania in 1934, whereupon he joined the staff of the Joint Com-

Modern Archives resulted from those lectures as well as from the earlier staff papers quoted in chapter 3. From 1956 to 1961 he lectured at American University, where since 1945 the National Archives had joined with the Library of Congress and the Maryland Hall of Records in giving courses on archival and records administration. He directed institutes there in 1957 and 1958, and in 1960 at the University of Texas. This teaching experience required that he expand his expertise and background to cover private papers and records. Before exposure to this broader teaching responsibility, he had completed his *Modern Archives* in September 1955.

In *Modern Archives*, Schellenberg's presentation of archival theory and practice in the public archives field was somewhat ahead of others, because no one who wrote on the subject demonstrated a firm grasp of the concept of a record level hierarchy and all that it entailed in intellectual control. In his treatment of private papers and records Schellenberg betrayed some lag behind Cappon in his view of private papers having integral characteristics. It is to his treatment of private papers and records that the following critique is addressed.

In distinguishing between manuscript holdings of libraries and archives, Schellenberg accepted the notion that manuscripts show a "more personal contact" with the subject, because they are "more likely to reflect natural human prejudices and feelings . . . and may present a more concentrated source of colourful data." Furthermore, "while archives grow out of some regular functional activity, historical manuscripts, in contrast, are usually the product of a spontaneous expression of thought or feeling. They are thus ordinarily created in a haphazard, and not in a systematic manner." He was willing to allow some deviation from this concept of historical manuscripts: when they are "part of the documentation of an organized activity—as, for example, when love letters are introduced as evidence in divorce proceedings—they also may be considered to be archives." He had not yet come abreast of Cappon in viewing historical manuscripts as being archival in character, independently of their personal content, just as long as they were integral in character. It should be noted that Schellenberg's belief in the uniquely personal element in manuscript collections would persist, unlike some of his other early attitudes. This deep reservation about the personal element also led him to deny a role for proper names as a mode of subject access. He was apparently more comfortable with the personal anonymity of institutional archives. For him personal names were of importance primarily to genealogists, antiquarians, and to those using literary manuscripts.[9]

As to the archival character of modern manuscripts, contrast the quotations

---

mittee of the American Council of Learned Societies and Social Science Research Council. In 1935 he became associate director of the Survey of Federal Records of the WPA. This led him into an illustrious career in the National Archives, culminating in the positions of director of the National Archives Division in the early 1950s and finally as assistant archivist for records appraisal. He retired in 1963 to concentrate on teaching and writing.

above from *Modern Archives* with the opening paragraph of his draft manual produced in 1961: "This book relates to the description of both private and public records. It is written in the belief that descriptive techniques that are applied to public records may also be applied, with some modification, to private records, and that they are particularly applicable to manuscript collections of recent origin, many of which have the organic character of archival groups." Note the reference to private "records," not "papers," illustrating a hesitancy to consider papers also under the term "archival." [10]

Between the appearance of *Modern Archives* and this draft manual he had taught, prepared syllabus items for courses sponsored by the NARS, and written some articles. All of this would be brought together in 1965 in *The Management of Archives*.

One of the syllabus items was "Arrangement of Private Papers." In it Schellenberg recommended that "large collections" of private papers that reflect "extended activity" be "broken down into series in the same way as an archival group." These series would be established on the basis of form or physical type (pp. 3, 9–11). [11] In proceeding directly to series formation he saw no need to apply the public archival practice of subgrouping series first. For example: "Most collections of personal papers are divisible into two groups: one relating to purely personal or family affairs and another the activity for which the person . . . became noteworthy. These groups may be regarded as series" (p. 11). [12] If he had rigorously defined subgrouping to apply only to record origins, Schellenberg would probably have recommended subgrouping those series which were generated from a particular line of activity. But in allowing, as he did in 1951 in *Staff Information Paper* no. 18, for subgrouping also on the basis of function and subject matter as well as administrative hierarchy, he provided no consistent basis for subgrouping even public records. If he had limited its application to hierarchy, subgroups would then be consistently formed on the basis of record-generating source; and when applied to personal papers, subgrouping would be on the basis of the agency for whom the person acted. Series would then be placed under the name of the agency for whom the person acted. By failing to make this recommendation (and extending its application to family papers)* series would thereby be formed without regard to their parentage and result in the dispersal of subgroups among general series. [13] By 1965, when *The Management of Archives* was published, he clearly limited the concept of subgrouping to the "records created by an organizational subdivision of the public agency that created an archival group" (p. xvi). [14] But he failed to see that it was similarly applicable to private papers having integral record characteristics.

---

*The family papers that often accompany an acquisition of personal papers may be subgrouped. For letters, grouping should be on the basis of recipient; diaries, according to their author; and other items, on the basis of other clues that indicate their origin. Lucile Kane recommended this practice in her *Guide to the Care and Administration of Manuscripts*, which will be reviewed later in this chapter.

The "personal" element about private papers is what deflected Schellenberg from applying the public archival practice of subgrouping; it also affected his treatment of other problems associated with manuscript collections. His descriptive program for personal papers in manuscript collections reflects the influence of the "personal" factor in his thinking.

While recommending that each accession be described according to public archival practice, in progressively greater detail, he nevertheless countered this advice by urging that the descriptive program should be adapted "to facilitate the particular uses to which particular collections of papers may be put." Consequently, "different types of finding aids are needed for different classes of researcher," one kind for genealogists, for example, and another for antiquarians, and another for scholarly researchers.[15] Thus, in trying to accommodate the idiosyncratic nature of personal papers to management by public archival procedures he became diverted from developing a potentially integrated descriptive program of the type that he had been instrumental in establishing in the National Archives.* Instead of describing papers first in terms of their actual serial management he would proceed initially to a content analysis of items and file units that make up series, keying the descriptive tool to the main type of user who is anticipated. Fragmentation of the descriptive program is the result. For example, he recommended that catalog cards be used "whenever it is desirable (1) to identify specific subjects . . . such as persons, places, things, topics, and the like, and (2) to identify specific or single record items." However, a page form should be used "whenever it is desirable to describe such papers collectively."[16]

Schellenberg also saw an independent role for indexes. He viewed indexes as easy to construct, since records need only be "identified" and "not described" in them. They are best adapted for subject references and personal names. He recommended a "combined" personal name index; also one for places. Topical subject indexes should have a "limited objective" because of the "unconscionable" expense in preparing them.[17]

In line with all of his contemporaries he accepted the idea that each kind of finding aid served a different purpose, and he found it unnecessary to integrate them in a single system. The potential role that a union catalog or "combined" indexes could perform as integrative tools did not loom forcefully enough in his thinking to advance him beyond his contemporaries in this respect.

As to *The Management of Archives* in general, it is unique in that it addresses problems in the arrangement and description of both public/corporate

* Although the National Archives had a program for integrating its finding aids system, its development was thwarted by the limited role of the catalog. Only "final" inventories" were to be cataloged, and since none were ever produced, there was no catalog. Potentially the catalog would have performed an integrative function by providing a single access point to all final inventories. The NARS A–1 automated system is an attempt to perform this function.

archives and manuscript collections. Schellenberg's was the first such attempt, stemming from his conviction that the principles and techniques of the public archivist were equally applicable, with some modification, "especially to private material of recent origin." As such, the volume attempted to relate controls to specific record levels in each of these archival subfields. That he only partly succeeded is less important than the stimulation he gave to others in expanding on his initial effort. He was more comfortable with the younger (and some of the middle) generation of archivists and curators than he was with his own. That his views made sense to a growing number in the field is testimony of the ultimate validity of the path he trod, often very much alone.

Since Schellenberg considered the archival methodology to be a "compound of the ideas of librarians, historians, and archivists" (p. 59), he first examined the development of library methodology. He then contrasted progressive librarianship with the laggard development of the archival profession and its methodology. Since his discussion was topically arranged, the historical origins of various practices, concepts, and their subsequent elaboration into principles were obscured. Such was the fate of the series concept (pp. 34–35). He noted, for example, that in the nineteenth century some private collectors and historical societies arranged their integral collections by series, as a purely empirical method, but he did not trace its subsequent development as it emerged under Norton's guidance. We have seen how her classification and cataloging committee of the SAA came to recognize the series as the focal "catalogable unit."

One does, however, get a general sense of the influence of librarianship on the archival field and that the latter did not become really differentiated from librarianship until after the establishment of the National Archives in 1934. Once having differentiated library and archival methodology, Schellenberg next concerned himself with recent changes in library management of manuscript collections. Among those changes, as described earlier, had been agreement about provenance, about record series constituting the main catalogable unit, and about the utility of the inventory, both as a supplement to the card catalog and as the best device for describing integral accessions having series characteristics.

In stressing this growing consensus, he advised: "Series within a manuscript collection are similar in character to those in an archival group" (p. 98). His contention that series in a manuscript accession should be kept intact for their value as documentation is similar to the justification for establishing series in an archival record group, "as a record of the activities to which they pertain" (p. 99). More pointedly, in his chapter "Arrangement of Manuscript Collections," he contended: "Unless series are established, it is necessary to deal with such collections on an item-by-item basis. Recent papers must be described collectively if they are to be described at all, and they can be described collectively by aggregations of items only if units of collective description, i.e., series, are established" (p. 182). Tolerantly, he contended that the principle of original order as applied to manuscript collections need not be as devoutly followed by manuscript curators as by public records archivists unless the papers are "the product of organic or extended activity." He advised that "usability" of the original order should be the test.

Schellenberg is ambiguous in his overall treatment, and this is attributable I believe to his handling of the record level hierarchy problem. His discussion leads the reader to seek a uniform level of control for all accessions in a repository, aiming for example for series level control of every accession regardless of its informational value (this was the National Archives objective in the 1940s). If, however, each accession is considered on its own merits, and if there is recognition that not all subgroups and series deserve elaboration, a different view of the record level hierarchy will obtain—one not entertained by Schellenberg. Given his presupposition, the effect is to give precedence to forms of content analysis before first recording and then extracting data by the objective method inherent in provenancially given data.

Although there are weaknesses in his writings, he had fewer than other writers. Fortunately for the field Schellenberg shared his views in abundant detail. He did not avoid controversy, he courted it—and imparted this attitude to some others. Without it there probably would have been even less progress than we have seen.

In one of his last articles, "A Nationwide System of Controlling Historical Manuscripts in the United States," [18] Schellenberg introduced a relatively novel idea for an archivist: broad topical subject headings that can be developed for only the main fields of human activity. Such headings could be developed first "to cover the holdings of most manuscript repositories [and later] a more comprehensive list should be compiled for a nationwide system." His list consists of twelve major headings: agriculture, business, education, fine arts, foreign affairs, government and politics, labor, military affairs, religion, science, social affairs, and travel and exploration. For him, this is the only practical course to follow, "for it is possible easily to identify the fields of activity that result in the production of collections; it is very difficult to identify the innumerable subjects to which they relate." He recognized, here, that the problem of topical subject access is the central problem of archival access generally. He also recognized it as the most expensive as well as the least reliable, because of its inherent subjectivity.

Lacking in his system was the keying of subject headings to specific record levels, and moving progressively, in terms of specificity, from the more general level to the more specific. That the archival field is only now addressing this problem in a general way attests to Schellenberg's insight. Librarianship/information sciences can provide the best guidance in dealing with this problem, but access to different hierarchical levels, progressively, is essential to a disciplined approach.

AMALGAMATION OF ARCHIVAL MODE WITH HISTORICAL MANUSCRIPTS
TRADITION, 1960–66

Schellenberg's earlier writings for the National Archives had already influenced public and institutional archival practices before *The Management of Archives* was published in 1965. Various programs at the National Archives generally served as models elsewhere. Its records management program was the basis for those in state governments and in some private organizations. Also, its finding aids system was imitated by the Library of Congress and other major manuscript repositories where papers and records of recent origin were common. By cribbing from the archival mode to deal with such collections they had created an amalgam that diluted the historical manuscripts tradition which all of them had inherited. The drift to a more purely archival mode is apparent in the writings to be examined. Those whose publications are selected for review are Lucile M. Kane, Ruth B. Bordin and Robert M. Warner, Carolyn A. Wallace, and Robert L. Brubaker.

It is significant that all the writers in this group wrote from an institutional base that provided them with a perspective that harmonized with the one expressed by Lester J. Cappon in his article on historical manuscripts as archives. They and their respective institutions had been heavily engaged in collecting twentieth-century papers that bore little resemblance to the category of material connoted by the term "historical manuscripts." Each had also been familiar with changes that had occurred in the National Archives and the Library of Congress, and had been influenced by those institutions.

First in this group is Lucile M. Kane,* writing from her position as curator of manuscripts of the Minnesota Historical Society. Her *Guide*,[19] produced for the American Association for State and Local History, systematically takes the reader successively from accessioning, appraisal, and preservation to cataloging. The flow of work is crystal clear; no cataloging takes place while arranging is in process. After accessioning, one must first respect the "integrity, or basic structure, of the collection, and [one must have] consideration for those who will use the materials" (p. 337). "In deciding upon the organization of a group of papers, the first point to determine is whether the group contains more than one catalogable unit. If two or more units are discovered, they may be treated as separate collections or as distinct sections within a collection, depending upon the relationship of one unit to another" (p. 340). In the Weyerhaeuser Company records, twenty-five such units were easily identified, one for each distinct subsidiary. The same principle was applied to the Gilman Papers. They contained two units "with subunits so closely related

---

*Lucile M. Kane had succeeded Grace Lee Nute in 1948 and had written the best historical account of manuscript collecting in the United States for Hesseltine and McNeil's *In Support of Clio* as well as updating the published guide to the society's collection in 1955. She closed out her archival career as state archivist in 1979. She is now joining in a cooperative history of Minnesota, specializing in the Progressive period.

that they are treated as distinct sections within one collection" (p. 341). The Gilman Papers were subgrouped in the second unit on the basis of the Gilman family papers collected by her and on the basis of the separate corporate activities conducted by Mrs. Gilman (pp. 344–46). While not enunciating it as a general principle, Kane had done in practice what Schellenberg hesitated to do: establish subgroups in personal/family papers (see also pp. 18 and 23 of the 1966 edition). Because she did not state this practice as a principle, those who would follow her recommendation would do so by imitation, but not consistently. Consistency would follow only when the principle was recognized. When it was not recognized by practitioners, they would confuse series with subgroups. For her in practice the subgroup first and then the series within are the basic catalogable units.

As to arrangement within the unit, a chronological order is only one of a range of options. An alternative is the "alphabetical-by-author arrangement" (p. 343), following the method developed at the Bancroft Library.[20] But in a "large" collection Kane advised retention of any existing series. She strongly opposed imposition of "subject-matter filing" on an unorganized collection (p. 343). An unorganized collection, she recommended, is best arranged according to document type, such as deeds, contracts, and general correspondence.

"Cataloging is the final step in processing," she wrote (p. 371). "In large collections . . . it is necessary to stress group description and general expression of subject matter rather than individual item cataloging" (p. 374). In developing a "compromise" between these two methods, group and item cataloging, she incorporated the following elements: (1) For group description a register or inventory is used. (2) A "main" or "collection" card and added entries are made and filed in a dictionary catalog. (3) "Special catalogs, indices, calendars, and shelf-lists" are prepared to "provide detailed information on particularly important manuscripts, or to fill a special or administrative requirement."

In gathering information to prepare the register and catalog, the processor takes content notes for items on cards, recording author names and subject matter. These are for entering in the catalog. For series and containers, content notes are recorded on sheets of paper, to be incorporated into the register (pp. 375–76). These two procedures are consistent with Schellenberg's views, as noted above. In presenting a bifurcated finding aid system, Kane does so in clearer terms than any other writer. Like Schellenberg, she also insisted that arrangement and description are inseparable stages of a single process, that of establishing intellectual controls.

Another major contribution toward amalgamation of archival and library principles and practices was that of Ruth B. Bordin and Robert M. Warner* in

---

*Bordin had been curator of manuscripts since 1961, while Warner was assistant director of the Michigan Historical Collections. Warner became the SAA's first executive director, later its president, and is now archivist of the United States.

their *Modern Manuscript Library*.[21] The authors were associated with the Michigan Historical Collections at the University of Michigan. The collection, born in 1935, combined records of the university and state historical materials. Its organization also benefited from the work of the Historical Records Survey. Like Kane, Bordin and Warner take the reader step by step in a workflow sequence, beginning with collecting and continuing through processing, preparation of finding aids, administration, and reference services.

Bordin and Warner first distinguish between archival management and "manuscript librarianship." The former primarily serves its agency, while a manuscript library serves the public at large, especially scholars. They concede, however, that because many manuscript materials are akin to archives, "the archivists' techniques will prove of value" (p. 7).

Like Kane, they suggest that "cataloging units" will become apparent during the preliminary sorting and they subgroup materials first in order to establish the units and then by arranging series within each subgroup: "Do not artificially create separate cataloging units. Instead, keep papers from a single source together whenever possible" (p. 40). Although the last sentence was meant to apply to the individual accession as a whole, it could have been stretched by them to cover subgroups of a corporate body's records, inasmuch as their subgrouping seems to have been done largely on that basis. For example, institutional or business records "may fall into broad categories reflecting the agencies creating them such as: executive board, committees. . . . Within these will come types of records" (p. 44). Unlike Kane, they did not apply subgrouping to personal papers, only to corporate records. But like Kane, they had not elevated the practice of subgrouping to the level of a concept that would lead to consistency when applied.

In addition to respecting provenance, Bordin and Warner advised retention of an original order if one had been preserved. For unorganized papers they preferred the chronological ordering within series: "No system of arranging personal papers other than the chronological one comes as close to life as it is experienced" (p. 44). When the original order is retained, the "manuscript group" should be described in an inventory (p. 45). "The inventory is almost the only manageable finding aid for the large collection of twenty-five to a thousand or more linear feet" (p. 54). But there are other finding aids to suit different kinds of accessions and user needs: calendars, the general catalog, supplemented by shelf lists and indexes. "The manuscript library with a great preponderance of personal papers will choose between the general catalog and inventory or a combination of both" (p. 51). "The catalog will need to be supplemented by calendars or inventories to certain collections, but it is the only manageable scheme for retaining complete control over a large number of collections" (p. 55). They recommended a bifurcated system of finding aids, as a practical matter. Further illustration of this bifurcation is found in their attitude toward indexes that are made for each inventory. They cited as a "disadvantage" the fact that "each index to each collection must be consulted individually" (p. 54). It apparently did not occur to them that these index en-

tries might be systematically cumulated or incorporated into the general catalog as name and subject added entries. If they had done so, the result would
have been a single integrated system, and it would only have required recognition to have been elevated to the level of a concept for guidance in general
practice.

In cataloging, library methodology remained unaffected by archival principles and practices. "After a collection is sorted, arranged, and boxed it should
be read" by a staff member with an appropriate subject background. Content
notes should be taken on a selected-item basis: subjects, place names, and
proper names as subjects. A "selected list of correspondents" is "perhaps"
most important, "noting the dates and sometimes the subject of individual
letters when the subject occurs rarely." The usefulness of the resulting name
index is dependent "on the cataloger's wide acquaintance with the names that
merit mention" (pp. 55–56). As can be seen, a certain randomness and subjectivity was introduced by the authors at the stage of cataloging. This resulted from not restricting their content analysis to a particular record level,
and because of their item orientation. Indeed, no attempt was made to key
controls to record levels, nor to move progressively toward more detailed
analysis. The kind of content analysis recommended by Kane and by Bordin
and Warner is the heart of the methods recommended by Robert S. Gordon
and Kenneth W. Duckett, as we shall see in the next chapter.

Bordin and Warner conceived of the catalog as being "no more than a master name and subject index to all the library's holdings" (p. 61). If they had
carried through from this observation, they might well have chosen to aban-
don the card catalog in favor of cumulative indexes (and with it traditional
cataloging itself), because they would probably have concluded that they
should index the inventories to circumvent the expense of cataloging items
and clusters of related items.

Another variant of an amalgamated system is that of the University of
North Carolina Library, described by Carolyn Andrews Wallace, curator of its
manuscripts department.[22] Its Southern Historical Collection was established
in 1930 from a nucleus of material acquired from the North Carolina Historical Society and from the materials collected by J. G. deRoulhac Hamilton in
the 1920s. During the 1930s the collection received the attention of the Historical Records Survey, benefitting it early in its career from new archival techniques that emerged from that program. In 1943 one of its new staff members,
Anna B. Allan, having attended the first archival institute given by Ernst
Posner at American University, introduced "many improvements" in processing, organization, and description (pp. 431–32). Following provenance each
"unit is given the name of its creator and is filed as a separate group within the
Collection." After accessioning, "general loose papers of each group are arranged in chronological order, with undated material filed alphabetically by
name of writer at the end. Large groups containing a variety of different types
of materials may be divided into several chronological series" (p. 433). It is
not clear that "different types" refers to physical type such as diaries, corre-

spondence, deeds, minutes, and so forth, but we can assume that it was meant as a nontechnical substitute for "series."

"Reference aids" provide access to the collection. The key element in the finding aid system is the "descriptive survey." It is analogous to the register or inventory. In it "a chronological analysis shows the more important individuals, places, and activities. . . . An effort is made to point out any unusual items that the reader would not normally expect to find within the group" (p. 434).

From this inventory and accession records other finding aids are prepared. One of these is the "master catalog," a main entry or collection card. Another is a "geographical file" which "indexes the Collection according to geographical areas." A "chronological file," divided into eight periods, provides a different route of access. Another file is an "index to proper names." Still another file is a subject index using a relatively small number of selected subject headings: "Subdividing of headings and more precise content descriptions will probably be taken whenever feasible, and these should result in a more useful subject index" (pp. 434–35). In essence, the system approximates a single integrated one in which the descriptive survey is indexed to provide different routes of access to the survey itself and from there to the material. But it is not explicit in establishing controls that are keyed to different record levels. No recognition, in fact, is given to record levels.

Robert L. Brubaker's* writings represent the view of a very knowledgeable, interested observer, rather than that of an active practitioner. Responses to a questionnaire led Brubaker to conclude in 1964 that "most libraries [have devised] methods of group description for most manuscript collections." In addition, owing to the limitations of the card catalog, "libraries have also developed various types of more detailed guides to individual collections," usually a "register or inventory." He commented that many such systems were in existence "long before 1954," when the NUCMC cataloging rules were agreed on. Briefly, he noted the prevalence of a bifurcated system in most large manuscript libraries, one that combined modifications of both library and archival methods.[23]

Brubaker delivered an important paper at the 1965 annual meeting of the Society of American Archivists. Schellenberg's *Management of Archives* was the focus of the session, which included as panelists Ruth B. Bordin and Schellenberg himself. Brubaker noted perceptively: "Early archivists, in effect, assumed that manuscripts were hopelessly lost to the librarians, and as part of their battle to prevent the same thing from happening to archives they emphasized the differences between historical manuscripts and archives" ("Archival Principles," p. 507). We have already seen that Gaillard Hunt, of the Library of Congress, conceded these differences in 1910 and how that concession contributed to the separation of public archives and historical manu-

---

*At the time, Brubaker was curator of manuscripts of the Illinois State Historical Library. He is now director of the library of the Chicago Historical Society.

scripts. Once separated, each camp reinforced its exclusiveness to the detriment of both until Schellenberg brought them together in a modern context in the late 1950s and early 1960s.

Brubaker noted the various forms of group description employed by librarians, such as collection descriptions (main entries) and added entries for a group of letters by a single correspondent. He drew special attention to the potentiality of a "comprehensive index to the holdings of an institution or a nation, [particularly] for manuscript collections (a) [because they] generally have less unity than archival groups, (b) there are generally many more manuscript collections in a major manuscript depository than there are record groups in an archival institution, and (c) a sizable proportion of manuscript collections consists of the papers of individuals or families who were relatively obscure but who corresponded with someone of importance or whose records contain information of value on various activities, localities, historical developments, or other subjects" (p. 511). He cited as examples of comprehensive indexing programs the one at the University of Washington Libraries and the beginning of one on a test basis at the Library of Congress (1965). The latter was the experimental SPINDEX computer program which will be discussed in chapter 6.

While commending *The Management of Archives* as a "remarkable achievement," Brubaker criticized Schellenberg's comparative indifference to the control of "major correspondents." This is a valid criticism and has already been commented on. But Brubaker was mistaken in judging Schellenberg as regressive for advocating the use of a limited number of broad subject headings. Instead of being "regressive," the idea marked a beginning of a more systematic attempt to provide better subject access to archives. Schellenberg's shortcoming was in not relating subject references to specific record levels, and in not recognizing the potential need for a different vocabulary for each level.

ASCENDANCY OF THE ARCHIVAL MODE

Another line of development extends the Schellenberg approach, wholly within the archival mode. It leads to the 1978 consensus of the SAA's Finding Aids Committee, wherein it was decided that the inventory should be the basic finding aid and that indexes to inventories should be created to afford access from a single point in the system.[24] Among those contributing to this result were Oliver W. Holmes, Frank B. Evans, David B. Gracy II, and the author.

Schellenberg's pioneering work pointed both manuscript librarians and archivists away from traditional methods for handling modern manuscript collections and institutional archives. In the National Archives the concept of different record levels underwent refinement, emerging for wider public consumption in 1964 in Oliver Wendell Holmes's influential article.[25] Mario D. Fenyo in 1966 published a critique of the record group concept,[26] tracing its origins and subsequent development. In this context, Frank B. Evans's article (1966) on the arrangement of archives is particularly valuable for its larger historical perspective and for its detailed examination of the changes that had occurred in the National Archives revolving around the record group concept.[27]

While practical refinements were being made within the National Archives, the concept of control at different record levels was being extended to manuscript collections. The leading proponents were me initially then David B. Gracy II, who wrote the SAA's basic manual on arrangement and description.

Let us turn first to the National Archives, focusing on Holmes's article, which is supplemented by the Fenyo and Evans articles. Holmes in 1941 had been a member of the National Archives Advisory Committee on Finding Mediums and was director of the Division of Research and Records Description. This unit registered the record groups, primarily for administrative control. To do this, record groups first had to be defined. Collective record groups proved particularly troublesome and complicated. Memorandum A-206 in October 1942 decreed, "in case of doubt the record groups should be more inclusive, so that they might be broken down later if warranted."[28] According to Fenyo, Holmes "recognized that no scheme based upon precedence or hierarchical considerations could be carried through consistently." It should be pointed out here that the emergence of a subgroup concept as a distinct level was postponed, because while some subordinate agencies were properly subordinated, some were clustered under a collective record group. Holmes's real advance over Schellenberg lay in the basis for subgrouping. Schellenberg had allowed for subgrouping on the basis of function and subject matter, whereas Holmes insisted that series and functional file units must have parents and must be classed accordingly. Given the practices in the National Archives, it is understandable why neither Schellenberg nor Holmes ever isolated the subgroup as a distinct record level, and why Schellenberg never applied it to manuscript collections. Fenyo concluded that "the concept of the record group has little or no history since its inception" (p. 235). Holmes, in apparent anticipation, sought to meet Fenyo's criticism two years earlier by his article on archival arrangement.

Holmes began by distinguishing between two broad levels of archival arrangement. At the "upper level" provenance is the basis, while at a "lower level" within the agency, arrangement becomes "the task of determining and verifying the original order, filling and labeling the archival containers to reflect it" (p. 23). Put differently, at the upper level arrangement is on the basis of record-creating activity, while at the lower level it relates to file order within the record group and subgroups. Whether Holmes understood the basis of this differentiation is not clear, since he did not elaborate on this distinction (the author eventually did so in 1975). Holmes's emphasis would be exclusively on the hierarchical relation of record levels. Remembering that his institutional framework is the National Archives, we note that these levels are arrangement (1) at the depository level, (2) at the record group and subgroup level, (3) at the series level, (4) at the file unit level, and (5) at the document level.

Although "this control may never be established completely, . . . it must be established to an acceptable degree before records description work is possible *because finding aids have to refer to specified units in an established arrangement*" (italics mine). This procedure and traditional historical manuscripts practice, as outlined earlier, are poles apart. One is item oriented while the other is oriented to aggregates of items that are filed in filing units, that are arranged in series, that are linked with other series—all produced by the same record-creating agency. Control in the latter proceeds successively from the upper level (record-creating agency) through the lower level as represented in the series, file unit, and item levels. Furthermore, description follows arrangement. We saw earlier and will see in Chapter 5 that description in the historical manuscripts tradition is done while arranging papers and is done directly from analysis of the manuscript items themselves.

Holmes considered that divisions of some kind within the depository are inevitable in larger archival depositories. Depending on the particular depository, these divisions might be on the basis of broad subject areas, geography, broad functional areas, chronological periods, hierarchy, or levels of government or administration—all for administrative convenience. At the second level is the record group. This "principle as defined in the National Archives united the records of subordinate offices under superior offices, usually up to the bureau level." Records of many smaller agencies "were grouped together . . . as 'collective record groups. . . .'" thus, the National Archives, partly for administrative convenience, has aimed at the intermediate level in establishing record groups" (p. 26). Holmes contended: "Some such concept is needed in all archival depositories having the care of records created by many different agencies and organizations. Once established, record groups are usually the basic units for administrative control; that is, for arrangement, description, reference service, and statistical accounting and reporting." Establishment of a record group "is the first real professional operation as one moves downward in the arrangement function" (p. 27).

Although he did not graduate the subgroup to individual status in the hierarchy of levels, Holmes urged that "all natural subgroups" be recognized at this processing stage: "Records of each field office ought properly to be considered a subgroup" (p. 28).

Holmes defined series as the next hierarchical stage of the arrangement pattern. It should be noted, however, that the record groups and their associated subgroups were, in fact, constituted by assigning particular series to them on the basis of the agency that created the series: "A true series is composed of similar filing units arranged in a consistent pattern within which each of the filing units has its proper place" (p. 30). "Once all series are assigned to record groups and subgroups . . . the archivist looks within the group or subgroup and works out a logical arrangement sequence for the series so assigned" (p. 32). This procedure is of the utmost importance in all cases where definable subgroups are present. If series are established without reference to their related subgroup, the series of the particular subgroup will be scattered among the general series of the parent agency instead of being physically linked with its originating subgroup. For example, if a series of general correspondence or of minutes includes those of two or more record-creating agencies, it becomes impossible to identify and describe the individual agency's records coherently, because subgroup-level control is not achieved in the arrangement process. Control at that level would have to depend on a careful analysis of each record series for the purpose of identifying each subgroup that is included within each general series of the superior parent agency as well as the quantity and content of materials represented by each subgroup. By contrast, if subgroup-level control is achieved in the arrangement process, the records of any one subgroup will be together as a unit, each with its own series of general correspondence, minutes, and so on. Consequently, the kind of content analysis required of each general series for the subgroups it contains becomes unnecessary: it has been taken care of without such analysis by having first arranged the records into subgroups. To do so enables the repository to realize more fully the advantages of the "provenance method," * as described later in this chapter in relation to the BRISC program.

This is why Holmes advised the grouping of each series first on the basis of its parentage. Once all series of common parentage are grouped on this basis, the record group and its subgroups are thereby established. The difficulty in grasping this principle is, I believe, that although series appears as the third step in the hierarchy of record levels, in work sequence, series should be grouped by parentage *as a first step*: the origin of the series must first be determined, and subgrouped accordingly.

Arrangement of file units within series is a level that Schellenberg neglected. Without it, there is no consistent way of locating a file unit with reasonable precision. Within a series a file unit usually has a logical place, as the product either of an originally orderly file or of one that has been established during processing. Once the files are logically arranged, the finding aid(s) can lead the user to the requested file unit. To do so represents file-level control. For Holmes, this logical ordering within series "is best done in connection with boxing and labeling" (p. 33).

Arrangement at the item or document level is largely self-evident. Concern is for "checking and arranging, within each filing unit, of the individual docu-

---

* The provenance method essentially outlines the arrangement of records by sequentially listing file units by their actual headings. These headings in turn supply index terms. No content analysis is required to reveal this information. Series descriptions that are synoptic narratives represent incipient content analysis, but fall largely within the compass of the provenance method. Series descriptions in narrative form to describe function and other characteristics are necessary only for those that are not made self-evident in the inventory listing. By observing this as a rule, redundancy in description can be minimized.

ments, enclosures and annexes, . . . that comprise the filing unit and the physical placement of each document in relation to other documents in some accepted, consistent order" (p. 24). For modern records this level of control should be discouraged until priorities allow item description. A primary consideration lies in deciding how much is inferred by file heading listings about the content of items within file units.

It should be emphasized that Holmes directs his attention to arrangement, and not to description. Description, for him, would follow after arrangement has been completed to any particular level. If only a record group registration or collection description has been done, a description of the record group as a unit will be the result. It can be incorporated with other similar description, together constituting a repository guide. The catalog equivalent of the registration would be a main entry or collection card. Holmes only implies what the description process might be.

Frank B. Evans* thought it timely in 1966 to generalize from Holmes's article. Although the focus of his "report" on modern methods of arrangement was the National Archives experience, the report was "based upon the conviction that it is of less value to know how many depositories practice each type of classification or arrangement . . . than to understand the reasons for the still existing diversity and the nature of the efforts made to develop a practical degree of uniformity." [29]

Like Holmes, Evans concentrated on arrangement, implying that description would automatically follow. Given the descriptive program of the National Archives at the time of his writing—its plethora of unintegrated finding aids—his emphasis is understandable. "Arrangement" could be summed up, but "description" would have required a preliminary evaluation of the entire descriptive program of the National Archives. In any case, the purpose of his article was to offer the experience of the National Archives as a general model in matters of archival arrangement as well as in its potential application to the control of manuscript collections.

Evans traced the early history of archival administration in the United States. He showed how archivists, and inferentially manuscript librarians, had moved away from "classification" as a concept and substituted "arrangement." Evans attributed this substitution to the absence of archival registry systems in the United States and to the "lack of a strong tradition in recordkeeping" (p. 242). In the National Archives it had been planned that classification in the tradition of the Iowa and Illinois state archives had to be based on analyses of agency histories: "After 5 years' effort the Division of Classification had produced classification schemes for the records of less than half a dozen agencies . . . and the work of the other units had similarly fallen be-

---

*Evans was director of the archival management institutes offered at the American University in the 1960s and early 1970s, serving as academic liaison for NARS. He is the main bibliographer of the profession. Before joining NARS he had been state archivist of Pennsylvania.

hind" (pp. 255–56). He then outlined the internal reforms that have been described in chapter 3. Instead of trying to classify records on the basis of rarely produced agency histories, in the future records would be assigned by the archivists to record groups on the basis of record-creating agency. He then expanded on Holmes's article, giving special attention to series because of the difficulty in establishing them: "It is at this point that the archivist must have a knowledge of the administrative history of the agency and of the records themselves. He must first determine what are the series in any given record group and subgroup. . . . The final arrangement of series should be 'not only logical but revealing of any agency's history and accomplishments.' . . . Arrangement at this level must be a constructive rather than simply a preservative kind of arrangement. It is this kind of constructive arrangement that characterizes the task of the American archivist, and it is his major contribution in making archives usable while still preserving their integrity" (p. 261).

The above system of the National Archives is the theoretical model that Schellenberg, in trying to reach manuscript librarians, applied to the control of modern manuscript collections. The author, beginning as an assistant of Schellenberg's when he taught at the University of Washington School of Librarianship in 1962, undertook the refinement of this model as a result of Schellenberg's stimulation and leadership.

The University of Washington system is derived from both the principles of librarianship and those of public archives. It accepts archival arrangement in which the principle of provenance and the record series concept are basic. It accepts the archival inventory as the principal finding aid. But it borrows from librarianship the union card catalog concept, by incorporating the card catalog function in a simple index format. The analog for this is the cumulative index to each NUCMC volume, in which the index provides a single access point to all entries. It also borrows from librarianship a disciplined approach to topical subject control by using scope notes for their determination. But these subject headings are keyed to specific record levels (record group/accession level and subgroup level) which are archival in conception, and topical subject analysis does not go below the subgroup level. In addition, the system applies rules for establishing the proper form of corporate entry, a library technique that few public archivists use. It expands on the critical importance of proper-name control, the importance of which had been recognized at some manuscript libraries such as the Bancroft and Clements libraries and by Philip Brooks. In a broader sense the University of Washington system tries to accomplish what Schellenberg sought to do in his *Management of Archives*, bringing together essential elements in these two traditions that began to be differentiated as early as 1910, and evolved separately.

To help accomplish the latter purpose, I conducted a survey in early 1970 to learn about the general relationships between manuscript catalogs and other finding aids at different repositories. Results of the survey were published in 1971 as "Manuscript Catalogs and Other Finding Aids: What Are Their Relationships?" In answering the question "to what extent do you believe that the catalog serves as an index to the finding aids," only sixteen respondents "leaned" toward the affirmative—that it does serve as an index. "Leaned" is apt, because it was clear that this indexing function of the catalog was probably discovered by most respondents while answering the questionnaire. Only four of them stated clearly that they consciously used the catalog as an index to the other finding aids. It was interesting to find that only seventeen respondents indexed their finding aids. Particularly striking was that although all collections surveyed were in libraries or were organizationally associated with libraries, they did not use the concept of a union catalog, which had originated in the world of librarianship.

The survey apparently made some impression on the field, because David B. Gracy II, as chair of the SAA Finding Aids Committee, formed a subcommittee for "finding aids relationships." When I succeeded him as chair in 1976 (through 1979) that subcommittee's work was continued. It concluded in 1978 that the inventory should be regarded as the basic finding aid, and that access to the inventories should be by means of cumulative indexes. The format for the inventory itself had been decided earlier, when the committee was chaired by Frank G. Burke. It was embodied in a model register as the first publication in this area by the new full-time secretariat of the SAA.[30]

Three more recent publications of mine constitute a unit, and should be considered as a refinement of the earlier articles.[31] In these articles I attempted to discuss more fully what is meant by "control to different record levels" and to describe the procedures for gaining control. The *Drexel Library Quarterly* chapter adapts the procedures to the field of manuscript librarianship, for those who would adhere to cataloging and the card catalog format. Because the *DLQ* chapter was to be of practical guidance, it was devoid of any explicit theoretical apparatus. Its theoretical underpinning was explained in the article, "Perspectives on the Record Group Concept." Record levels had previously been seen by writers on the subject as having only a hierarchical relation. Although Holmes had hinted at a parental relation as well by his characterization of "upper" and "lower" levels, he did not pursue the point.[32] He moved on to discuss only one aspect of their hierarchical relation. My argument associated the record group and subgroup levels with record-creating activity (provenance) while linking series, file unit, and item levels with filing activity—more precisely, their arrangement after their parental origin has been determined. This recognition is essential for establishing a progressive sequence in arranging papers and records, and the logic becomes clearer for associating series with their appropriate subgroup as a first step in arranging papers having subgroup characteristics. No one will seriously dispute the association of series with record group. But their linkage with parental subgroups had not gained legitimacy, although the procedure is based on the same principle as in forming series for a record group, on the basis of record-creating activity: provenance.

By distinguishing the subgroup as a definite record level, I believe that a useful preliminary control can be devised. In establishing subgroups initially in processing, all series are arranged into subgroups on the basis of record parentage (every series has a parent). In this procedure, information about each series is conveyed without narrative; the mere recording of the arrangement implies information about their contents. For the manuscripts field this principle was defined as a practical concept for the first time. Under the concept, all records of that subgroup will be found together as a unit within the larger record group or manuscript accession. If this procedure is not followed, general series of the record group must be analyzed by a content analysis or indexing method in order to locate the subgroups within those series (see Appendixes 7, 8, and 14 for illustrations). In the subgrouping procedure all series that are not subgrouped will, almost automatically, become the series of the subgroups' parent, those series of the larger administrative unit of which the subgroups are subdivisions. For an accession of personal papers having subgroup characteristics, those series of the "parent" would be the residue of series not already subgrouped on the basis of the separate corporate activities of that person.

In the inventory of that record group or manuscript accession, subgroup-level control would be reflected by listing the papers in their arrangement sequence, beginning with series of the parent (person or corporate body) and following with a listing by subgroup name. If series for the parent and each subgroup are arranged logically, not only could they be listed appropriately, but their bibliographic elements could be listed in cumulative indexes or as added entries in a card catalog. Those entries would refer the user back to the inventory and the particular series from which the entry was derived. Control to the file folder/unit level would be similarly reflected. The user, on consulting the inventory and its own index, would identify the precise file folders that are wanted within the series itself.

By beginning with controls established first at the subgroup level and postponing further processing until priorities justify it, two major goals are achieved: the accession is made usable in the shortest time possible, with the records of any one subgroup found together and not scattered randomly among general series throughout the entire accession; and a more rational basis is provided for assigning processing priorities for the collection as a whole.

The following are the basic elements in the University of Washington system (see Appendix 9 for illustration):

1. *Data sheet* (one for each accession). This contains accession name and number, type of documentation, inclusive dates, size, location, source of acquisition, biographical or agency sketch, restrictions, literary rights, names of some major correspondents/authors, subgroup names, and topical subject headings. The latter appear only on the data sheet, like tracings on a main entry catalog card. Topical subject headings appear only on the data sheet.

2. *Inventory/guide*. This is used for all accessions that cannot be described adequately on the data sheet. It reflects the level of control achieved in the

arrangement process. Index terms are increased proportionately at each successive level. Only the guide portion is truly narrative, providing information on provenance and other features that are not self-evident in the inventory listing.

3. *Cumulative indexes.* There is one for proper names and some place names, one for topical subject headings, and one for chronology. These are derived from the data sheets and inventory/guides. By referring the user back to them and to the level from which they are derived the indexes constitute a single point from which the entire collection or archives can be approached. These three indexes could be combined in one, but the different structure of each makes them more easily read separately; conceptually they are one.

4. *Scope notes* for subject headings provide a basis for disciplined subject control to the subgroup level. Only the primary topical subjects acted upon are noted; peripheral subject matter that is reflected in series and file units lies outside the scope of analysis.

5. *A corporate entry guide* provides for uniformity of corporate name entry in both arrangement and description.

In late 1977 the Society of American Archivists began publishing a *Basic Manuals Series* dealing with special archival problems and fields. Though intended primarily for the novice, these publications also challenge veterans to reevaluate their programs in light of a fresh statement on the state of the art. The manual on arrangement and description is by David B. Gracy II.*[33] Comparison of his manual with state-of-the-art productions of the mid-1950s gives a measure of how far the field has come. The chief difference between his manual and the relevant articles in the *Library Trends* issue on "Manuscripts and Archives" (January 1957) is that he finally gives recognition to the full range of record levels. In the *Library Trends* issue acknowledgement finally had been given by the authors to the record series as the "main catalogable unit," twenty years after Margaret Cross Norton, the HRS, and the National Archives had already recognized this feature of controlling archives and manuscript collections.

Gracy starts by recapitulating Holmes's five different levels.[34] But he does not share Holmes's grasp of the subgroup level. For example, "A subgroup of the president's ofice records—a major subject division with the group—could be fund raising, another academic affairs" (p. 5). "Within the papers of an individual, one subgroup might contain all the documents relating to the person's authorship of a book, another to his teaching career" (p. 6). The groupings he suggests above are subject groupings and are series, not subgroups; for Holmes, subgroups are formed on the basis of administrative organization—that is, provenance. Gracy needs to identify the parent of each of these series, first. Subject series like those above simply reflect the idiosyncracies of a filing order. This failure is one that Gracy shared with Schellenberg—the

---

*Gracy had been head of the Southern Labor Archives at Georgia State University, editor of *Georgia Archive*, and is currently state archivist of Texas.

confusion of subgroups with series. Subgroups become dispersed among general series when series are not linked with their parental subgroup as a first step in the process of arrangement. (See Appendix 12 showing the mixture of subgroups with "subject files." If they are not differentiated by their arrangement, there must be information telling the user that they are subgroups. This has not been done for most manuscript collections because subgrouping is not generally practiced.) Gracy did use subgroup correctly sometimes, however, as when he discussed a governor's office record group. Here, he would establish "one subgroup for each staff officer" (p. 6). Also, "An archivist prefers arrangement by administrative hierarchy." But he continued the sentence by suggesting that subgrouping be done also on the basis of function, "placing those [files] covering more than one function ahead of those documenting a single activity and those of a former stage of a sequence before those of a later stage (as applications before discharges)." Applications and discharges are series, not subgroups, they belong to a parent. The question that must be asked of series is: What is their provenance, their parent? Subgrouping, if done according to Gracy, tends to be arbitrary, because he does not consistently subgroup by provenance. Sometimes it might be done according to Holmes and provenance, and sometimes by subject or function, with function being subject-laden, as in "applications" and "discharges." In differentiating subgroups from subject series, for example, the mere listing of them under the "subgroup" caption tells the reader directly what they are, and this is done without narrative.

Because of this confusion over the subgroup level, series would be established directly within the accession of the general parent instead of first linking them with their appropriate subgroup in accessions that contain subgroups. On this point Holmes is clear: "Once all series are assigned to record groups and subgroups so that the boundaries of these are finally certain, the archivist looks within the group or subgroup and works out a logical arrangement sequence for the series so assigned." [35] Gracy, on the other hand, maintained, "Subgroups often are not finally established until the series have been confirmed" (p. 10). It is not clear what he means by "confirmed." As a procedure, the first step should be to identify the parent of the series. Apart from his ambiguity in handling subgroups and series, Gracy's presentation about series, file unit, and item levels is straightforward and of positive benefit.

As for description, Gracy recognized the inventory as "the first document produced after a collection/group has been processed, and it is generated specifically to record the information developed during processing. . . . It reflects arrangement. . . . It combines data on both arrangement and contents [and] is produced for every body of records" (p. 21). He outlined the SAA's manual on *Inventories and Registers* as a procedure to follow.

On the role of the card catalog, Gracy commented: "The catalog operation has fallen into disfavor because of the harm it did to the integrity of collections. The index function, on the other hand, is being pursued in greater depth than library cataloging methodology permits" (p. 30). "The objection of archivally trained curators to the [cataloging] system is the added entries are too few in number and often too general. The archivist needs . . . specific names, places, and events that the user of archives more often seeks" (p. 31).

Gracy advocated using a variety of indexes to provide access to the collection or archives as a whole. Most "common" and "basic" is the "subject index." He advised the indexer to make "too many entries than too few." They are "gleaned from the inventory or directly from the manuscripts." He discouraged creation of a "master name index" or one for "geographical points," because they "fragment the index system and increase the number of locations a searcher must look for the same information" (p. 33). One of the weaknesses in Gracy's system is the minimal role for proper names and the maximum emphasis on subject content. He does not differentiate between the incipient content analysis of series descriptions that are recorded in an inventory and analysis of the actual files. As we shall observe in describing the work of Richard Lytle, Gracy failed to see that he advocated two methods: one is the provenance method; the other is the content indexing method. The former is based on an analysis of the finding aids, while the latter analyzes the actual files.

In general, the absence of any systematic discussion of how controls are actually achieved at specific levels makes it difficult for the novice to conceive how this complex procedure can be accomplished. Consider the following illustration. If the inventories are the main finding aids and if they are indexed, the indexes will refer the user back to specific inventories. The inventories will record the level of control that is achieved in the arrangement process. If control is only at the subgroup level, the inventory will direct the user to specific containers holding the subgroups that probably contain the series they need. If control is at the series level, each inventory for such accessions will probably have its own index, in which entries will be recorded that are derived by the indexer from the series description itself. The index entry of the inventory will then refer the user to the specific series that probably contain the file units that are needed. The user will probably want to read each inventory for more clues and also to analyze the relations of the various series to one another. If control is at the file unit level, the user, after being directed from the general repository index to the inventory, will probably find in the inventory's own index references to specifically numbered file units. At each level of control there is also a higher probability that the user will find what he hopes to find, because there are increasingly more references and the references are more definite at each successive level. By following this kind of procedure, full advantage is taken of provenance. Instead, the absence of this kind of information in detail and supported by graphics limits the usefulness of the manual. If Gracy had, for example, used the SAA's model register as a basis, he could have extrapolated the kind of suggestions above. And some attention should have been devoted to establishing some principles of description, such as provisions of access points. Users of the manual might then be persuaded to follow the example, and move toward standardization more consciously. To do so would make automation ultimately easier at every level within the repository and extending to a national level.

One of the most promising ventures in automated programs for archives is that of the Baltimore Region Institutional Studies Center (BRISC). Its ARCHON program* has stimulated Richard H. Lytle to examine it for its theoretical implications and to envisage a theoretical model for improved subject retrieval. Lytle, archivist of the Smithsonian Institution, has written an article in two parts.[36] In the first he establishes his theoretical model, and in the second he tests it on their ARCHON program.

Lytle distinguished the provenance method (P Method) from the content indexing method (CI Method), but recognized that they are complementary approaches to the same material. The former is archival in derivation, while the latter is rooted in librarianship: "Subject retrieval in the P Method proceeds by linking subject queries with provenance information contained in administrative histories or biographies, thereby producing leads to files which are searched by using their internal structures." Information provided in inventories and other finding aids also falls within the framework exploited by the P Method. Index terms are derived from the listing of file folder/unit headings seriatum, including subject terms, proper names, and so forth. They become part of the data base. A superficial test has presumably been made by the processor to verify the validity of the file headings, but stopping short of content analysis. The quality of the finding aids determines the effectiveness of the P Method.

By contrast, in the CI Method subject retrieval is done by matching questions with index or catalog terms that are "gleaned by an indexer who examines the records." The real distinction is that in the P Method inventories are indexed, while in the CI Method index terms are derived from an analysis of the items or folders themselves—or as in the BRISC experiment, an analysis of the file folders for their contents.

Lytle outlined the four elements constituting the "archival system": the materials, the users, finding aids, and the reference service. He contends that because archives are used primarily by their creators, a "strong creator-orientation" has become a basic part of archival doctrine. Users are directed to documents for their probable content, not because the specific information they seek is definitely there. Secondary users have tended to be ignored, but they have accommodated this by tolerating imprecision in satisfying most of their retrieval requests. Browsing, as a factor, is given importance in this con-

---

*Although ARCHON is an automated program, it is its manual characteristics that are the subject of the following analysis. H. Thomas Hickerson describes the ARCHON program in the SAA's forthcoming basic manual on archival automation. He supplied me with a draft copy of the first three chapters.

text—browsing of the "files" themselves, and of finding aids before the materials are served up. That he should find that "apparently browsing and broad subject questions are related" should come as no surprise if the user has first examined the finding aids. In testing the merit of the P Method, Lytle concedes the circularity of the problem: user demands are generated by the system and fed back into it. As a consequence, users cope by asking for files mainly by proper names, sometimes by topic, and so on, as noted in finding aids, supplemented by leads from nonarchival sources as well (colleagues and bibliographical citations mainly). Administrators who use their own government or institutional archive usually know beforehand the names of agencies whose records probably relate to the functions about which information is needed.

Let us turn to the BRISC experiment for the results of Lytle's study. Fifteen collections were used in the project. "Rudimentary P Method finding aids existed." They had been indexed also. Fifteen questions were run, twice each, using both methods. Ten of the questions were selected from BRISC's record of past questions, and five from current demand. Altogether 897 folders were retrieved from 380 cubic feet of records. Lytle found that both methods yielded poor results, about equally. The CI Method showed wider variability. "This was a surprising finding, considering the inadequacy of the P Method finding aids and the apparent high quality of the CI Method indexes at BRISC. The P Method may have greater strengths than even its advocates have imagined." Indeed. It was because of the poor and uneven quality of finding aids that the SAA Finding Aids Committee under Frank G. Burke made its first goal the creation of a model register. The crux of the problem, therefore, seems to be associated with the need to improve finding aids generally, using the model register as a standard. To do so would result in fullest use of the P Method, and maximize cost benefits in the process. The CI Method is significantly more expensive.

The low scores recorded in using the CI Method were attributed to the absence of index entries for the subjects the user was seeking. This failure, "constitutes a warning for those designing subject access systems, where the demands on the system are poorly defined. On the other hand, if the system vocabulary *can anticipate user demands*, the CI Method has considerable potential as indicated by its high scores [also] in this experiment" (italics mine). Such anticipations are a hazardous undertaking because of their subjectiveness and ephemeral nature. Consequently the CI Method requires repeated analyses of the same files in order to satisfy changing user needs. For voluminous modern manuscripts this is not a probability. (See Appendix 22, "Provenance as an Inferential System.")

Not tested was comprehensiveness of coverage. But Lytle volunteered, "A large number of files strains the P Method approach, but the CI Method alternative becomes quite expensive when applied to large accumulations of records." This expensiveness of the CI Method was pointed out in the Cornell University pilot project using SPINDEX II.[37]

From this experiment, Lytle contends that in any archival system that is designed, the users and what they demand of the system must be part of the design. I agree with Burke that the P Method would be enhanced by improving finding aids that fully exploit the advantages of arrangement by provenance.* Only then can we begin to see the real limitations of the P Method and tailor other finding aids as complements to the basic system resting on provenance. Two basic considerations are required. One requires that useful file folder titles must be developed for current records; this requires articulation of RM and archives. The other requires refinement of indexing methods for improvement of access to existing finding aids that are based on deficient file unit titles. If we do not proceed in this direction we may well move in an opposite one, as illustrated by Phyllis Platnick.[38] She argued from the assumption that archivists and manuscript librarians cannot agree on methods of arrangement, and they spend so much time on arranging materials that they find no time for indexing them: "Yet indexing is the real key to the contents of the collections." By not bothering to arrange them, indexing can move along unhindered: "Each item can be numbered, recorded, analyzed, and filed as it comes to hand." The indexing data can then be "recorded in machine form, pertinent material in all holdings of the institution can be retrieved at one time, and from many aspects. Yet all the data is recorded only once, and in one place." Here we have echoes of calendaring and of archivists versus librarians on the issue of collective description versus item description. It need not be "versus" but instead, each in its place, in complementary relationship. Platnick's kind of item orientation that slights arrangement ignores the great amount of information that is conveyed by orderly arrangement and description—file and informational relationships that no quantity of narrative and cross references can supply economically or reliably. Waldo G. Leland's original advice to describe records in progressively greater detail still applies. The P method is essentially an inferential system. Descriptors imply that there is information about which the user is searching. Probability of success depends on the level of control attained. At its best, the system is free of redundancy and uses narrative sparingly. Ideally, the arrangement itself will imply informational content if the arrangement is faithfully recorded in an inventory. The CI method is applicable, but in its place and as priorities allow. The CI method is inappropriate if it is applied uniformly to all accessions in an archive or manuscript repository unless some degree of access has already been provided to all other accessions. Even within a given accession it is unnecessary to analyze the content of all subgroups and series unless they probably contain information to justify the effort.

---

*This point is succinctly stated in the introduction to the *Descriptive Inventory of the State Archive of the State of Illinois*, vol. 15 (1978): "But we have allowed the contents of the state's archives to speak for themselves, and in their own language."

5

The Historical Manuscripts Tradition to 1979

Although the first section of chapter 4 was entitled "Twilight of the Historical Manuscripts Tradition," the tradition has nevertheless persisted as a pure strain. It is like the twilight of a summer Arctic night. Writings during the period that best exemplify this tradition are those of Robert S. Gordon and Kenneth W. Duckett.[1] Each presents an excellent general statement of these practices, and is selected for that reason. For Gordon, the institutional setting is the smaller local historical society. For Duckett, the settings seem to be manuscript collections within special collections units of private and academic libraries as well as collections of state and local historical societies. Duckett's recommendations also owe their origin in part to the requirements of specialized types such as literary and subject collections. Neither author addresses the problems of controlling integral accessions of recent origin, those which drew the attention of Schellenberg and others described in chapter 4. Indicative of Duckett's frame of reference is his first chapter, "Manuscript Collecting." In distinguishing different categories of collectors, he gives the institutional collector less than a page while private and autograph collectors occupy more than ten pages out of eighteen. Because it is the institutional collector that has most of the "modern" manuscripts, it is striking that so little attention is devoted to that type of collecting agency, considering the title of the book, *Modern Manuscripts*. It is well to bear in mind Duckett's orientation when an assessment of his contribution is made.

A corporate/institutional perspective at the national level is reflected in the NUCMC rules for descriptive cataloging. In chapter 3 their origin was traced. They had evolved wholly within the framework of librarianship. Their application will be reviewed after examining the writings of Gordon and Duckett. These rules, in turn, became the basis of the *Anglo-American Cataloging Rules* for manuscripts. The larger purpose of the American Library Association, in monitoring the development of the NUCMC rules, had been to use them as a national standard. The AACR made them an international standard as well.

ADVICE TO LOCAL HISTORICAL SOCIETIES

Let us turn, first to Robert S. Gordon's carefully wrought article.[2] In observing that many local historical societies, despite staffing handicaps, had developed "remarkably efficient" systems of control, Gordon saw the need "to develop a uniform set of rules of organization and description . . . as guides [for the societies] in their archival work." As a first measure, he advised dividing a society's holdings into three categories: papers of individuals, those of corporate bodies, and the official files of the society itself. This division parallels that of Grace Lee Nute, whose writings were examined in chapter 2. Papers should be accessioned into one of these categories and should be kept intact, not distributed among subject categories.

For papers of individuals, "each item should be examined carefully; the date, name, and subject should be checked and noted," then placed in its appropriate classification (pp. 23–24). Gordon recommended as the next step a calendaring of letters (pp. 25–28): "When the subject merits it, the entry should be more detailed and exhaustive and may take up one or several sentences." All important topics should be dealt with, and it takes skill and experience to cover the contents of a letter in a few words (p. 27). Although he advocated a chronological arrangement for most correspondence, "the alphabetical arrangement . . . is suitable for bulky and relatively unimportant papers. It calls for grouping together in one entry all letters written by one person, giving his name, the inclusive years . . . , [general subject matter], and page numbers." By contrast, in the chronological arrangement each item is recorded individually in the inventory (pp. 28–29). In dealing with "personal" papers (pp. 30–31), a chronological arrangement is judged best. From his example, items are recorded chronologically in abbreviated calendaring style, without regard to record type or series characteristic. In other words, series is not recognized as a step in the arrangement process; the item is the catalogable unit.

It is in the category "occupational papers" that Gordon approached a concept of the subgroup—arrangement on the basis of separate corporate activities. But, unlike Kane, Gordon handled all correspondence as one "unit" (p. 33), even when it was produced from activity for one of the subgroups for which the person was the agent. Kane, by comparison, respected the integrity of each subgroup.

Other "groups" potentially among "papers of individuals" were "land papers," "legal" papers, and "civil and military affairs offices," "societies and organizations," "accounts and receipts," and "miscellaneous" papers. "Series" as a concept was but dimly recognized; "unit" was used in its stead. Subgrouping as a practical matter also was inconsistently applied. Kane, by contrast, was consistent in her application of the subgrouping method. Gordon's method of organization is reminiscent of practices in the United States before the influence was felt of practices established by the National Archives and used in the HRS. Gordon's presentation was the clearest and broadest in this genre of archival arrangement and description.

One must ask of Gordon, considering the typically niggardly staffing of local historical societies, how such a high level of expertise can be expected? How, also, can the relatively high expenditure of staff time on item description be justified in the absence of some prior preliminary controls? These questions might also be asked of Duckett.

ADVICE TO CURATORS OF MODERN MANUSCRIPTS

Some preliminary remarks about Kenneth W. Duckett's* volume are in order. The American Association for State and Local History (AASLH) was the sponsor of his book, as it was of Lucile Kane's *Guide* in the 1960s. The Council on Library Resources supported the research and publication. The AASLH sought to produce a work of broader scope than Kane's booklet to meet the demands activated by more extensive manuscript collecting programs nationwide. It is well to bear this in mind with respect to Duckett's discussion of "bibliographic control," which will be the focus of our attention. Remember that Kane had a clear grasp of the record series as the key catalogable unit, and as a practical matter she advocated subgrouping mainly on the basis of separate corporate activities, without defining the concept. Inherent in her practical recommendations was the concept of controls keyed to different record levels. Missing was a crystallization of these elements into a general system that could serve as a theoretical model to guide practice. Kane nevertheless made a significant advance in bringing modern manuscript collections under control.

Duckett intended his book for the novice curator of manuscripts, "to serve as a practical guide, not as an exposition of theory" (p. xi). Unlike Schellenberg, who recognized that practice presupposes methodology or theory, Duckett wrote as though practice has no theoretical basis. The reader is left with the problem of uncovering the presuppositions of these practices and their theoretical implications as well. The critique that follows is directed only at Duckett's handling of bibliographic control, and should not be construed as a general criticism. In almost every other respect the book makes a major contribution.

Duckett recommended a preliminary overview of the entire accession, making as little disturbance of its organization as possible, but taking notes in the process. From this initial survey the processor should prepare "a simple

---

*A historian, Duckett had been curator of manuscripts of the Ohio Historical Society and at the time he wrote his book was curator of manuscripts at Southern Illinois University. At present, he is head of the Special Collections Division of the University of Oregon Library.

outline showing the major series in the collection" (p. 119). Following the principle of provenance, the collection should be kept intact according to record-creating source. In addition, Duckett alerted the processor to the possibility of an original file order waiting only to be discovered. But in the absence of orderly files, "the simplest method of arranging manuscripts is chronological [because it] shows the relationship between documents and the events to which they relate" (p. 120). He advised against subject arrangement, because it "tends to fragment a set of papers." But he advised acceptance of subject files that already exist. He cautioned against an alphabetical arrangement by writer because of the "inherent difficulty of . . . determining whether letters should be gathered under personal names or the names of firms, governmental units, and other organizations" (pp. 120–21).

In processing, two forms of notes should be taken: sorting notes and content notes. The first relate to arrangement, the second to identification of subject matter and other substantive data. This information should be recorded on data sheets, which in turn provide information for compiling an inventory. The data sheets are also useful "as a secondary finding aid when the researcher wants more details on a collection." They are "most useful in arranging large modern collections that are to be retained in original order" (p. 121). "The process of taking content notes is an attempt by the curator to abstract what he thinks is the important information in the collection so that he can synthesize it for the researcher." He recommends, for example: "During the first sort . . . he did see a group of letters from an author and another smaller set from an inventor. He will want a complete list of all those letters by date, with content notes on at least some of them. . . . With these and other thoughts in mind, the curator starts the second sorting. . . . By this time he will have determined whether the papers will be perfunctorily or intensively cataloged" (p. 128). In this second sort the curator will be "looking for letters with content. He will be looking for both the expected and the extraordinary. . . . The curator must alert researchers that they may not find what they expect, as well as point out the unexpected which would otherwise be overlooked" (p. 129).

Before we pass on to Duckett's discussion of finding aids, the reader should notice the great emphasis on the attention to be devoted by the processor to item description compared with the minimal attention given to series beyond accepting those that exist. Kane, at this stage, would have recommended, for disorderly files, their placement into series on the basis of physical type. Also there is an aspect of this work that has to do with the division of labor between the manuscripts library and the researcher. Duckett's recommendations on such extensive notetaking overlap with the researcher's area of responsibility, and could well lead to the researcher placing too much reliance on those notes once they are transformed into catalog entries. In recommending this extensive notetaking procedure, Duckett overlooked the advantages of arranging papers in series as a method of revealing, by implication, the probable content of items and file units that make up series—a self-accessing quality, in fact. To have done so would have capitalized on the "provenance method" as characterized by Richard Lytle. We will see from Duckett's comments on name indexes that he would not couple them to series by means of catalog or index references as a vital part of this self-accessing quality of series arrangement.

"Having settled upon a system of arrangement," Duckett wrote, "the curator now must describe the collection in one or more of the commonly used types of finding aids—calendar, name index, register, inventory, or card catalog" (p. 135). He dismissed calendars, appropriately, as an impracticable method. Name indexes of a comprehensive sort he also gave short shrift, although conceding that "all collections deserve a selective name index of some degree" (p. 135). "But whatever form they take, they are very time-consuming to produce. . . . In preparing a name index the curator should equip himself with a box of catalog cards and an alphabetical card guide," and begin recording the information. "If the completed index is to be an in-house finding aid, these rough cards will do; but if it is to become part of the inventory, it can be typed on other cards or in sheet form" (p. 123). Duckett, here, did not deal with the various arrangements in which names of writers appear: chronological, alphabetical, chronological/alphabetical, numerical, and so forth. In a numerical or chronological arrangement, for example, the subjective and expensive elements in selection are at their highest; whereas in an alphabetical arrangement these are minimized. For example, if one were to use as a rule of thumb, "Enter in the index all writers to whom an individual folder is given," this would be a fairly automatic procedure, and objective besides. It also is the least time-consuming and least expensive. Coupled with his attitude toward the cost of making name indexes was his nonrecognition of the proper name/subject association, and the use of proper-name control as a mode of subject access—a mode that is not dependent on the kind of intensive content analysis that Duckett recommends, and that can lead users directly to series and file unit levels least expensively.

Duckett acknowledged that "the inventory is the best tool yet devised for maintaining bibliographic control over huge twentieth-century collections; and in condensed form, it is useful in describing collections of one box or larger" (p. 135). Apart from his description of the inventory's makeup he added nothing with respect to its relation to other finding aids in the repository. This is consistent with the writing of others. The result is a bifurcated system: "The co-ordinated inventory and unit catalog system . . . forces the researchers to use two bibliographical tools" (pp. 141–42). He recommended the use of unit cataloging over analytical cataloging, because the latter requires the typing of individual cards for each entry and is unbearably expensive for that reason (pp. 139–45).

The highly subjective controls recommended by Duckett, combined with the absence of any controls at intermediate record levels between collection and item levels, lead to randomness. The effect, at the level of the card catalog, could be almost kaleidoscopic if his recommendations were to be followed. Cataloging in the Duckett mode begins, for all practical purposes, in the "first sort" stage, when content notes begin to be made. The result is that cataloging is done from the manuscripts themselves while they are being arranged, and not from information provided in an inventory. Lacking is a control device, such as an inventory, that records precisely what has been first arranged then described and that indicates what the next step in description should be. In the absence of such a control device, items are cataloged without relation to the larger accession of which they are only a part; description is of the trees first, not of the forest, then its constituent parts. Compare this procedure, for example, with Kane's treatment, by which cataloging is done after arrangement, and each step in the process of establishing controls is clearly distinguished. But Kane, for all her clarity, is imprecise about the content notes that she recommends. Notes for her are made for preparation of both registers and catalog cards. They are prepared in the course of arranging the accession, and thereby represent also cataloging directly from the manuscripts themselves. This ambiguity is one shared with all other writers described above. The practical exclusion of series in arrangement procedures leads the cataloger to seek items and clusters for entry independent of their series relationships. From the archival mode Duckett would consider only the principle of provenance and the inventorying technique by itself as applicable.[3]

CATALOGING RULES FOR HISTORICAL MANUSCRIPTS: NUCMC AND AACR

Evolution of the NUCMC[4] cataloging rules has been discussed in chapter 3. The Library of Congress had acted as the surrogate of the American Library Association in their development. The latter adapted them to its *Anglo-American Cataloging Rules*. The NUCMC rules and their application are examined before analyzing AACRs 1 and 2.

Reporting to the NUCMC began in 1959 and the first volume was published in 1962, covering the reports that were cataloged by the NUCMC staff during 1959–61. It is a project that is apparently endless. Reporting institutions followed the "preprint rules" of September 1954 and their supplements.

Originally the promoters of the NUCMC considered publishing a book catalog in addition to a catalog in card form. It was not until the "union catalog" feature failed in card format that the book format was adopted. Through the "union" feature of a catalog, users are led to sources wherever they are located geographically. The degree of effective representation is determined by the number of institutions who report their holdings and by the number of subscribers, and by their accessibility. By 1961 there were only nine subscribers to the complete union set of cards, thereby defeating the purpose of a union catalog in its card version. Other repositories subscribed only to cards of their region or cards of even smaller scope. Contributing to the defeat of the union purpose was the additional workload, at the repository level, of typing added entries and maintaining the catalog. For already understaffed manuscript units this was an impossible undertaking that ought to have been anticipated by the planners. The union catalog feature could be achieved at the national level only by going to the book format exclusively. This has been coupled now with the provision of complimentary cards to the cooperating repository for collections reported by it.

Another original feature of the NUCMC that was significantly modified was subject headings. Subject headings in the first volume were derived from the Library of Congress's own *Subject Headings List*. The difficulty lay in making the headings specific enough. To do so required making many subdivisions, some running to three lines, a cumbersome added entry to say the least. The editorial advisers decided to use topical headings instead. Volume 1 was redone to incorporate topical headings, and subsequent volumes have continued this use.

One of the purposes of the NUCMC rules had been to establish national standards for cataloging manuscripts at the repository level. This standardization would be applied in those repositories that prepared catalog cards for use by the NUCMC office. Those who chose the NUCMC data sheet for reporting could, it was felt, avoid being locked into using the NUCMC rules in their own repository. That locking into NUCMC standards has indeed occurred in the local repository, however, is confirmed by Terry Abraham's * study published in 1977.[5] The result has been to perpetuate, uncritically, the bifurcated system of finding aids by encouraging cataloging from the actual manuscripts and not from other finding aids. By not cataloging the latter, the resulting catalog ranks as only another aid and it serves no integrative function. Particularly odd is the fact that the NUCMC volumes themselves represent an integrated system, wherein the entries are indexed and the references refer the user back to their source. At the national level an integrated system is represented, while a bifurcated system is promoted at the repository level. So preoccupied had the promoters of national cataloging standards become with promulgating catalog rules, they did not and still have not recognized this truly significant, innovative feature of their own creation.

In each volume the cumulative index does the integrating by simple end-of-book-like indexes devoid of analytical paraphernalia. The individual entries are indexed for proper and place names, and for topical subjects. If all entries had been done from data sheets, it is the data sheets themselves that would have been indexed. Viewed as a theoretical model, these volumes represent something quite different from the intent of the rules. While the rules perpetuate a bifurcated system for the repository to follow, the volumes offer an integrated one if used as a practical guide. Bear in mind Duckett's passing but perceptive comment that in a unit system "the dictionary card catalog is essentially an index to the inventory" (p. 141). The data sheet is the analog of the inventory in this conceptual framework. That the NUCMC volumes have not instead become the model for repository-level description attests to the pull of traditional cataloging.

The descriptive rules for cataloging entries in the NUCMC are for collection-level cataloging. In other words, description, in its cataloging version,

---

*Terry Abraham is curator of manuscripts at Washington State University, Pullman.

attempts only to note principal characteristics such as bulk dates, subject content, geographic area, and names that are significant for the collection.[6] Any attempt to go beyond that level to other levels in the hierarchy is negligible, but there is nevertheless some encouragement or accommodation to repository vanity: "If a collection contains some particularly important item . . . , an analytic entry may be prepared for it according to the rule of entry for single manuscripts and RDC 6:1–2."[7] To what extent this has been done is not clear. It is an inducement to individual item cataloging, the very kind of reporting that the proponents of the NUCMC had wanted to exclude. In another view, this kind of random item cataloging is done independently of a process of progressively cataloging through the hierarchy of levels of an accession and *concluding* with the cataloging of items.

The rules themselves are straightforward cataloging rules for author, title, size, and so on. As such, they deserve no substantive criticism. It is for what they do not include that they need examination. Most critical in this connection is the absence of any discussion of record levels between the collection and item levels. All that is required by the rules is a mere reference that other finding aids exist. The inventory format for finding aids, particularly, is a structured instrument that records the level of control that is achieved in the arrangement process. If it is used as the basis for cataloging, it is possible for catalog entries to reflect the level of control. The rules, in neglecting to link cataloging with other finding aids in this fashion, imply only one alternative: to catalog from the actual manuscripts. (AACR2, which is based on the NUCMC rules, recommends that the "whole collection" be employed as the cataloging source. AACR2 is discussed below.) It is no excuse that these intermediate record levels were only dimly recognized at the time the rules were being formulated. These levels are now recognized, but the rules have not yet been modified. In their modification it would seem advisable that they specify that the inventory be used as the cataloging source. Otherwise there is no simple and easy way to develop progressively refined controls, either at the repository level or at the national level in the union catalog. This end result of the NUCMC rules is probably more than what their makers intended, for they lead back to manuscript librarianship, "before Schellenberg." Instead of continuing to incorporate relevant elements from public archival practices, the NUCMC rules lead away from these influences. This tendency has been reinforced by the *Anglo-American Cataloging Rules*.

Before turning to the AACR, we should note an oversight by the developers of the NUCMC. It had been presupposed that the unit "card" would usually be confined to one card and could be used for making added entries. This had proved unfeasible for collection descriptions that run to two or more cards. As a result, the repository must create a new card to handle added entries. In addition, the unit card, even when it is only one card, is not readily adaptable to any but an added entry that directs the user to a collection-level description. The rules provide no guidance in this vital matter. If advice had been given to indicate how added entries referring to the series level could be made by the repository, the rules would have immeasurably helped the local repository. To have done so might also have alerted the uninitiated to the series concept and to record levels generally. Such information might also have dissuaded repositories from cataloging directly from the manuscripts themselves, by suggesting that collections not be reported unless they are arranged first into their basic series units. (See Appendix 14 for an illustration of the problem and a recommended solution.) That these instructions or some kind of information was not incorporated reveals the hazards of trying to separate the inseparable, arrangement *and* description. Cataloging, as a form of description, became insulated from other descriptive instruments and from that other element of intellectual control—arrangement. The AACRs further alienated cataloging from that intellectual process.

The two editions of the AACR are companion volumes.[8] Guidelines for treating nonbook materials in the second edition were determined "primarily from a consideration of the published cataloguing rules of the Canadian Library Association, the Library Association, and the Association for Educational Communications and Technology" (p. vii). The American Library Association appears to have had a minimal role in treating manuscript collections, although it did revise chapter 12 of AACR1 on motion pictures and filmstrips. Unlike earlier editions of the ALA rules, which were limited to author and title entries, AACR1 embraced rules for description. The latter are "essentially" the *Rules for Descriptive Cataloging in the Library of Congress* (Washington, D.C., 1949) which were adopted by the ALA. Rules for manuscripts (items and collections) "have been drawn up in such a way that the entries are compatible [with those for published works,] thus permitting inclusion of all, or as many as may be desired in the same catalog" (AACR1, p. 2). Basic to using the rules is an understanding "that each rule dealing with a specific problem is to be understood in the context of the more general rules" (AACR1, p. 6).

A bifurcated system of finding aids is reaffirmed in the introduction to part 2, "Description": "It is recognized that descriptive cataloging is not the only method of making library materials accessible, and that, in dealing with some types of them, guides, calendars, indexes, inventories, etc. may be preferable" (AACR1, p. 189). In other words, the catalog does not integrate the other finding aids, but stands independently with them. Chapter 10 of AACR1 deals with problems of entry for both single manuscripts and collections. Single manuscripts are handled like books. "Collections of manuscripts" are the focus of our attention. Conforming to provenance, the *Rules* define a manuscript collection as "a group of manuscripts or typewritten materials formed by or around a person, family, corporate body, or subject" (p. 265). Straightforward instructions are given for establishing the main entry. It is with added entries that there are problems. Although added entries for subjects have been traditionally a part of manuscript cataloging, no provision is made for them. Rule 206C advises, "An added entry may be made under any person or corporate body that has a significant relationship to the content or origin of the collection, including a donor, former owner . . ." (p. 267). Missing is any specific reference to "major correspondents" or proper names generally, although "significant relationship" might imply that to the experienced manuscript librarian. But how is the novice to know this? It is through added entries that multiple access points are given to an accession and to the repository's entire collection. The two main routes of access for users of manuscript collections are by proper names and topical subjects,[9] yet the AACR1 provides only the scantiest instruction about added entries. There are no specific instructions for identifying the main topical subject characteristics, or the names of major correspondents or other significant proper names, despite a long tradition in the manuscript field of making catalog entries of this sort specifically.[10] Yet it is through added entries for proper and geographical names, and topical subjects, that the integrative function of the catalog is performed. Without such a function for the catalog, it is of questionable value.

The AACR2, like its 1967 predecessor, seeks to provide general guidelines for cataloging normal library materials and also "uncommonly collected materials of all kinds and library materials yet unknown." With these standards, all library materials will be represented in a union catalog. Special libraries and archives, if they use the rules, are advised to use them as the basis of their cataloging and augment them as needed (AACR2, p. 1). In each of its two parts the rules proceed from the general to the specific. Part 1 relates to description. Part 2 is of main concern to manuscript librarians, because it deals with the problem of access points to the holdings. There are three access points: the main entry, added entries, and alternative heading entries. The latter provide opportunities for local options, and potentially offer some flexibility in the application of AACR2.

An opportunity was provided in AACR2 to compensate for one of the deficiencies in AACR1. As noted above, AACR1 made no attempt to integrate cataloging and the catalog with other finding aids, but simply acknowledged the catalog as their coequal. The AACR2, in its first general rule, "Sources of Information" (1.0A), could easily have proceeded toward cataloging the other finding aids by recognizing them as the chief source of the catalog's information. In moving from this general rule to the specific one for manuscripts (4.0B1) it recommends: "For collections of manuscripts, treat the whole collection as the chief source." The implication is that the information should be derived from the actual manuscripts and not from a secondary source such as an inventory or other finding aids. In rule 4.0B2, "Prescribed sources of information," in the column opposite "Physical description" and "Note," there is no specific reference to what might be the information source.* By this

---

*Cf. Lydia Lucas, "Efficient Finding Aids: Developing a System for Control of Archives and Manuscripts," *AA* 44 (Winter 1981): 21–26. Lucas, in her work as director of Technical Processes for Archives and Manuscripts at the Minnesota Historical

inattentiveness to the existence of other finding aids specifically, as a source, the AACR2 missed the opportunity to employ cataloging as a device to integrate all finding aids. We cannot even be certain that a repository that had produced these other finding aids would employ them as the information source, since there is no specific reference made to them. Furthermore, unless they are used as the source, there is no possibility of linking entries to the specific level from which the information was derived. Since one of the objectives of AACR2 is to ease the transition to automated catalogs and on-line access to them, its incapacity for hierarchical searching of archival finding aids is a definite handicap. This difficulty would be overcome if it specifically made the other finding aids the basis of its information. As the rules are now, the user will be led to arbitrarily selected manuscript items as well as other unstructured sources for the information.

In turning to part 2 for instructions about providing access points (headings), we find special sections for artworks, musical works, and other forms of material, but not for manuscripts. For them, general rules must suffice. In rule 21.0B we are told: "Determine the access points for the item being catalogued from the chief source of information." Instructions follow for determining the composition of the main entry. For developing added entries one proceeds to rules 21.29 and 21.30 for guidance. Rule 21.29D tells the reader: "If, in the context of a given catalogue, added entries are required under headings and titles other than those prescribed in rule 21.30, make them." If this rule seems too general, if not opaque, one can turn to a more "flexible" option, rule 21.29G: "use explanatory references in place of added entries in certain cases (see 26.5)," entitled "References Instead of Added Entries Common to Many Editions." For manuscripts, 26.5 proves a dead end.[11] Compared with AACR1, the second edition appears less useful in the matter of added entries. And the device of alternative heading entries remains underdeveloped in providing flexible options.

Both editions of AACR suffer more than the NUCMC rules from having separated description from arrangement. There is no evidence that the rule makers are even aware that arrangement is relevant to cataloging. Unless a radical accommodation can be made in a special supplement, it is questionable that AACR2 can benefit the manuscript librarian who deals with manuscript "collections" (as distinct from "items"). A special supplement will need to focus on two problems: (1) the relation of cataloging to its information sources, specifically to inventories and other finding aids, and (2) access points to holdings (this necessarily entails references to the different hierarchical levels from which the information is derived).

Thus far only the inventory provides a disciplined control device for estab-

---

Society, has made the archival inventory the information source for cataloging, thereby establishing an integrated system and culminating the work of Lucile Kane in this respect.

lishing controls at different record levels. If the actual manuscripts in an accession are used as the information source for cataloging a given accession, the result will inevitably be random, as we have already noted in our critique of Duckett's *Modern Manuscripts*. In contrast, the inventory will record the level of control achieved by the arrangement process, and the information derived from it will inevitably reflect that level of control. If, for example, a proper name or topical term is abstracted and entered from a series description or from a file unit in the series, the added entry will refer the user to that specific series or file unit as described in the inventory. The inventory, in turn, will show the relation of that added entry (or index entry) to the accession as a whole. But a catalog entry that is derived randomly will refer only to the item or clusters of selected items, and is incapable of showing the wider range of information relationships and the relevant clues that are found in a normal search process. By contrast, a catalog entry that is derived from the inventory to an accession is under control throughout. The inventory serves as an authority document. Information in it is hierarchically arranged, and more information and catalog terms are supplied at each successive level in the hierarchy. From whatever level the catalog entry is derived its source will be identified—by a control number in automated programs, for example. By using the inventory as the authority document for catalog entries the status of cataloging is known at all times. In addition, the user is thereby referred back to the inventory itself for examination and for expanding the search for related file units. In failing to deal with the problem analogously (as just outlined), AACR2 seems to have barely begun to identify the archival search process and the issues involved.

6

Automated Archival Systems

Automation has proved to be a stimulant to archival finding aids systems. Automation is also revolutionizing information access in libraries as well as effecting economies in their administrative operations. In librarianship, AACR2 attempts to ease the transition from the card to other media by homogenizing information about all forms of library-held material, including manuscript collections. Various library networks in conforming to these rules hope to include reports about manuscript collections. Whether these networks can accommodate data produced from different hierarchical levels, such as those derived from series descriptions and from file unit analysis, is a serious question. An alternative to cataloging is SPINDEX,[1] if such information cannot be integrated into library networks. SPINDEX is an automated system that specifically accepts information about manuscripts collections and public and institutional archives, and has other computer applications as well in the archival field at large. The system can accommodate data from every record level and was designed to do so, in contrast with existing library networks.

In the archival field in some institutions, and in the National Archives and Records Service (NARS), systems have been devised to provide better means of access for administrative purposes.* In NARS, for example, its A-1 system has this as its main function. Whether it can be extended to provide in-depth information by indexing series and thereby serving an intellectual purpose as well as an administrative one remains to be seen.

To make any of these systems effective, however, the data must be organized manually at two levels unless it is already in machine-readable form. One level is the physical arrangement of the papers themselves, and the other

*These administrative needs are for the following kinds of data: name of accession, provenance, quantity, series types, location, administrative level in a corporate body, terms of access, literary rights, and supplementary data, but not the intellectual content. The latter comprises subject information, names of principals, and other data that are derived from an analysis of the actual records for the information they contain.

85

is their presentation in a descriptive format, such as an inventory. The archival profession is only now coming to consensus on uniform manual finding aids. There are programs to record in automated form the data presented in these manual finding aids. All that is needed is for the data to be put in the computer systematically for each level of record control. The lack of standards in the past makes it particularly difficult to report about accessions that have not been organized according to these levels of control and that have not been inventoried to reflect that degree of control.

This chapter is organized to reflect the status of automation in the archival field before and after SPINDEX.

BEFORE SPINDEX

The first substantial project for automated programs in archives was the Presidential Papers Program of the Library of Congress, which began in 1958. It was in the historical manuscripts tradition, involving item indexing. In 1965 two projects in an archival mode were independently conceived. One was at the Hoover Institution and the other at the Library of Congress.[2] Before we turn to the archival projects, some passing observations are warranted about the Library of Congress presidential papers project.

The project directors decided against extensive subject indexing because of its expense and the difficulty of constructing an appropriate thesaurus. In addition, "It was their experience in the Library of Congress that the queries of most users related to sender or recipient." Another factor was that arrangement for microfilming was the paramount consideration. This, combined with the legislative mandate for "definitive indexes," limited the range of computer applications. The project "was undertaken before anyone fully appreciated the potential of automation." Today "it is unlikely that an item index of comparable size would be attempted. . . . More commonly, directors of large-scale indexing projects have tended to limit themselves to folder-level indexing."[3]

Since the project at the Hoover Institution adapted the SPINDEX II program in the 1970s, let us examine its early program before outlining the evolution of the three SPINDEX programs. Rita Campbell, archivist of the Herbert Hoover archives in 1966, conceded that some minimal arrangement according to provenance was desirable, but she insisted that indexing for retrieval was not dependent on arrangement. For example, without any regard to record series, "the indexer takes a group of papers, sorts them so that he will be able to group together 5 or 10, hopefully even more, pieces of paper on some general subject into a single folder." The folder is then given a unique number for retrieval identification. Then "the indexer selects from the authority list the descriptors or keywords."[4] For Campbell, a controlled vocabulary is essential in an archival setting, and it must go beyond the broad subject terms associated with the provenance method, to "subjects peripheral to the known subjects of interest in the collection" ("Automation," p. 281). If the subject matter is peripheral, does it deserve mentioning, particularly if the primary subject matter is not first revealed? The keyword list itself "may suggest new relationships to the research scholar" (p. 282). She advised that costs can be minimized by indexing at the folder level instead of the item level. Folder titles, at least for unarranged items, are invented by the indexer. This is the primary base of the Hoover system (p. 285).

More details are provided in an unpublished handout that traces the Hoover Institution program to 1976.[5] For one, the authority list includes terms for document forms, subject keywords, geographical names, and proper names. The indexer is free to add terms as indexing progresses; these are reviewed for possible adaptation in the initial list. The computer program converts unauthorized words to synonyms, makes cross references to synonyms, corrects misspellings, and indicates the frequency with which keywords appear.

Although the program could produce strings of keywords derived from folder headings, no coherent series descriptions could be produced, nor could printouts of collection-level data be generated. To do this the Hoover had planned to supplement its program with the Library of Congress's Master Record of Manuscript Collections (MRMC) and SPINDEX. When the latter migrated to the National Archives, the Hoover Institution began experimenting with it as SPINDEX II, "with good results." This had led to the publication of its general guide in 1979. Its main goal is to convert folder-level data to a computer-based file for immediate access to all accessions for which folder-level control has been established.

SPINDEX I AND MR II

SPINDEX I originated in the Library of Congress in 1966. Frank G. Burke states that it "was designed initially to fill the gap created by question 11 on the NUCMC data sheet," which asked for a description of contents and the scope of the papers reported.[6] SPINDEX I was not implemented at the Library of Congress but was applied experimentally to only twenty-five collections. Instead, the Manuscripts Division modified the Machine Readable Catalog program (MARC). Burke, who was the key figure in developing SPINDEX I, initiated SPINDEX II when he transferred to the National Archives in 1967. When Burke became executive director of the National Historical Publications and Records Commission in 1975, SPINDEX went into its third stage. With this sequential framework in mind let us examine SPINDEX I at the Library of Congress.

At the Library of Congress in 1965 a Master Record of Manuscript Collections (MRMC) was developed to provide administrative information about the holdings. This program was expanded in 1966 to include content information, using the technique of keyword-in-context (KWIC). The result was a "selective permutation index" (SPINDEX).[7] The keypunch operator "translates the container lists verbatim into a punched-card format." Verbatim folder unit titles proved to be one of the weaknesses in SPINDEX I, since titles were, too often, not informative. At the time of Burke's article "Application of Automated Techniques" (1967) the program details were in flux, but the long-range purpose was clear, and has continued through the second and third stages. The program continues to have the capability of analyzing collections at all record levels. In addition, container lists can be reconstituted from the index to each accession. This means that repositories with catalogs, but not inventories, could have an inventory or container list compiled by the computer. The program was written to index finding aids, but will also produce finding aids from the indexes. The latter feature would become more important as an objective at the second and third stages. The program is also adaptable for use at the repository level and for larger networks and records management uses. These are the larger objectives.

After Burke transferred to the National Archives, the Library of Congress staff continued work on their primary program of extracting content information from the many data sources at the Library of Congress. They devised a modified MARC program, to be called Master Record of Manuscripts II (MR II). John Knowlton, head of the Preparation Section at the Library of Congress, describes MR II as "a MARC-based system for the collection-level description of manuscripts and manuscript collections." He says that it is based on an identification and tagging of the crucial elements of description: "Upon this tagging structure then is hung a NUCMC-style catalog entry. Subjects and name index entries . . . are then made upon the basis of the collection description in the scope and contents note. The catalog records are then input and processed by the computer programs." This gives a "complete name and subject index to the cataloging." Knowlton stresses that these are indexes to the cataloging: "The cataloging is a summary of the registers and the registers are a summary of the collections." [8] (See Appendix 5 for an example of the MR II entry form, and Appendix 12 for register pages.) By the end of 1980 the Manuscripts Division had substantially completed the indexing of the card catalog preparatory to its permanent retirement. The total system will be on line. The Manuscripts Division still has a bifurcated system and suffers by failing to extricate their program conceptually from the card catalog configuration. By not indexing the Library of Congress registers directly, and enriching the index with as many entries as information in the registers can provide, a severe restriction is placed on the growth of the system. An examination of the catalog entry form in Appendix 5 for the Charles J. Bonaparte Papers reveals that the source of this stricture seems to be the vestigial catalog card, in that the quantity of name entries is confined by the card configuration and the desire to limit the number of continuation cards. Depending on the kind of records arrangement of the papers, the register will contain either much or little detail in its container listing. For example, the incoming letters in the Bonaparte Papers are arranged chronologically and no attempt is made to note major correspondents. The "scope and contents note" does list fifteen names for the catalog entry, but there are probably well over a hundred major correspondents that merit index entries. By way of contrast, in the register to the Carl W. Ackerman Papers (see Appendix 14) the general correspondence (1907–70) is alphabetically arranged and every correspondent is listed who is assigned an individual folder, a total of about 250 names. In addition, the "subject files" in the Ackerman Papers are also alphabetical by name, containing about 600 more names. The scope and contents note, however, mentions about 35 names to be indexed. If, instead, all names appearing in the register were indexed, there might be more than 800—a very rich source. These file folder headings when listed provide substantial series information in objective, nonnarrative form inexpensively, because content analysis of series is largely superfluous. Through automated indexing, in contrast with the obsolete card catalog, these 800 names in the Ackerman register could be entered relatively cheaply and considerably enhance user access. To do so more fully realizes the potential of the provenance method.

Appendix 5 illustrates the MR II system. By referring to it and the above comments the following assessment will be more useful. For one, a repository need not automate its finding aids to use the elements in the MR II program. MR II provides only a collection-level access, a standard that is met by manual systems as well. The criteria used by the Library of Congress to establish subject entries are unclear but seem unrelated to record levels, and entries are uncontrolled if that is true. Proper names, the other main mode of access, would seem to pose no special problem at the Library of Congress regardless of the vast increase in number as analysis moves to other levels. But if the Library of Congress is to increase proper names in recognition of their importance, the registers must be indexed directly, and they in turn need to accommodate more detail for all series in which proper names are a key feature, but which are obscured if their arrangement is chronological, for example. When the Manuscripts Division proceeds to series level analysis, it will undoubtedly benefit from experiments now in progress in the development of SPINDEX III, and SPINDEX II at Cornell University, Wayne State University, and South Carolina State Archives. The big problem for the Library of Congress lies less in description—particularly if the registers are indexed—than in the area of arrangement. In arranging papers, subgroups still are not being isolated as integral subunits within a given accession. Instead, they are submerged in general series. See Appendix 12 for an illustration from the register of the Bonaparte Papers, showing the submergence of subgroups among series. In the more recent register to the Ackerman Papers in which subgroups are included in the "subject file" series, Ackerman's reports as dean of the journalism school are in containers 190–91 while the subgroup for that office is in the "subject files" in containers 64–97 (see Appendix 14). Treating subgroups as subject files makes it impossible to distinguish subgroups from subject files, and limits the self-accessing value of provenance as a method—not a fault of the method but of its application. As we have seen in an examination of Gracy's recent manual and of Schellenberg's writings, this weakness at the level of arrangement is endemic in the manuscripts field.

Will other repositories follow the lead of the Library of Congress in this new form as they followed the earlier model which was established in the early 1950s as the NUCMC program?

SPINDEXES II AND III

Before we follow the course of SPINDEX's development at the National Archives, an outline of its features is in order. SPINDEX II is a system that contains eleven programs with three modules. One module is for input and files management. Input can be in the form of punched paper tape, punch card, or magnetic tape. Other input programs for specific data-entry devices or media have been independently developed by individual users but are not part of the standard program. Data can be merged, updated, and modified. A second module can produce a basic finding aid. The third module indexes. There are three indexing programs. One, the keyword generator, searches the data fields for indexing terms, and it records each term that is found. The term is associated with the particular level in the record-level hierarchy from which it was selected, and the index term will refer back to that level by its control number. Also, each word in the data field can be indexed as one term, and dates can be indexed. A second indexing program is for sorting keywords in alphabetical order or numerically (in the case of dates). A third indexing program is for printing the index in different formats that are user controlled. Each user designs a data base to fit specific needs. Most users are now using their own input programs and using a wide range of data entry devices. A "level designator" is part of the control number, and is the feature that permits the "formulation of hierarchical structures" and potentially the production of finding aids from the indexes.

A crucial precondition that SPINDEX developers had to contend with was the lack of standards—the lack of uniformity in content and format. Archives and manuscript collections are not arranged and described like publications. The latter are in standard format with title pages, tables of contents, and other shared characteristics that can be readily cataloged, and the cataloging can be shared by all institutions holding copies of that publication. Because of these uniform features of publications, it is easy to provide for user access to the data bases that contain this information. The information is also displayed at the terminals in a standard cataloging format established according to international standards. The user can interrogate the data base at the terminal. Library networks have been established that use various systems that are largely compatible with one another, and consequently pave the way for easy user access. The absence of comparable features for archival sources has required the development of systems that can record raw data whether they have been organized intellectually or not. And because these data are derived from different levels in the record hierarchy, they must be coded to reflect this information, since the search becomes more definite and the probability of success increases at each successive level in the hierarchy. Archival information is also more complex than information for standard library source materials. It was because of these problems associated with variations in intellectual control and formatting of the information that SPINDEX took the form it has. This also accounts for its flexibility, its adaptability to a wide range of archival and records management needs. Unlike an archivally oriented system that deals with information that is hierarchically arranged, library systems have been devised to handle information at the collection level, not below (items are treated like books and not as part of the hierarchy). Frank G. Burke, the father of SPINDEX, volunteers that if on-line access were provided it would be to a data base that is so large it would "make library networks pale by comparison."[9] He implies that the very size of the potential data base has inhibited the National Archives from applying SPINDEX to its own holdings. SPINDEX is, however, being applied to holdings of more than twenty institutions that have formed a SPINDEX User's Network, which publishes a newsletter (*SUN*) and holds annual technical meetings.

To follow the career of SPINDEX we need to migrate with Burke to the National Archives.[10] Beginning in June 1967 with a two-year grant from the Council on Library Resources, tests were conducted to improve the SPINDEX system. The goal was to make it work for collections of varying sizes, and to accommodate information from a wide range of collection descriptions from different kinds of institutions. Nine institutions with computer capabilities cooperated in the subsequent experiments that ended in October 1969.

After CLR funding had ended in 1969, some of the original participants continued their own experiments. At NARS five SPINDEX II applications were initiated between 1969 and 1974. From its experiments NARS produced a draft of the system documentation in 1973. This served as the basis for a conference of the program's users in June 1973. International Nickel Company, South Carolina State Archives, and Cornell University experimented with the program and documentation. Each modified the program to suit its specific needs.

At Cornell University the presidential office records were used to test the program. During 1969–73 a "computer-compatible format" had been developed. This was applied to the records of President Edmund E. Day's administration (1921–52), "indexing the contents of 4,985 individual folders." The index contains subject, personal and corporate names, and topical keywords arranged alphabetically. Since the analysis was of individual folders, folder-level control is achieved. Under each keyword, folders are arranged chronologically. The following information is printed for each folder: full folder title; series, box, and folder number; hierarchical level number (indicating that the unit described is a folder or a collection, series, box, or item); physical and intellectual record types, by identification number; and repository identification number for use in the production of multi-institutional finding aids. The latter point is especially important because the system's users particularly wanted to see the creation of a national data base, beginning with their efforts.

It should be noted that folder titles were not indexed because they were not consistently informative. Consequently, "it was necessary to supply at least one keyword for each folder to appear in the index." (Presumably, folder contents had to be examined to determine keywords.) As to subject analysis for subject keywords, Cornell found it unjustifiably expensive: "This option should be adopted only when the information retrieval clearly justified it, [as] when easily derived personal name and organization keywords are not available" or when a wide range of subject matter is represented. Of the 11,359 keyword terms used, proper names (personal and corporate) represented 60 percent, while topical terms made up about 40 percent.

The South Carolina State Archives illustrates another adaptation of SPINDEX II. Unlike the collections at the Library of Congress and the Cornell University Archives, here strict attention in arrangement is paid to distinct record levels, in the manner prescribed by Oliver W. Holmes. Coupled with this is a program for establishing progressively refined controls by record levels.[11] As a reminder of what is implied from a hierarchical standpoint, by following Holmes, series are first placed with their parent subgroup or agency. This grouping is done as one of the first steps in arranging records containing the work of a parent agency and its subagencies. Series within each subgroup and the administrative records of the parent agency are then refined to the folder level, once they have been linked to their record creator.

The South Carolina Archives has a three-stage control system made up of (1) a general Temporary Summary Guide, (2) a much more detailed computerized Descriptive Guide, and (3) a computerized consolidated index to many of the most important records at the document level. The Summary Guide represents one level of control. It is manually produced, being a simple list of record series that are arranged under each record group and subgroup. Quantity and inclusive dates of each series are noted. The Descriptive Guide represents a second level of control; it uses the SPINDEX programs. From the series descriptions topical keywords are selected as indexing terms, of which there are four types: subjects, types of documents, personal names, and geographic locations. Cross references lead the user from the broader to narrower topics and to proper names. Indexers select from the thesaurus the topic "at the lowest level of specificity which is applicable." This indexing procedure is followed for both series and document-level indexing.

Some series are being identified for more detailed indexing, and isolated items or clusters of importance are indexed, such as a constitution, a petition with supporting papers, and the like. A third stage of control is represented by this level of indexing. In general "content analysis and subject indexing at the document level [is limited] to those voluminous series which contain extremely significant, multi-subject documents, and for which . . . [it is felt] description and indexing at the series level is inadequate for retrieval and use." A forerunner of this system is the one advocated by Sherrod East and Ken Munden in the early 1950s and which is described in chapter 3. Different levels of access controls are indicated in the introduction to the index by showing "which series have been indexed to personal names, geographic locations, types of document, and/or subject topics."

An additional feature of the South Carolina program is its integration into the overall records management program. Provision is made for records to be added to series as soon as current use of them by the agency of origin is terminated, and they are accessioned by the archives.

Of the original group of SPINDEXers, one was from private industry: International Nickel Corporation. INCO uses SPINDEX for a number of records management functions and is extending its applications throughout its subsidiary network.[12]

SPINDEX III improves on II while remaining compatible with it, by "offering much greater sophistication in both the register (text) listings and the index listings" by using "electronic photo-composition for its listing." This feature "will permit selection of up to twenty-five data field types from each SPINDEX hierarchical level." But photo-composition is the only output for III and it is expensive relative to line-print composition. In addition, III permits dual-level indexing. The primary term is indexed, and secondary keywords can either appear independently or "in the context of the primary index term." With respect to the master file, a user of II has to process the entire file; whereas III allows the user to select a limited portion of it.[13]

In Washington State a substantially different application of SPINDEX II has been made, influencing its modification and leading to its third generation. Financed by the NHPRC, the State Historical Records Advisory Board began a statewide survey in April 1977 that included public and private archival sources, most of which were in archival custody. The survey data have been coded and entered into the national data base of the NHPRC. The state's own data base provides access to the collection and record group level, but is capable of providing access to other levels.[14]

Still another application that demonstrates the versatility of the SPINDEX system is Portland Oregon City Archives/Records Management, also funded by the NHPRC. Like the South Carolina system, it is linked with the general records management program, and can incorporate data for active series which are identified on record schedules, as well as accommodate them when they are transferred to archival custody. (See Appendix 20 for an illustration of series-level control in the Portland City Archives.) Like the Washington State project, it incorporates data from the initial city records survey.[15]

The largest program is the one in the Midwest involving four state archives: Wisconsin, Minnesota, Illinois, and Indiana. It also is funded by the NHPRC. Series indexing for subject content is a main focus. Compatability of terminology for series of the same or analagous content is intended to result in a thesaurus that should be useful to all state archives, particularly for "long data" series.* The first objective is to create a nucleus for a regional data base. These data, of course, will be brought into the NHPRC's data base if it pursues its long-range goal.[16] But in the region, access to the series level can be provided before the NHPRC is prepared to do so nationwide.

In all these projects funded by the NHPRC a cassette or a magnetic card is produced by the project agency and sent to the NHPRC office, which processes it and returns a nine-track tape for incorporation into the project agency's SPINDEX program. There it can be used for whatever needs it can serve, fulfilling the purpose of the SPINDEX system.

Four other state projects are in progress in Kentucky, Tennessee, Delaware, and New York. Each is using the program for different purposes: Kentucky for a guide to manuscripts and archives; Tennessee for a guide to manuscripts in the state archives; Delaware for control of state and county records; and New York to survey cultural records in the state.[17]

The Historical Department of the Church of Latter Day Saints first applied SPINDEX in 1977, automating its manuscript catalog. At the same time the department produced an automated catalog for the General Church Records and for photographs. More applications are in progress.[18]

The first product of SPINDEX III was the *Directory of Archives and Manuscript Repositories in the United States*.[19] Begun with the II program, the *Directory* was completed under III. The volume represents the first stage in the development of a national data base under NHPRC auspices. This program at its second stage will gather collection/record group level data. Between the series level and collection/record group level is that of the subgroup. Ideally, the subgroup level should be represented, but few manuscript repositories recognize that level; consequently, that control would of necessity be bypassed for most manuscript collections. Subgroup-level control for most state archives will be possible because subgrouping is normal in such repositories. Until the NHPRC publishes the next volumes for collection-level description, the NUCMC volumes for manuscript collections will continue to be the effective national control for all collections that have been reported to it. But far more repositories are in the *Directory* than report to the NUCMC. Unlike the NUCMC, the NHPRC *Directory* includes institutional and public archives; thus it is more comprehensive in scope.

As users of SPINDEX increased in number and as the variety of specific adaptations and innovations broadened, they decided in 1978 to form the SPINDEX Users Network (SUN). SUN's first newsletter was published in November 1979 in order to share experiences and to inform the interested public. The computer program is owned by NARS and is being promoted by

---

*Long data series are represented by series that have the same kind of organized information repeated, as in tax rolls, audit records, financial records, and census records. The subject data in such series are substantially the same from state to state and could be made part of a general thesaurus for public records.

the NHPRC through its goal of developing a national data base. At present SUN is seeking from NARS information as to its long-range commitment to the program.[20] What that is remains to be seen.

In a discussion of SPINDEX, serious attention should be given to David Bearman's criticisms of SPINDEX III.[21] SPINDEX, he contends, has limitations derived from its orientation to the printing of finding aids. The data base cannot be searched, because it is not on line: "It is not merely the case that the software to retrieve data from the SPINDEX system has not been written; it seems very likely to those who have studied the problem that such on-line access to the data will be prohibitively expensive because of the very structure of the system. . . . The purpose of the directory is to serve as the backbone of a national archival data program. To plan such a program and knowingly commit ourselves to a system which prints guides but cannot be searched on-line, is folly." Bearman explains that efforts to produce traditional repository guides are misspent, and urges that effort be directed instead to making collections accessible in the same depth as finding aids make possible. This would be at series and folder levels in many repositories. Guides are too superficial. On-line access to a national data base that can be searched is the direction in which Bearman points.

Richard M. Kesner also criticizes SPINDEX for being too rigid in its demands for hierarchical control, which in turn act as a pressure for standardizing finding aids. The recent experience of the Minnesota Historical Society with SPINDEX reinforces Kesner's observation. Lydia Lucas of the MHS reports that after the MHS cancelled its original participation in the SPINDEX program it improved its manual finding aid system by making the inventory the core of the system and integrating it by use of repository indexes. When MHS returned as a SPINDEX participant in the Midwest State Archives Project, Lucas comments about the "ease with which we could prepare automated input from manual finding aids." [22] In the light of these two observations perhaps greater attention might be given to the standardizing manual systems in preparation for automation.

In defense of the developers of SPINDEX it should be noted that it was the lack of finding aids standardization that led them to choose the batch processing mode instead of an on-line system. This has meant the recording of data according to the SPINDEX tag structure. By assigning each individual data element a tag number, the data can then be sorted sequentially and hierarchically and the information can then be produced in a recognizable format such as a repository guide or a container list. In either case the user will be led to the record level from which the data were derived. Access is off line, but Burke contends that an on-line system will not produce information "much different from information in the off-line, batch processing, printed output system now being employed [by the NHPRC]." [23] These are serious questions that require prompt examination.

Although NARS owns SPINDEX, it has applied the program only to limited projects, such as indexing the Central Files of the Kennedy White House, the Papers of the Continental Congress, and the Guide to Cartographic Records in the National Archives, and compiling the *List of Microfilm Publications in the National Archives*. Most recently, a cumulative index to more than sixty Guides to German Records has been produced.[24]

NATIONAL ARCHIVES AND RECORDS SERVICES A-1 SYSTEM

The NARS A-1 System is computer assisted and depends on batch processing to bring together all series descriptions into a single master file.[25] A standard format was designed to record the highly varied series descriptions that had been compiled since the 1940s. Because the main purpose was for administrative needs, the extraction of the informational content within the series descriptions has been postponed.

The absence from the data base of index terms derived from series descriptions limits the use of the system for intellectual purposes. The master file is never on-line; only the tapes/discs that are produced in updating inventories are on-line. To have a particular series description displayed at a computer terminal one must know the series storage number. Without this number the user needs to scan all preceding series descriptions to find the one desired. The record group and/or subgroup and/or subsubgroup (and so on) number that contains the series is also required for the search. The printouts present the data in the traditional hierarchical format.

There is limited on-line capability provided for the NARS staff when an update computer tape is created and entered in the system; at that time the identification number can be obtained for future use.

At the time Alan Calmes wrote about NARS A-1, subject indexing was considered prohibitively expensive because of all the problems associated with indexing languages and thesaurus construction. Under the new administration in NARS this problem of providing subject access is being reconsidered. Meanwhile the National Archives still has no unitary system of finding aids, because there is no master index to the master inventory file.*

PARADIGM

PARADIGM (Programmed Annual Reports and Digital Information Matrix) is an automated data processing system developed in 1971 at the University of Illinois.[26] It was established to "maintain administrative and subject control." In the words of Assistant University Archivist William J. Maher: "For administrative purposes we have placed all series and collections within a hierarchi-

---

*The *Descriptive Inventory of the Archives of the State of Illinois* (1978) illustrates this point. The scope and contents note for each series contain proper names and topical references. In my spot-check of the index all proper names and topical references are indexed. The index is relatively short—131 pages—yet is able to effectively index to the series level.

cal numbering system that reflects a major administrative unit . . . , secondary unit . . . , and series/collection name. We treat personal papers as record
series."

"Subject descriptors are selected and coded for 900 record series in the
University Archives." Of these descriptors 76 percent are proper names.
These index terms are selected from a control card, finding aids, "and the
content of the collection" (i.e., some form of content analysis of the actual
series). There is no thesaurus. The system is on line, and it constitutes a single
integrated system that provides access to the series level—using the term "series" conventionally.

Because of the ambiguous use of the term "series," a commentary is in
order. In the above hierarchy the record-group level is the "major administrative unit"; the "secondary unit" is the subgroup level. But series includes not
only the typical series as conventionally defined but also collections of personal papers. This deviates from the customary practice, which is to consider
a manuscript collection (or accession) the equivalent of the record group. This
use of the series concept deprives it of any utility as an organizing tool. So too
would subgroup, record group/collection (accession) concepts lose their utility. Any repository wishing to adapt PARADIGM should bear in mind this
confounding application of the series concept.

NEED FOR COMPATIBILITY

At present the SAA's College and University Archives Committee is reviewing the application of the Ohio College Library Catalog (OCLC) and Research
Libraries Information Network (RLIN) computer systems.* Convenience of
access to terminals for these programs has induced an unreported number of
manuscript collections to add collection-level data to the OCLC data base, or
to consider doing so. OCLC has formed a task force to study its manuscript
format. It is expected also that the SAA's National Information Systems Task
Force will be working with that of OCLC. Among the serious questions to
consider is the adaptability of a library program that was developed primarily
for publications. Can it handle archival data derived from series and file unit
descriptions? If library networks can only handle accession- or collection-
level data, it might be more cost effective for each repository to produce its
own collection-level guides, which in turn would reach a wider community
than is served by the library networks.† This guide information could then be
put into any automated system that wanted the data. Also, an index term or
descriptor from a published work will have an implied meaning different from
the one it has for a manuscript collection or institutional archive. Indicative of

---

*The OCLC is the first national automated network for libraries. RLIN is compet-
ing with OCLC for customers, claiming to have improved on OCLC's program.

†I am indebted to Charles Palm, deputy archivist of the Hoover Institution, for this
suggestion.

the concern for mixing these source data is the long-standing taboo in the archival field against including data from both the manuscript collection and the archive of the same institution in the same catalog. Curiously, some of these same institutions add data to national networks, such as the NUCMC, while at the home base they have no union catalog that would serve the same purpose locally for the holdings of their own organizational archives and manuscript collections. The NUCMC responds to this tradition by limiting its coverage to manuscript collections. We are now witnessing erosion of this taboo through networking and the search for compatibility. If the data are mixed, however, coding will be needed to differentiate them for intelligent use.

In all of this, compatibility is the key to cost-effective archival information systems. Cost effectiveness, in turn, must be subordinated initially to getting a program that can handle archival data from all record levels. If the library-generated programs are not compatible with this need, then it would not be cost effective to put archival data into their data base if the process would have to be repeated for an archival data base.

Richard H. Lytle observes that one assumption shared by archivists is that archives and manuscripts are not for everyone—unlike other library materials. He writes, "the national information system for archives and manuscript collections might well be affected drastically by considering whether many potential users would be better served by another information source altogether." He further contends that the kind of indexing will be conditioned by the characteristics of the user audience. The quality of the subject indexing certainly will be determined by this factor.[27] The broader the user population the more detailed are the information requirements. Skeletal data of the sort found in most inventories will be insufficient for the more casual user. This deficiency leads back to the question about standardization of finding aids and to noting the experience of the Minnesota Historical Society with its SPINDEX participation. Standardization might well be the key, but there is a great inertial drag to be overcome—an anarchy of independent systems and a commitment of resources to their maintenance, come what may.

ARCHIVAL–RECORDS MANAGEMENT RELATIONS AND AUTOMATION

The nature of the archival–records management relations that must be established for effective automation is illustrated by the following problem: File titles must be converted into useful indexing terms if the original headings are not useful. This conversion issue was noted by Richard Lytle in his experiment with the BRISC program wherein poor file headings contributed to the low performance of the content indexing method in comparison with the provenance method.[28] To make useless file titles useful requires that they be converted to terms that can be incorporated into an index. There are two aspects of this problem; one is retrospective and the other leads directly into records management.

Accessions that are received bearing titles that are without good indexing characteristics will require title conversions. If the headings are to be used as the source of index terms, the topical subject of each folder's contents needs to be reflected in the title. In addition, proper names need to be correctly identified, and special attention must be given to proper use of corporate entry, to designate a corporate body by the same term consistently. Most files that are being accessioned in archives are deficient in both respects: poor subject designations and inconsistent identifications of corporate bodies.

While the problem just outlined is one concerned with retrospective conversion of useless file headings, the issue can be dealt with effectively in the future, and eliminate the need for conversion, if there is a close articulation of archives and records management. Only through records management programs that respond to this problem can the need for conversion be eliminated. Titles that are useful as indexing terms and properly identify names must be installed in files management systems if this need for conversion is to be minimized or avoided altogether. As the archival profession deals increasingly with the papers and records of contemporary society, this issue of coordination between archives and records management will become more evident. It is not a matter that can be addressed piecemeal, but only by cooperation between the two fields.

7

Archival Education and Training, 1937 to the Present

In retrospect it should be clear that progress in gaining a consensus on theory and practice in the archival field has been remarkably slow. Considering that Waldo Gifford Leland's opening address at the first Conference of Archivists was in 1909 and tht Victor Hugo Paltsits's outline of a manual on archival economy was presented and accepted in 1912, time has dragged indeed. It may be granted that it did not help matters when Leland, Dunbar Rowland, Arnold J. Van Laer, and others in these early years emphasized the inapplicability of library principles to the management of public records archives. It may also be granted that Gaillard Hunt and other manuscript curators conceded too easily to the public archives group in their feeling that archives and manuscripts should be handled differently. In fact, the common ground had not yet been established, because few manuscripts that were being collected had "organic" or integral qualities that would lend themselves to handling in a public archival mode. We have noted, for example, the cross membership of these persons in the same professional organizations, and that they served on the same committees in these organizations. Each group moved apart, independently developing its own tradition, but the representatives continued to share platforms at the same meetings. Rarely was a potential commonality sensed at these meetings, and when sensed there was too little reinforcement of the kind that would guarantee continuity of systematic development. Significant contributions and observations were not incorporated progressively into a growing intellectual corpus. Witness, for example, some of the writings in the late 1930s by Margaret Cross Norton and Augustus F. Kuhlman, by John R. Russell in the National Archives before its reforms of the 1940s, and later by Ellen Jackson, Sherrod East, Lucile M. Kane, and particularly Theodore R. Schellenberg.

Once the National Archives was established in 1934 there was a sudden demand for archivists. There were few in the United States, and they were already working as archivists. These few did not constitute a labor pool. Fortunately for the National Archives the depression created a pool of unemployed and underemployed librarians and historians. The backgrounds of those who were trained in either of these two professions were relevant to archival work, but they needed on-the-job training to become archivists. Thus the education and training of archivists was almost wholly a catch-up effort until the late 1960s. Even now, the education and training of archivists has been of the postemployment variety, and associated primarily with the individual motivation of the job holder for self-education and economic improvement. Coupled with this has been a tradition of apprenticeship and advancing upward by cumulative practical experience.

Since there was no formal academic program for educating archivists, it is understandable that a truly professional literature was slow to develop, slow to focus on the essentials of archival theory and practice. We have seen the consequences in tracing this history: after some seventy years we are still fumbling for a hold on these essentials.

A continuing theme in the literature is who should provide the education, library schools or history departments. Linked with this choice is the relevance of each curriculum core to archival education. The professional associations in both fields have generally ignored the issue, with but one weak exception currently in process: in order to find nonacademic employment for aspiring historians the American Historical Association and the Organization of American Historians are now trying to identify a new subfield for the "public" historian.* Initiative in librarianship has come from individual library schools, often in conjunction with a history department. Instructors have been drawn from a pool of practicing archivists, usually the nearest one available. If, as is true in most cases, the instructor is drawn from an already understaffed operation, that program suffers even though the time lost to the operation might only be actual teaching time. Moonlighting like this cannot produce the best results no matter how gifted the instructor.

That this argument about who should be responsible for archival education has taken the form it has is unfortunate because the discussion started harmoniously at the 1937 annual conference of the American Library Association. Convenor was Augustus F. Kuhlman, head of its Archives and Libraries Committee, a position he would hold until 1940. At this first meeting of the committee Margaret Cross Norton led a discussion on archival training.[1] In addition to talking about a suitable teaching site, she spoke about the "dearth of technical professional literature" and the prospects for remedying it soon with the publication of the syllabus on classification and cataloging that her committee in the Society of American Archivists was preparing. She also submit-

---

*The term owes its origins to the increasing employment of trained historians by federal agencies, which employ them as agency historians. With the decline in number of academic positions, other fields are being identified for potential application of the historians' craft. The archival and preservation fields have been so identified.

ted a curriculum outline that enlarged on Victor H. Paltsits's proposed archival manual, originally presented in 1912 at the Conference of Archivists.

In view of the exclusion of manuscript collections from consideration in the future Bemis Report (presented at the 1938 meeting of SAA and published in the *American Archivist* in 1939), a particularly notable reference was made by Norton to the need to "include training not only for archivists but also for curators of manuscripts and librarians for historical societies." She said, "There is at present no special training for such positions but [there is] a growing demand for library school graduates who can fill such places." Norton made this recommendation because "at present there are few positions for trained archivists and no trained archivists because there are so few positions."

The dilemma plagued the field from the beginning. Archival education had to be taught as a subfield of another profession, because there was little effective demand for archivists as such. And when positions became open, there were few or none among the applicants who had the qualifications. Consequently, until recently, postemployment training and self-education have been the only ways of learning.

Kuhlman, in reporting on this 1937 meeting, pronounced that the first task of the committee was educational and promotional: "The interest of librarians and of the public needs to be aroused, directed and motivated in the care and preservation of archives—public, institutional and family records." It should be remembered that he was responding to the immense potential of the ongoing Historical Records Survey, a subject that remained in the forefront of this committee's work while he was its head. He continued, "Funded knowledge as to acceptable methods for handling archives should be made available and should be diffused." [2] Obviously he saw a vital role for the American Library Association in the effort, but unfortunately his ALA colleagues did not share his enthusiasm or his broad vision. Instead, the ALA narrowly focused its effort on developing a cataloging code for manuscripts that is more of a handicap than something of positive value. [3] The ALA ignored its broader responsibility to expose future librarians to the special requirements of administering manuscript collections and to stress the responsibility of librarians for their institution's own archives. Contrast the ALA's future indifference to Kuhlman's closing remarks:

> . . . social scientists, directors of library schools, librarians, and archivists have common interests in recruiting and training new archival workers. Should not the several hundred public document librarians and curators of historical manuscripts and of near-print materials have the same fundamental pre-professional and to some extent professional courses as public archivists? Both need the same thorough grounding in all of the social sciences including some law if they are going to become competent to appraise, select, and organize wisely for use the materials to be preserved for the future. Both must become the peers of social science scholars and learn to talk their language if they are to be worthy of

their trust. . . . It is also recognized that there are certain problems peculiar to the organization and administration of public archives that can be approached more effectively by the American Society of Archivists than by the A.L.A. Committee on Archives and Libraries. Gradually the similarities and differences between archival economy and library economy will become defined and established in a body of funded knowledge—that is, a communicable technique that is one of the prerequisites in placing the work on a professional level.

Following this conference, Kuhlman wrote to Carl Milan, executive secretary of the ALA, "I think there is room for organizing in the A.L.A. a powerful group that is concerned with public and private archival matters including every kind of manuscript material and near-print material." He had earlier written of the need to "tie [the SAA] in with the A.L.A." [4] Whether he had in mind the subordinating of SAA to the ALA or working closely with SAA is less important than that he saw the need to work together whatever the organizational relationship. His record bears this out. He expected the National Archives to lead the way in developing an "archival economy," "principles that should govern the organization and administration of archival and historical manuscript collections." [5]

In his last year as committee head, Kuhlman remained ebullient about the potential of the HRS, writing to the new ALA president, Charles Brown, "an enormous amount of interest in the proper collection, organization, and preservation of historical manuscripts [has been activated by the HRS] and it is appropriate that this committee should devote a goodly part of its energy . . . to the subject of historical manuscripts." Later that year funding of the committee's operations ceased and Kuhlman resigned. [6] With his resignation also ended any serious effort to involve the ALA in archival education for librarians, although Roscoe Hill, the committee's leader from 1943 to 1947, reported in 1944, "At the Princeton meeting of the archivists the opinion was expressed that library schools were neglecting greatly an opportunity opened to them by the need for trained archivists and manuscript custodians." [7] As we shall see, this experience with archival education would be repeated in different form and circumstances in 1970.

If the ALA in 1940 saw no role for itself in promoting archival education among librarians,* some influential historians saw a role for their profession, if not for the AHA as an organization. When the Society of American Archivists was established in 1936, it formed a Committee on the Training of Archivists, headed by a diplomatic historian, Samuel Flagg Bemis. Its members were primarily historians with an interest in archives. One was R. D. W.

---

*John J. Boll wrote about education in librarianship in 1972: "Unfortunately, by custom and voluntary abdication, we must exclude archival materials from this list." See "A Basis for Library Education," *Library Quarterly* 42 (April 1972): 200.

Connor, archivist of the United States, who was a historian before ascending to that lofty position. Another was Theodore C. Pease of the University of Illinois history department, who had contributed to the archival field as early as 1915. The two other members were Herbert E. Bolton, historian and director of the Bancroft Library, and Ralph H. Lutz, director of the Hoover War Library. The Bemis Report emerged from the committee at the 1938 meeting of the SAA.[8]

The Bemis Report ignored manuscript collections and their proper administration, choosing to concentrate on the training of public and institutional archivists. Taking inspiration from the Prussian State Archives program, "toward which our instruction might strive as an ultimate goal," Bemis saw historical training as providing the best background. "It is the historical scholar who dominates the staffs of the best European archives," he said. "We think it should be so here." He drew attention in Prussian training to the relatively little emphasis on "so-called library science." Apparently, the committee, for good reason, had been disenchanted by the record of librarians in mistreating archives, and assumed that it would always be thus, despite the accommodating leadership of Kuhlman as long as he was head of the ALA's Archives and Libraries Committee. At that time there was a clear opening for interdisciplinary and interprofessional collaboration. This crack in the doorway would be closed after issuance of the Bemis Report and the resignation of Kuhlman. Bemis saw librarians as performing a useful role, "but it should always be a subordinate role." He would not concede that interested, motivated librarians might have the capacity to grow with compensatory education.

Training recommended in the report was for two different classes of archivists. The first class ("exalted").should be for directors of "major municipal, state, and national archives." For them a doctorate in American history was essential. The second class of archivists need only have a master's degree in the social sciences, "with a support in library technique." Training for both classes should include study in history (including use of archival sources) and relevant social sciences, and exposure to library classification and cataloging, government documents, and reference materials. The committee's affirmative attitude toward the relevance of library classification and cataloging is puzzling, since these elements in librarianship had been recognized as the principal source of previous mishandling of archival materials by librarians.

Of some relevance also is that the originally keen interest of the AHA in the work of its Conference of Archivists had tailed off abruptly with the nation's entry into World War I. That interest continued feebly until the AHA's Conference of Archivists was succeeded by the SAA in 1936 (an act that was promoted by the AHA). Given the declining interest of the AHA in archival matters it seems that the Bemis committee expected the SAA to assume leadership despite the absence of any academic connection for the SAA. This inconsistency was not addressed. Historians never stepped forward in the training role until 1962, when Wayne State University's history department did so.[9]

It is particularly ironical, in light of the Bemis Report, that the first archival course in the United States was given in the library school of Columbia University during fall and spring of 1938–39. Solon J. Buck of the National Archives was the instructor. Margaret Norton followed Buck the next summer. H. G. Jones, author of the first history of the National Archives and state archivist of North Carolina, noted in 1968 that almost all the shorter courses to date had been given in library schools. For the SAA not to have worked at that time to support this initiative through Kuhlman's Archives and Libraries Committee of the ALA is also curious. The timing was opportune, but the SAA leadership did not push its opportunity with Kuhlman. Perhaps the SAA was deflected from this effort by the entry of Ernst Posner on the scene in the summer of 1939. Posner had been an archivist in the Prussian Privy State Archives and also had taught the subject. He was immediately appointed professor of archives administration in the American University, where the National Archives would jointly offer a course on "The History and Administration of Archives." Considering the small demand for archivists nationally, this one course probably sufficed for a time. But the larger issue of exposing librarians formally to the subject was lost once Posner filled the immediate need, primarily as an adjunct to the training needs of the National Archives.[10] On the other hand, this development was consistent with the thrust of the Bemis Report. The combination of these two factors reinforced the separatism that had begun in 1910. Overlooked in this concentration on vocational training was the intellectual discipline of archival work. In a vocational setting the substance of the education is inevitably practical in immediate emphasis. As such the theoretical basis and broader implications of practice rarely are explored systematically in the actual workplace. A survey of the literature reveals that a recognition of this deficiency in the education and training of archivists has been lacking.

Buck's own attitude about the training and the required background of archivists was consistent with the Bemis Report, but was tempered by experience. The recommendations offered in his article, "The Training of American Archivists" (1941), constitute the elements of a curriculum core to this day.[11] The archivist should be "well-grounded in history, and especially the history of the country or district he serves." He should also know the "current workings of his government" and "needs to understand the historical method." He should "know something about the special fields of knowledge to which the documents in his custody relate" and have a "broad general education and the ability to orient himself in any field of knowledge when the occasion arises." Finally, the archivist must have special training in archival administration. Buck lists fourteen components of this course in archival administration. Coupled with this theoretical education must be a practicum in the form of in-service training or an internship. Nowhere in his article is there a role for librarianship, not even a reformed librarianship, if indeed reformation was possible after Kuhlman's departure from the archival scene.

We have already traced some of the subsequent history of the National Archives and American University program in describing the metamorphosis of T. R. Schellenberg. He had participated with Posner in teaching the general course, and then had directed the summer institutes in the late 1950s. Schellenberg became the principal advocate for conducting courses on archival administration in library schools after teaching such a course at the University of Texas in 1960. He continued these summer offerings throughout much of the 1960s. Because of his advocacy, the SAA decided to feature a session at its 1966 meeting, with H. G. Jones defending the traditional view about the primary relevance of historical training. Jones's paper provided a thorough history from an archivist's side of the subject, and of the subject as an issue.[12] His treatment will not be recapitulated here. While conceding that library schools are one appropriate place for such courses, given the continued indifference of history departments since the recommendations in the Bemis Report, Jones insisted that library schools must have archivists as instructors. And students must be allowed historical training. For Jones, another appropriate place for archival training is history departments. He preferred this alternative and outlined a proposed curriculum. Noting that the SAA had "done little officially to encourage the establishment of training courses," he concluded: "For more than 30 years we have been talking about the need for more and better training. It is time for us to stop complaining and get to work."

Schellenberg agreed with Jones about the need for a thorough foundation in history,[13] and for the same reasons that Jones, and Buck before him, had given. All agreed about the content of the archival component of the curriculum. But Schellenberg added the necessity for auxiliary training in records management, and some courses in librarianship, especially classification principles and systems, reference sources, and government documents. He saw the need for "active collaboration of several departments." But library schools ought to have responsibility for the courses, because historians "are not concerned with methodology," with the application of archival principles. Librarians, on the other hand, have mistakenly applied their own techniques to archival materials with poor results. But given the will to learn archival methodology, library schools should do the training, because librarians *are* concerned with methodology. The methods of the two disciplines Schellenberg regarded as complementary and having the common goal of making materials available for research. He concluded that "since neither profession has developed adequate training programs, each profession should welcome training developments within the other."

John C. Colson, of the University of Maryland Library School, responded to Jones and Schellenberg.[14] He wisely observed that too much emphasis had been placed by librarians and archivists on the differences in the materials that each dealt with. Instead, he pointed out, both are engaged in interpreting information and making it available for use: "Unity among archivists and librarians can best be fostered by developing a program for preparation . . . that emphasizes our joint concern for the systematic organization of knowledge regardless of its origin or its format. . . . The common profession of archivists and librarians is that of making information available for use." Colson urged the development of library schools into schools of archives and library administration to help achieve this common goal. In making all of this information accessible, he saw a key role for the computer, and for reprography. History departments are not prepared to offer this kind of education because it is not germane to the history curriculum, Colson contended, and that is why no history department had established an adequate training program for archivists.

Philip P. Mason, as chair of the SAA's Committee for the 1970s, reported in 1972 that the SAA had taken no leadership, given no direction to education and training.[15] It was this lack in SAA of a sense of responsibility for education and training that led me in early 1967 to seek formation of a unit for manuscript librarians within the ALA structure. Arline Custer, editor of the NUCMC, joined in this effort, and arranged for an organizational meeting at the ALA's 1967 annual meeting.[16] The unit was formed within ALA's Association of College and Research Libraries (ACRL) by expanding its Rare Books Section to include manuscript librarians, and to change its name accordingly. (The SAA responded later by creating a Joint Committee on Archives-Library Relationships.)

It had been our purpose to develop programs for educating and training librarians in administering manuscript libraries. A manual was needed and its preparation became a high priority. The manual could well become a text for use in library schools and as an operations manual.[17] Work on it proceeded. Custer first invited the SAA and the Manuscript Society (and later the AASLH) to participate in its compilation. At the ALA's annual meeting, June 21, 1969, she called for consideration of a committee to study manuscript training in library schools. Mr. Kahn, representative of the SAA to the committee, told of the study by SAA of all types of manuscripts and archival training. Custer stated that the Committee on Manuscript Collections wished SAA success and offered "any help necessary."[18] Since the manual was considered part of the education program, Howard Applegate was delegated to seek funding, aiming first at the Council on Library Resources (CLR). Verner W. Clapp, director of CLR, later expressed an interest, the ALA Publications Department head gave the project high priority, and Custer wrote to William Alderson, director of the AASLH about the manual.[19]

A sudden turn then occurred. The Council on Library Resources had been funding a project by AASLH for "a manual on collection and servicing of local history materials in libraries." Its author, Joseph Wheeler, had died, and according to Clapp, in a letter to the executive secretary of ACRL, Alderson decided to approach CLR with a proposal to "re-orient the project so as to develop a handbook for the acquisition, custody, organization and care of manuscript collections." Clapp went on to say, "The Association is of course aware of the interest in such a handbook on the part of ACRL . . . and would be very happy to have the collaboration of ACRL and/or the Committee on the project" through an advisory committee. Clapp concluded this account of recent events, "Accordingly, I now write to you to ask whether ACRL would wish to collaborate. . . . May I express a hope that it will wish to do so?" [20]

Probably unknown to Alderson at that time was a series of events within the SAA during the preceding months. Clapp, in the summer of 1969, had met with the SAA president, Herman Kahn, to learn whether the SAA would sponsor such a manual. Kahn's response was affirmative, and he named a potential author for it. The nominee accepted the offer, but Clapp was then persuaded by a former SAA president to withdraw from the proposed project, because it was believed no one in SAA was qualified. Alderson then approached Clapp. [21]

The result, in any case, was to end the work of the ACRL's Manuscripts Committee on the manual, and to terminate the potential involvement of the ALA itself in support of archival education. The AASLH contracted with Kenneth W. Duckett, who produced *Modern Manuscripts* in 1975. In a general way, this potential involvement of the ALA in such a program parallels the experience of 1939–40. In all of this, the SAA had remained cool to the idea of training archivists and manuscript librarians in library schools, while continuing to offer only limited workshops mainly for postemployment "archivists." [22]

Robert M. Warner, as chair of the SAA's Education and Training Committee, reported in 1972: "Increasingly, these courses are being established in library science schools rather than in history departments, although a number of schools today list the course in both areas. A contest between disciplines does not seem to exist, regardless of where the course is given." [23] Perhaps this observation of the educational leaders in the field marks the end of the mystique surrounding the theme of the Bemis Report. At least the trend sharply departs from that shackling manifestation of elitism, for Warner concluded, "Archivists today seem to concentrate more on being the link between primary sources and the historian rather than being scholars endeavoring to build comprehensive collections that reflect particular themes in American history." [24] It could be added that if many archivists had not been infatuated with the mystique of the Bemis Report—that archivists should consider themselves scholars primarily—they would have dealt more directly with archival problems and helped to bring the profession along faster in its development. The snobbishness that was cultivated by the report carried with it an unwarranted contempt for librarians and librarianship, and came unfortunately at a time when the opportunity for fruitful collaboration was most promising.*

---

*A casualty of this elitism was the Library of Congress, where the scholar-as-archivist concept had led to the chaos that faced Solon J. Buck in 1948 when he took charge of its Manuscripts Division and led it to the modified archival form of administration it now has. The Library of Congress had had an uninterrupted series of historical scholars in charge before Buck. Buck himself had been an academic historian before he assumed direction of the Minnesota Historical Society in 1914, where he activated a program of collecting organic papers and records of twentieth-century origin. None of his predecessors had his combined background of scholarship and experi-

While the SAA's committee continued its work in developing specifications for formal archival education as a subfield of an established academic discipline such as librarianship or history, the committee also addressed the well-known fact that most practicing archivists had been self-taught. Consequently, it promoted postemployment training programs. The SAA, responding to the initiative taken in this area by some of the regional and state archival associations, began to sponsor short institutes and workshops, frequently in cooperation with those associations. Its *Basic Manuals Series* is intended to introduce students and practitioners to the full range of archival practices. This is consistent with Frank Evans's recommendations about postemployment training. Also it recognizes that the registrants are rarely interested in academic credit, and therefore the SAA does not need academic affiliation to pursue this part of its program. Most of the SAA's efforts are in this area of training.

To deal with formal academic programs, the SAA assigned its Committee on Education and Professional Development the task of developing guidelines. These were approved in 1977 as "Guidelines for a Graduate Minor or Concentration in Archival Education." [25] These guidelines have been supplemented recently by a proposed practicum. [26] Their aim is to influence the quality of formal academic programs, all of which lie outside the SAA's authority. To gain authority, the society plans to use accreditation as its means— not only accrediting institutional offspring, but individual archivists and archival programs. How it is to give effect to this authority remains to be seen. In turn, its *Basic Manuals Series* will need outside review if it is to serve as a basic reading core. There is already a serious need to upgrade the quality of some of these manuals. They are being used now by teachers of archival administration, some of whom lack archival training and the background essential to evaluate course material, organize practical exercises, and compensate for deficiencies in the literature.

Concurrent with these developments inside the community of archivists have been changes in both library education and the history field. Some library schools are moving toward two-year programs that allow students to take outside electives. History departments are now beginning to prepare their graduate students for nonacademic careers as applied historians. [27] Lawrence McCrank sees these developments as mutually beneficial. He points to the double master's degree program at Case Western Reserve University as a model. Case Western students register for two years of interdisciplinary training, improving their career choices accordingly.* They can choose public his-

---

ence as a true archival administrator. They had been historical scholars who brought prestigious reputations with them to the Manuscripts Division, and were expected to apply their erudition to the Library of Congress's manuscript collection itself. They brought distinction to the office but little or no archival expertise. They contributed nothing to development of the archival profession except their own good works—editorial products for the most part.

*Since the above was written, Case Western has abolished its program, and there is one now at the University of Maryland.

tory, librarianship, or an archival career. McCrank sees a weakness in the continued reliance on practicing archivists as adjunct faculty, because he fears it overemphasizes practice at the expense of "theoretical research and retards the profession by not providing the pool of research scholars available to other professions" (p. 449). But it is precisely these archivists who have made the major contributions to the literature; certainly no library school or history faculty has made notable contributions. That the quality and breadth of their writing has not been as satisfactory as it might have been had these adjunct faculty been fully engaged in teaching and research is obvious. It is this feature of McCrank's recommendations that sets the leadership of the SAA on edge in the matter of archival education. The laboratory and practicum, essential for archival education, require library school faculty who have undergone the experience of archival work in substantially all its phases. This would hold true for historians as well. Given these requirements the only teaching pool at present is those practicing archivists who are themselves teaching and doing research. For the near future, there will continue to be dependence on them to do the job until an alternative teacher pool is developed.

McCrank also belittles the introductory courses that have as their objective "archival awareness" for administrators who deal peripherally with archives. It would have been better all around, I feel, if present library administrators had been sensitized when they were students. But these introductory courses will continue to fill a real need through consciousness raising if nothing else.

To recommend as two writers have done recently, that a basic cataloging course should be the "cornerstone of any archival education program" is to ignore the past history of failure that has resulted from assigning a central position to cataloging.[28] Cataloging gives a wrong direction to the major archival enterprise, which is first to bring into archival custody all such documentation that is worth saving. This means massive accessions over which effective intellectual control must be established. Cataloging must accommodate that process, and it has not thus far. It must become part of the whole workflow involved in establishing intellectual control and no longer stand independently or at the center—it is in fact an end product. Interdisciplinary and interprofessional collaboration of the highest order is required for building an adequate curriculum. A series of regional and national colloquiums would be a healthy first step, and a necessary one. To take it requires leadership. The ALA, AHA, SAA, AASLH, Organization of American Historians, and the Association of Records Managers and Administrators would form a nucleus for such symposiums. Who takes the initiative in this vacuum remains to be seen.

8

Hindsight, Foresight

The archival profession faces major tasks and decisions in several areas: automated systems and subject access; collecting and appraisal in relation to intellectual control and records management; education and training; and archives as part of information science. The importance of some of these areas has been acknowledged by the appointment in recent years of appropriate ad hoc committees or task forces by the Council of the Society of American Archivists. This does not mean, however, that there is general agreement on what the next steps should be. A summation of the historical background should be helpful for those who are addressing current archival problems.*

The historical manuscripts tradition (HMT) was shaped by two factors: the collecting of the accidental documentary remnants of the remote past, and an orientation to item control instead of control of items as integral record series. (In the latter case the general subject character of the item is implicit in its association with the other items in the series.) But the HMT was fated to deal with items as items because only rarely were series ever collected intact.[1] The nature of the collecting of manuscripts and of the methods for their intellectual control were in harmony. Later, when repositories turned to collecting the more integral records and papers of the recent past, the sheer mass of paper defied techniques of control that were concerned with single items rather than items as parts of a collection. In the nineteenth century, when the HMT took root, the only systematic method of intellectual control was that provided by librarianship. What documents were collected had usually been separated from other records with which they had originally been linked. They normally came under some form of library administration, either in a historical society

* "Foresight," as used in the chapter title, has a limited meaning; no predictive connotation is intended.

A slightly modified version of this chapter, under the title "Toward National Archival Priorities: A Suggested Basis for Discussion," appears in *AA* 45, no. 2 (spring 1982): 164–74.

or library. Preconceived classification schemes that had originated in the library field were applied to give the collected items an apparent unity they lacked. Items were usually grouped by subject and arranged chronologically within each group, and cataloging was done directly from an examination of the manuscripts themselves. If calendaring was the goal—and it usually was—the items would be arranged and listed chronologically, the listing accompanied by a synopsis. A proliferation of finding aids resulted: catalogs, calendars, shelf lists, special subject indexes, and other aids. Moreover, this array of finding aids could not be approached from a single access point such as a union catalog; each aid stood on its own.

After World War II major manuscript repositories began collecting manuscripts of recent origin. State archives, following the lead of the National Archives, became more oriented toward contemporary records and applied techniques of records management to assure their integral character. Major manuscript repositories borrowed heavily from concepts and techniques that were being developed at the National Archives. They were forced to borrow from the Public Archives Tradition (PAT) because the HMT was item-oriented and thus incapable of dealing effectively with the extensive, integrally related manuscript collections they were acquiring. This amalgamating process led manuscript curators successively to accept the principle of provenance as the basis of arrangement, the series concept as the main unit of control, and finally, in the 1970s, the concept of a hierarchy of record levels over which controls would be established progressively, beginning at the record group/accession level and ending at the item level. This concept of establishing progressively refined controls had its beginnings in the United States with Waldo Gifford Leland in 1909[2] and was expanded by the National Archives staff after the reforms of its finding aids system that began in 1941.

Knowledge of these archival traditions makes it possible to view pressing archival problems of the present in both an historical and a theoretical context that can in turn provide a basis for determining national archival priorities.

AUTOMATED SYSTEMS AND SUBJECT ACCESS

Our earlier preoccupation with traditional cataloging and the card catalog format has obfuscated an objective analysis of the whole array of finding aids and their relationships: what they are and what they might become. Traditional cataloging has led to the separation of the technique itself from the total process of control that begins with accessioning and ends with description. Such automated library networks as the Ohio College Library Center (OCLC, now called On-line Computer Library Center) and the Research Libraries Information Network (RLIN) represent a continuation of the HMT. *Anglo-American Cataloging Rules* (AACR) is intended to ease the way toward the use of these automated systems, but these rules seriously restrict the adaptability of these networks to the cataloging of modern manuscript collections.

In following AACR, one uses the whole collection as the source of cataloging information. In other words AACR is in the HMT because cataloging is done from the actual manuscripts and not from a control device, such as an archival inventory, that records each successive stage of control.* Archivists should be wary of becoming locked into automated systems without deciding what the source of cataloging information is to be and what level of detail a national system should be prepared to handle. If these library networks cannot handle archival data that are hierarchically arranged according to record levels and are progressively brought under control, the expenditure might be a complete waste.

Analysis of fundamentals is needed before major commitments of resources are made. For example, such pilot projects as that for President Edmund E. Day's papers at Cornell University and the BRISC project[3] proceed directly to file unit analysis without having first taken advantage of the information that is provided by the provenance method. These experiments ignore the cost-beneficial results that the provenance method provides in a self-accessing manner, and they closely resemble features of calendaring, a technique that has been considered antiquated since about 1950. If scale alone is considered, it is highly doubtful that these pilot projects are relevant. To become even moderately effective in dealing with the archives of 20th-century society, pilot projects like these must move into the records management field. They must become part of the files management process, devising useful file titles and standard entries for proper names instead of passively accepting and coping with what they find when records are received in the archives. Neither of these two pilot projects even takes this aspect of the problem into account, although in each of them dissatisfaction is expressed about the descriptors with which they had to deal.

Archivists should also postpone a decision about automated systems until

---

*Since writing the above text in 1980 some important changes have occurred during 1981–82. A group headed by Steven Hensen of the Library of Congress's Manuscripts Division has drafted a revision of the AACR2 rules for cataloging manuscript collections. On page 3 of the draft is the statement: "In actual practice these finding aids . . . are, in effect, the only practical equivalent to a chief source of information." This postulate represents a potentially new basis of consensus from which an integrated system can be structured, if the inventory/register is the agreed upon format, and if there can be agreement on its basic structure and purpose (to serve as the source of catalog/index terms).

Some principles of inventory construction are now incorporated in the second edition of the University of Washington Libraries *Manual for Accessioning, Arrangement and Description of Manuscripts and Archives* (1982) and a paper bearing that title was co-authored with Uli Haller for the October 1982 annual meeting of the SAA. These principles, as enunciated, have been submitted as a basis for development by the archival profession. If they are adopted the next step is for the profession to develop a clear understanding of the concept of "establishing progressively refined controls." The manual referred to above is the most recent attempt at clarification.

we have more fully considered the feasibility of and need for on-line access.* At the national level, do we need to provide users with as much information as the repository has established for any or all of its holdings? Perhaps yes, perhaps no; but the question should be addressed. For example, because of their smaller compass, statewide and regional networks might permit faster progress in recording data from series and file unit levels than would networks that depend on the initiative of a central national office. Many repositories can provide access to a substantial number of their accessions at file unit level for on-site users. They can input this data into statewide and regional networks directly, in the way that the Midwest State Archives Project is now doing.† This same degree of access should be considered in an automated system at the national level when a national network is prepared to handle data below the collection/record group level. A manual equivalent of this is achieved now when copies of inventories are sent to off-site users who respond to information they derive from NUCMC or other union catalogs and subject guides. At the repository level, it would seem shortsighted and not cost-effective to feed data into a program that cannot handle data below the accession level, and to do this simply because a terminal for that program is conveniently available. Also, can archival data be mixed with publication data when the reference terms imply something quite different for each category? And, as the quantity of data from archival finding aids is much larger than that for regular library materials, how much of the archival data can be accommodated without constituting an overload of the system? My impression is that in archival history, a fear of overloading the catalog is what limited its role as a finding aid and denied to it a comprehensive integrative function in the manner of a union catalog. Decisions about automated programs should be made with deliberate speed, but with an emphasis on deliberation. Consensus on construction of the manual systems that are to be automated must precede the adoption of automated systems.‡ This proscription does not preclude experimentation of the type now in progress with SPINDEX. There is, however, an element of finality about inputting data in OCLC or RLIN that ought to be guarded against if joining the network means a long-term commitment of resources that might better be conserved until the issue has been examined more fully.

---

*Critics of SPINDEX object that the system is off-line. But SPINDEX has its defenders. See *AA* 44 (Winter 1981): 5–7, for a debate among David Bearman, Nancy Sahli, and Frank Burke. Recently, an attempt was made to merge some of the different data bases using the SPINDEX program and this proved infeasible because of the lack of standards in finding aid construction.

†The Washington State survey project, although using the SPINDEX program, has not provided for reporting below the accession level for manuscript collections. The finding aids are cataloged and the catalog entry is then indexed. This parallels the MR II program of the Library of Congress, and represents bifurcation, not integration.

‡The SAA's National Information Systems Task Force is currently dealing only with the problem of formatting information. It has not yet addressed the fundamental issue of whether the actual manuscripts or the finding aids are to be cataloged. And, among

For progress in the matter of subject terms, for example, we must accept a pace that proceeds by record levels instead of skipping to content analysis at the file unit level. Present practice in subject analysis is too undisciplined to be usefully continued, unless a larger purpose can be served, such as a general thesaurus. In proceeding by record levels, primary subject characteristics down to the subgroup level should be noted first; these are relatively easy to establish. It is at the subgroup level that provenance is most helpful in implying subject matter acted upon. To provide topical subject access effectively, a thesaurus of primary subject terms for each archival field might be developed: one set of terms for state and local public records, one for college and university archives, one for business archives, and other sets of terms unique to other archival fields. A composite of all these primary topical subject terms could constitute the basic list of subject terms. Experience with establishing these lists for all archival fields should be instructive for establishing lists for use at the series level. To deal systematically with these problems will require attention to indexing languages and thesaurus construction. As a guide, Dagobert Soergel's pioneering work will provide a good starting point.[4]

This raises the general issue of subject access. Subject access is the heart of the problem. The different modes of subject access ought to be more clearly

---

finding aids, it has not yet been agreed that the inventory should be the control document.

The NISTF has chosen the MARC program for manuscripts as its format and considers a single data element capable of providing substantially all of the intellectual content data needed. This single data element is the equivalent of the scope and contents note in the NUCMC format and corresponds to a prose description of a record group or subgroup. Being in prose style this format is incapable of incorporating the specific context in which a catalog/index term occurs. A properly constructed inventory will register context simply by its format; e.g., whether the term is that for a subgroup, or is a correspondent name in a series, or is a subject. The promoters of the NISTF defend their use of the MARC format because their objective is limited only to informational exchange among institutions, and it is not intended to serve the users of archives and manuscript collections. But what are the possible consequences of this commitment to the MARC format for manuscripts; is it temporary, transitory, or long-term, and what is its nature? Recall that the NUCMC rules have had a long-term effect on repositories. (See Terry Abraham "NUCMC and the Local Repository," *AA* 40 [January 1977]: 31–42.) Logically the profession should be moving toward accepting as a first principle the idea of entering data directly from a control document into the data base. This is a trend only, however. Direction is needed to give coherency.

A further question arises: For what purpose are institutions exchanging information if not for the end user? And if it is the end user who is to become the ultimate beneficiary why not build on this fresh consensus about "source of information," which is also consistent with the recommendation of the SAA's Finding Aids Committee in 1978: that the inventory be considered as the main finding aid and that a cumulative index to inventories should provide access to all holdings? See Lydia Lucas, "Efficient Finding Aids: Developing a System for Control of Archives and Manuscripts," *AA* 44 (Winter 1981): 21–26, and Mary Jo Pugh, "The Illusion of Omniscience: Subject Access and the Reference Archivist," *AA* 45 (Winter 1982): 33–44.

One of my students, Uli Haller, helped in the formulation of this footnote.

recognized. As Richard H. Lytle indicates, provenance itself provides a high degree of self-access to orderly papers and records.[5] The name of the record creator, whether a person or corporate entity, private or public, implies something about the subject matter acted upon. For example, in the records of the Forest Service we can expect to find an array of forest resources subject matter. Subject content at this level does not depend on content analysis for its revelation; it is implied without such analysis. An inventory will record the arrangement of record series, along with a brief series description if one is needed. Relationships among series, and of the file units comprising them, can be studied in an inventory. For example, if there are gaps in a correspondence series but none in the minutes, then the minutes can be searched for information missing from the correspondence. If the minutes refer to a relevant subject report, then the inventory of the report series can be checked to see whether it is present. If there are subject series—and in most twentieth-century collections they abound—the series description or file unit headings can be checked for clues. Characteristics of a series are made known by describing, in an inventory format, the order of the file units that comprise the series. This process represents description according to provenance. Provenance in this context serves as an inferential system of information, and this usage conforms to Lytle's meaning when he distinguishes between the provenance and content indexing methods of subject retrieval.[6] At each successive level of control there is a higher probability that the information being sought is there. This probability depends on the record level from which it is derived; if it is derived from the file unit level the reference will carry a higher predictability of success in the search than it would if the term had been derived from a subgroup description. The content indexing method should be employed only with an awareness of what kind of information is needed that the provenance method has not revealed, and only when there is a high probability both that the information is there and that it is needed. If the information is not needed, it would seem to be unnecessarily expensive to extract it.

Another mode of subject access also takes advantage of two elements that are given. One element is provenance, and the other is the methods users employ in approaching manuscript collections and archives. This mode recognizes that users normally will have done background reading about their chosen subject before approaching archival sources. In the course of this reading users will have associated proper names with the topical subjects of interest. In this way users provide their own mode of subject access; the repository can take advantage of this by maximizing its control over proper names to provide users with a higher degree of precision in their search.* This is relatively easy if at least some of the records are arranged alphabetically. Provenance is less helpful as a self-accessing method where files are arranged

---

*To my knowledge I am the only archivist to have incorporated this proper name-subject linkage into a finding aid system; it is a cornerstone of the University of Washington system.

chronologically. To reveal proper names in such arrangements requires analysis of the files themselves for their primary content, including proper names. In all of this it is important to recognize the complementary relationship of the provenance and content indexing methods. Hindsight provides a lesson here. If the disciplined standards of "describable item cataloging," as outlined by Sherrod East in 1953 and Ken Munden in 1956, had been broadly practiced since 1956, we would now be in firm command of the problem, instead of having to start almost from scratch.[7] East and Munden placed item cataloging within the framework of establishing progressively refined controls.

COLLECTING AND APPRAISAL IN RELATION TO INTELLECTUAL CONTROL AND RECORDS MANAGEMENT

The persistent inability of archivists and manuscript librarians to process and describe papers and records of recent origin for effective access has adversely affected collecting and collection development. Arrangement and description have too long been harnessed to expensive cataloging principles; this has contributed to the lag in collecting of contemporary archival documentation. Traditional cataloging has not only been expensive, but its undisciplined character has made it relatively unreliable as a method for providing comprehensive access. While granting that lack of proper storage is a second major factor in retarding collection development, the primitiveness of our methods for intellectually controlling materials of recent origin has been a strong primary inhibitor in its own right.*

There is a definite relationship at another level between intellectual control and collecting of contemporary archival documentation. Effective standards of appraisal are essential if we are to pursue our mission of collecting all that is worth preserving. Yet these standards depend upon a qualitative assessment of the documentation already in archival custody. Qualities in papers or records are hidden by the way they are arranged and described. We need to be aware of significant gaps in the collected data if those gaps are to be filled in. We need to know where collected series leave off so that we can insure their continuation. We need to know the quality of archival sources in custody, how they have been used, and their potential not only for continued use but for new uses—e.g., for other categories of scholars, different research methods, and for more uses in administration. Above all, we must work to minimize the element of chance in collecting, and move into more systematic collection development, following the lead recommended by Mary Lynn McCree in defining collecting objectives.[8] In this, the goal should be nationwide archival coverage, and the various archival societies should take the lead in coordinating this collecting activity. Coverage must aim at comprehensiveness in

---

*A hidden factor is a psychological one associated with the false notion that only old or rare documents qualify as "historical." In reality any current papers or records having potential archival value are historical and researchable.

scope, and at consecutiveness for major archival series within record groups and manuscript accessions.

As an accompaniment to these considerations, we must be more selective about what we acquire. Collecting is initially an appraisal decision. Standards of appraisal are crucial to the implementation of this goal. We must decide what to keep and what to destroy. For archival documentation to be as authoritative as it should be, it must not only be comprehensive in scope and consecutive in sequence, but it must exclude useless and/or minimally useful series and file units. Historians and those from other academic disciplines, administrators, and individuals who depend upon archival sources will be handicapped to the extent that this larger goal is not accomplished. However, all those who create, work with, or use archival sources need to engage in the appraisal process together, each bringing his or her perspective to bear upon the documentation requiring evaluation. In addition to historians who use traditional methods of research, those who employ techniques of quantitative analysis must be involved. Similarly, other kinds of users, both actual and potential, need to be identified and brought into the decision-making process. The professional organizations, whose constituents either are major users of archives or are concerned with their collecting and organization for use, ought to become involved in the appraisal process. At a minimum, those professional associations that represent historians, political scientists, public administrators, records managers, archivists, and librarians ought to join the effort. The contemporaneity of modern archives also poses special problems in historical evidence that historians have yet to deal with systematically.

Machine-readable records in particular need attention because they are being produced in enormously increasing volume and there are few programs set up to deal with them as archives. Those series that are archival in quality can be identified at their creation and be earmarked for archival retention. In appraising machine-readable records, records managers will have to be consulted and coordination with them will need to be undertaken systematically.[9]

Apart from the matter of machine-readable records, archivists who are not responsible for overall records management at their institutions need to work closely with the people who are assigned that responsibility if they are to assure the preservation of archival records. Institutional archives depend upon close articulation with records management. Like machine-readable records, other archival record series need to be identified in records schedules so that they can be scheduled for either archival review or definite retention. In an institution that has an archives but no records management program, the archivist should seek to establish records management, preferably under archival control, so that a layer of administration is not imposed between the archivist and the records. The degree to which records management is influenced by archivists will largely determine the quality of the archives. Special librarians should do the same for the institutions they serve if there is no archivist.

Active involvement in records management is essential to the archivist's mission; records management is fundamentally a system of appraisal and it should be developed within that frame of reference.*

EDUCATION AND TRAINING

We archivists, manuscript curators, librarians, and historical society administrators would have functioned better in the past if we had all been formally trained either for archival work or at least in an appreciation of what it entails. To review the literature on archival training and education is disheartening. Who should undertake the training, the historical profession or schools of librarianship? The American Historical Association (AHA), the Organization of American Historians (OAH), and the American Library Association (ALA), representing their respective professions, have until recently almost completely ignored their responsibilities in this matter. The question, however, is not only the persistent one of who is to teach the subject, but, even more important, how it can be taught most effectively. Although the specific components will vary in accordance with the local situation, it is crucial that the historical perspective be taught, in particular for its value in collection development, appraisal, and reference service. Archival methodology has not been of central interest to historians, but it must receive primary attention if the advantages of an historical perspective are to be fully implemented in the archival context. The value of the historical perspective for the archivist is in improving his or her ability to bring researchers and their sources together, as Robert Warner suggested in 1972; this is preferable to Samuel F. Bemis's view that archivists should primarily be historians.[10]

Substantially all archivists, manuscript curators, and manuscript librarians (including the author) have taught themselves while learning the job. Most come from backgrounds in librarianship and/or history. Entering as neophytes, most have concentrated on learning the then current state of the archival art; the present state of confusion and disarray suggests what the earlier conditions were like. Too few have raised themselves above narrow mastery of mere techniques borrowed from myriad institutional settings. As a result, the literature has lacked general relevance, and we have muddled through. Acquiescence to the prevailing conditions has been typical. As an example, it took about two generations for the concept of different record levels to become part of our common language, and even now too few really know how

---

*In trying to establish a system that would assure the retention of archival records and the routine disposal of non-archival records, the National Archives invented records management. At its core this system has been concerned with files management at the point of operations, and with the scheduling of records for disposal or retention. In the later 1940s the staff saw the need for regional archives and records centers to implement the program. Records centers were established, beginning in the early 1950s, and archival components were added to them beginning in 1969. These are the three key elements of the appraisal system; most other elements in the spectrum of records management functions are intended to support these elements.

to translate this recognition into actual levels of control; an example of this lack of understanding is the slow progress of the National Information Systems Task Force and the debate about AACR2. If archival education had been formalized like that of other professions, the quality of the professional literature would undoubtedly have been higher. An academic program would not only have prepared most for a vocation, but would also have provided for the necessary continuing interaction between the practitioners and their teachers. The teachers, with their graduate students, could pursue problems that practitioners face daily but have little time to resolve with the needed care. This kind of interaction and research are what academic status for the subject would bring about. Without such status there is no reason to believe that the future will be different from the past.

There are encouraging signs, however. Both the history and library professions are awakening to the opportunities for a role in archival education. The AHA and the OAH are well on the way toward training aspiring historians for such nonacademic careers as archival work. Also, individual library schools * are responding with archival management courses, preparing recruits to librarianship for archival work, but the ALA is not involved in this effort. The kind of organizational leadership that characterizes the history field is lacking in the library field. Perhaps the initiative being exercised by these few library schools will stimulate the ALA finally to assume greater responsibility than it has since the "halcyon" days of 1937–40, when August F. Kuhlman and his Archives and Libraries Committee were trying in vain to activate ALA's interest.[†] There is a real possibility that this will happen as a result of the basic reorientation that is leading the library field to encompass all aspects of information control and access.

The role of the SAA in archival education has been largely peripheral. Lacking an academic link, the SAA has, for the most part, substituted archival workshops, beginning in 1964 with one-day sessions that were cosponsored by NARS and local institutions. After the SAA secretariat was established, education became a more definite program. The SAA's *Basic Manual Series*, which began in 1977, is intended to provide building blocks for the education process. Some are excellent, some are inadequate, and some are not really manuals.[‡]

---

*The University of Wisconsin, Wayne State University, and University of Maryland are examples.

[†]A. F. Kuhlman headed the ALA's Archives and Libraries Committee, 1937–40. He organized annual meetings that brought together manuscript librarians, public record archivists, historians, and others. The proceedings were published as *Archives and Libraries*. His efforts represent the nearest the ALA has come to being involved in archival education.

[‡]For example, the manual on arrangement and description (David B. Gracy II, *Archives and Manuscripts: Arrangement and Description*, Chicago: The Society of American Archivists, 1977) fails to distinguish successfully between series and sub-

More recently the SAA has considered accreditation as a means of influencing archival education, and in 1977 it approved some guidelines for that purpose. (See the *SAA Newsletter*, May 1977). However, the traditional bias of SAA against such courses being conducted in library schools is evident in this comment, quoted in the March 1980 *Newsletter*, that one of the problems of professional education is "keeping library schools from controlling archival education programs." I know of no attempt at such control.

Returning to the issue of who should teach, there seems to be no question that initially archivists should comprise the primary teacher pool. Archivists must be the teachers "initially" because the quality of archival literature is so uneven and diffuse that only an experienced archivist can compensate for its deficiencies. Instructors in "public history" should recognize their own limitations and those of the literature on the subject; they should also recognize the critical importance of including an archival practicum. Instructors in librarianship also should recognize their own limitations and be aware of the history of library catalog codes and of their shortcomings for modern manuscripts. In light of this history I find it absurd to make cataloging the cornerstone of archival education.

CONCLUSION: INFORMATION SCIENCE

Of primary importance to librarians and archivists is the impact that automation has had on both the production and storage of and access to information. This reorientation is leading to a redefinition of librarianship as "information science," which is concerned with access to intellectual information and is thus quite different from applications of automation for administrative data about records.

Automating access to information for intellectual objectives is non-routine and much more complicated than automating programs to handle library and archives business functions. To do it well, we need more studies of user behavior and a better understanding of the hierarchical structures into which information is organized, and we must continue to study the ways in which

---

groups; it does not show how to translate controls that are established in the arrangement process into a descriptive program; and it contains serious inaccuracies. That such a crucial manual as this one has just been reprinted without revisions casts doubt on the judgment of the editorial board. In the manual on business records (Edie Hedlin, *Business Archives: An Introduction*, Chicago: The Society of American Archivists, 1978; see p. 8, "Provenance") the editors allowed the author to equate the principle of provenance with the concept of original order. The editorial board's decision to include accessioning in the same manual as appraisal (Maynard J. Brichford, *Archives and Manuscripts: Appraisal and Accessioning*, Chicago: The Society of American Archivists, 1977) is questionable, because accessioning is a critical first step in establishing control and therefore should properly be included with arrangement and description. Brichford devotes only one page to appraisal in relation to manuscript collections.

these two features of information science affect each other.* Beyond the intellectual horizons of both archivists and librarians, it seems, is a clear recognition that they must devise ways to affect the quality of the information that is generated in the first place. Information quality is determined in the workplace by the kind of file headings employed, by the way(s) files are organized, and by other ways information is generated and managed. Librarianship has many of the essential tools required for these tasks; archivists (and records managers) can learn to use and adapt them. If archivists in particular do not pursue an active role in information management they must inevitably perform the role of "refile" clerks—making better sense of records that are poorly identified and organized originally.

Whether or not they assume this kind of active role it is nevertheless of utmost importance to learn how much information is provided in a cost-beneficial and self-accessing manner, as it is in the mere recording of useful original filing index terms in an inventory format. In addition, the very structure of the inventory format should convey the basic relationships of the series and of the file units that make them up. All of this can be done without the expensive and subjective type of content analysis employed, for example, in the BRISC project.

While there is some recognition of hierarchy of information among librarians (e.g., in analytical cataloging), with manuscripts and archives this feature is more significant. Librarians generally deal with each book as a discrete unit, and they impose relationships by means of subject classification primarily; whereas archivists must both arrange (the equivalent of publishing) and describe each accession in terms of its hierarchical structure which usually includes two to four intermediate levels between the accession/record group and item levels. As we prepare to automate archival and manuscript information, we must consciously shed the historical manuscripts tradition once and for all.

How difficult this is to do is indicated by the BRISC experiment, which Lytle analyzed. Although its creators believe that they are acting within the PAT, their practices represent a return to the HMT: they largely ignore the information that is easily provided by intelligent use of the provenance method and resort instead to content indexing in the tradition of librarianship, a tradition that is rooted in calendaring as well as in cataloging. Once the vestigial baggage of this tradition has been removed as a restraint, archivists and manuscript librarians can concentrate upon the central purpose of modern manuscript collections and archival management—the collecting or bringing into archival custody of all archival documentation of contemporary society.

---

*Richard H. Lytle, who is chair of the National Information Systems Task Force, and the task force itself are dealing with this problem. The SAA's Finding Aids Committee also dealt with this issue while under my chairmanship, 1976–78. See also Lytle's "Intellectual Access to Archives: I," 66–70.

The problems that have been associated with providing intellectual access will no longer be an impediment to such collecting goals if the HMT is abandoned. To do this effectively, sound records management principles must be developed as part of the general appraisal process and there must be interdisciplinary and interprofessional collaboration, brought together from a strong sense of urgency and a commitment to the end result, the systematic collection of the archives of contemporary society and their organization for use. It is high time that we move ahead.

Glossary

Terms and their definitions are selected from "A Basic Glossary for Archivists, Manuscript Curators, and Records Managers," Frank B. Evans, Donald F. Harrison, and Edwin A. Thompson, compilers; William L. Rofes, editor.* Commentary/extensions are by the author and are in square brackets. Some terms have been added by the author and also appear in square brackets.

ACCESSION. (1) The act and procedures involved in a transfer of legal title and the taking of records or papers into the physical custody of an archival agency, records center, or manuscript repository. In records center operations, transfer of legal title may not be involved. (2) The materials involved in such a transfer of custody. [Also useful as a substitute for the term "collection" when that term is meant to refer only to individual accessions that are part of a repository's manuscript collection as a whole. *See also* "Collection," "Papers," "Records," and "Record Levels."]

ARCHIVES. (1) The noncurrent records of an organization or institution preserved because of their continuing value; also referred to, in this sense, as archival materials or archival holdings. (2) The agency responsible for selecting, preserving, and making available archival materials; also referred to as an archival agency. (3) The building or part of a building where such materials are located; also referred to as an archival repository (or, in U.S. Govt., archival depository). In American usage, the term *archives* is generally a plural or collective noun, although the form *archive* has been applied to a number of special collections.

ARCHIVIST. A person responsible for or engaged in one or more of the following activities in an archival repository: appraisal and disposition, accessioning, preservation, arrangement, description, reference service, exhibition, and publication. *See also* "Manuscript Curator."

ARRANGEMENT. The process and results of organizing archives, records, and manuscripts in accordance with accepted archival principles, particularly provenance, at as many as necessary of the following levels: reposi-

---

*Published in the *American Archivist* 37 (July 1974): 415–33, and separately available from the Society of American Archivists; reproduced here by permission.

tory, record group or comparable control unit, subgroup(s), series, file unit, and document. The process usually includes packing, labeling, and shelving of archives, records, and manuscripts, and is intended to achieve physical or administrative control and basic identification of the holdings. *See also* "Processing."

CALENDAR. A chronological list of individual documents, either selective or comprehensive, usually with a description giving one or more of the following: writer, recipient, date, place, summary of content, type of manuscript, and page or leaf count.

CHECKLIST. (U.S. Govt.). A finding aid, usually for a particular accession, created by an archival agency and consisting of a preliminary listing of records with or without summary description of their informational content. With the development of the record group concept this finding aid evolved into the inventory.

CLASSIFICATION. (1) The predesignated filing system for a record series. (2) The act of identifying documents or records in accordance with a predesignated filing system.

COLLECTION. (1) An artificial accumulation of manuscripts or documents devoted to a single theme, person, event, or type of record. (2) A body of manuscripts or papers, including associated printed or near-print materials, having a common source. If formed by or around an individual or family, such materials are more properly termed *personal papers* or *records*. If the cumulation is that of a corporate entity, it is more properly termed *records*. (3) In singular or plural form, the total holdings—accessions and deposits—of a repository. *See also* "Manuscripts," "Papers," "Record Group," and "Records." [Used in both a singular and plural sense, the term is ambiguous and a source of confusion. Historically, papers and records were brought together by their collector as artificial collections. The term implies both plurality and artificiality; its use should be restricted accordingly. "Manuscript collection" is correct if used to connote the acquisition of two or more *accessions*; but "accession" should be used when referring to the individual accessions that make up a collection. Another alternative term that has been used is "manuscript group"; it is satisfactory except when applied to accessions of only one item or accessions of miscellaneous items having no integral relation. *See also* "Record Levels," "Manuscript Group."]

COLLECTIVE RECORD GROUP. A modification of the *record group* concept which for purposes of convenience brings together the records of a number of relatively small and short-lived agencies that have an administrative or functional relationship, the records of each such agency constituting a separate subgroup. *See also* "General Record Group," "Record Group."

CORRESPONDENCE. Letters, postcards, memoranda, notes, telecommunications, and any other form of addressed, written communications sent and received.

CORRESPONDENCE MANAGEMENT. Application of records management techniques to correspondence to increase efficiency, improve quality, and reduce costs. In Canadian usage, *treatment of correspondence*.

CURRENT RECORDS. Records necessary for conducting the current business of an office and which therefore must be maintained in office space and equipment. In Canadian usage, *active records*. In Canadian and U.S. Govt. usage records are regarded as current or active if there is at least one reference use per cubic foot per month; in business usage, four references per file drawer per month.

[DEPOSITORY LEVEL. Oliver W. Holmes defines "arrangement at the depository level" as "the breakdown of the depository's complete holdings into a few major divisions on the broadest common denominator possible and the physical placement of holdings of each such major division to the best advantage in the building's stack area." This is applied in the National Archives.]

DESCRIPTION. The process of establishing intellectual control over holdings through the preparation of finding aids [i.e., catalogs, inventories, registers, checklists, calendars, special lists, indexes, etc.].

FILE. (1) An accumulation of records maintained in a predetermined physical arrangement. Used primarily in reference to current records, the term in archival usage may refer to either a series or a file unit such as a folder or dossier. (2) To place documents in a predetermined location according to an overall plan of classification. (3) In machine-readable records/archives, two or more data records of identical layout treated as a unit. The unit is larger than a data record, but smaller than a data system, and is sometimes known as a *data set*. (4) Storage equipment, such as a filing cabinet. *See also* "Series."

FILES. A collective term usually applied to all records of an office or agency.

FILES ADMINISTRATION. The application of records management techniques to filing practices, in order to maintain records easily and to retrieve them rapidly, to ensure their completeness, and to facilitate the disposition of noncurrent records.

FINDING AIDS. The descriptive media, published and unpublished, created by an originating office, an archival agency, or manuscript repository, to establish physical or administrative and intellectual control over records and other holdings. Basic finding aids include guides (general or repository and subject or topical), inventories or registers, location registers, card catalogs, special lists, shelf and box lists, indexes, calendars, and, for machine-readable records, software documentation.

FONDS. A term widely used in Europe to designate for control purposes the archives of a particular type of institution or organization; a term comparable to the concept of the record group.

FORM. Any document, printed or otherwise produced, with space(s) for inserting information, descriptive material, or addresses.

GENERAL RECORD GROUP. Record groups with titles usually beginning

"General Records of . . ." established for most executive departments and several independent agencies as a practical modification of the record group concept. Such record groups include the records of the office of the head of the department or agency and the records of other units concerned with matters, such as fiscal and personnel, that affect the department or agency as a whole. Several of the record groups of this type include records that were produced by bureaus or comparable units but that were incorporated into central files maintained for the entire department or agency. [*See also* "Record Levels."]

[INTEGRAL RECORDS/PAPERS. That quality of documentation within an accession that approximates completeness, permitting an analysis of activity of the record-creator extended over time; aiming at authoritativeness of the documentation because of its substantial completeness. Used interchangeably with ORGANIC RECORDS in this book. It is this shared quality that justifies handling of personal papers according to principles derived from the public archives field.]

INVENTORY. (1) A basic archival finding aid that generally includes a brief history of the organization and functions of the agency whose records are being described; a descriptive list of each record series giving as a minimum such data as title, inclusive dates, quantity, arrangement, relationships to other series, and description of significant subject content; and, if appropriate, appendices which provide such supplementary information as a glossary of abbreviations and special terms, lists of folder headings on special subjects, or selective indexes. (2) In records management the term is used to describe a survey of records prior to disposition or the development of records retention schedules. *See also* "Register" (2).

ITEM. The smallest unit of record material which accumulates to form file units and series, e.g., a letter, memorandum, report, leaflet, photograph, or reel of film or tape.

MANUSCRIPT. A handwritten or typed document, including a letterpress or carbon copy. A mechanically produced form completed in handwriting or typescript is also considered a manuscript.

MANUSCRIPT CURATOR. A person usually engaged in one or more of the following activities in a manuscript repository: solicitation, accessioning, processing, preservation, reference service, exhibition, and publication. *See also* "Archivist."

MANUSCRIPT GROUP. An organized body of related papers or a collection, comparable to a record group, for control purposes. *See also* "Record Group."

MANUSCRIPTS. Documents of manuscript character usually having historical or literary value or significance. All manuscript records may thus be regarded as manuscripts, but generally the term is used to distinguish non-archival from archival material. Included in the term are bodies or groups of personal papers with organic unity, artificial collections of documents acquired from various sources usually according to a plan but without regard to provenance, and individual documents acquired by a manuscript repository because of their special importance. *See also* "Collection," "Papers."

[ORGANIC RECORDS. Used interchangeably with INTEGRAL REC-ORDS, q.v.]

[ORIGINAL ORDER. Relates to the original filing scheme employed by the person or record-creating agency. It is to be distinguished from the order/disorder in which papers and records are received. One of the first processing tasks at the accessioning stage is to learn whether there was an original filing system and, if there was one (or more), how it might be re-stored. Often confused with the principle of provenance, which relates to record creation not to the way records have been filed. *See also* "Prove-nance," "Registry Principle."]

PAPERS. (1) A natural accumulation of personal and family materials, as distinct from records. (2) A general term used to designate more than one type of manuscript material. *See also* "Collection," "Manuscripts," "Per-sonal Papers."

PERSONAL PAPERS. The private documents accumulated by an individ-ual, belonging to him or her and subject to his or her disposition.

PROCESSING. The activities intended to facilitate the use of personal pa-pers and manuscript collections generally comparable to arrangement, de-scription, and preservation of archival material.

PROVENANCE. (1) In general archival and manuscript usage, the "office of origin" [of] records, i.e., that office or administrative entity that created or received and accumulated the records in the conduct of its business. Also the person, family, firm, or other source of personal papers and manuscript collections. (2) Information of successive transfers of ownership and cus-tody of a particular manuscript. (3) In archival theory, the principle that archives of a given records creator must not be intermingled with those of other records creators. The principle is frequently referred to by the French expression, *respect des fonds*. A corollary, frequently designated as a sepa-rate principle, is the Principle of Sanctity of the Original Order (Or *respect pour l'ordre primitif*, *Registratur Prinzip*, or Registry Principle). [*See also* "Record Levels."]

PUBLIC RECORDS. (1) In general usage, records accumulated by govern-ment agencies. (2) Records open to public inspection by law or custom.

RECORD GROUP. A body of organizationally related records established on the basis of provenance with particular regard for the administrative his-tory, the complexity, and the volume of the records and archives of the in-stitution or organization involved. Collective and general record groups represent modification of this basic concept for convenience in arrange-ment, description, and reference service. *See also* "Collection," "Collec-tive Record Group," "General Record Group," "Manuscript Group," "Subgroup," ["Record Levels"].

[RECORD LEVEL(S). Record levels are recognized as the basis for establishing progressively refined controls over integral papers and records. Conceived in the National Archives, the concept has been subsequently refined to the point that the following levels are recognized: depository level, record group/accession level, subgroup level, series level, file unit/folder level, and item/document level. Depository level is dependent upon administrative convenience. Record group/accession level relates to provenance; whereas series and other levels relate to the way records and papers are arranged within the record group/accession and subgroups. In other words, series include file units that are made up of items; they are filed as records of the record-creating agency, which is either a record group or a subgroup. *See also* "Depository Level," "Record Group," "Series," "Subgroup."]

RECORDS. All recorded information, regardless of media or characteristics, made or received and maintained by an organization or institution in pursuance of its legal obligations or in the transaction of its business.

REGISTER. (1) The list of events, letters sent and received, actions taken, etc., usually in simple sequence, as by date or number, and often serving as a finding aid to the records, such as a register of letters sent or a register of visitors. (2) (U.S. Govt.) A term applied to the finding aid developed in the Manuscript Division of the Library of Congress to describe groups of papers, collections, and records by giving their provenance and conditions of administration; scope and general content including span and bulk dates; a biographical note about the person, family group, or organization whose material it is; its arrangement; a container list which is essentially a folder listing; and, on occasion, selective document indexes. *See also* "Inventory."

REGISTRY PRINCIPLE. The basic archival principle, sometimes referred to as the Principle of Sanctity of the Original Order, *respect pour l'ordre primitif*, or *Registratur Prinzip*, which maintains that archives should be retained in their original organizational pattern or structure and in their original filing arrangement in order to preserve all relationships. *See also* "Provenance."

SERIES. File units or documents arranged in accordance with a filing system or maintained as a unit because they relate to a particular subject or function, result from the same activity [this clause leads to confusion of series with subgroups], have a particular form, or because of some other relationship arising out of their creation, receipt, or use. Sometimes known as a *record series*. [Briefly, the file arrangement or system, if any, imposed by the record creator on items generated in conduct of current business. Also, series represents one level in a hierarchy of record levels—intermediate between the subgroup and file unit levels. In practice, series are assigned to their parent agency or to one of its subgroups depending on the source of their creation. *See also* "Record Level(s)," "Subgroup."]

SUBGROUP. A body of related records within a record group, usually consisting of the records of a primary subordinate administrative unit. Subgroups may also be established for related bodies of records within a record group that can best be delimited in terms of functional, geographical, or chronological relationship. Subgroups, in turn, are divided into as many levels as are necessary to reflect the successive organizational units that constitute the hierarchy of the subordinate administrative unit or that will assist in grouping series entries in terms of their relationships. *See also* "Record Group," ["Record Levels"].

[This term has been extended by the author to personal papers as well as records of corporate bodies. Its usage in this context is defined as the separate corporate activities for which the person was the agency of action. Persons often act as the agents of voluntary organizations, public bodies, and trade and professional associations as officers or in committee work. Records generated in that capacity quality for subgrouping under the name of the agency for which the person acted. To do so achieves subgroup-level control. This concept may also be applied to family papers in which items belonging to individual family members are represented. See the author's chapter in *Drexel Library Quarterly*, January 1975, and "The Record Group Concept," *Georgia Archive*, Winter 1976.]

[SUBJECT SERIES. File units for topical subjects are often established by the record creator. Included are all types of records: letters, clippings, pamphlets, telephone memos, and so forth. Current practice is to leave them intact but give them some logical arrangement within the subject file unit if necessary. Current practice opposes creation of subject files that do not already exist.]

SUBSERIES. An aggregate of file units within a record series readily separable in terms of physical class, type, form, subject, or filing arrangement.

SUBSTANTIVE RECORDS. *See* "Program Records."

SUMMARY GUIDE. A preliminary guide to the holdings of a repository, generally lacking in descriptive detail regarding the informational content of record and manuscript groups, subgroups, and series.

Appendix 1

Excerpt from *Catalog Rules: Series for Archival Material* (Illinois State Library, 1938)

2. Departmental Entry.

20.   Archival series are entered under the name of the department of origin. By department of origin is meant (in this code), the department which gathered the items into series as a record of its business transaction. The term does not apply to the department which was the author of individual documents in the series.

21.   The following rules for departmental entry apply to series only (including sub-series). They do not apply to analyticals for individual documents or groups of documents within the series.

22.   Library rules for entering printed "public documents" are based upon the author relationship while the archival catalog entry is based upon the collecting activities of the department. Theoretically, therefore, library entry rules cannot be followed; practically, however, many of the forms of entry worked out through long experience are analagous and can be applied to archival departmental entry.

23.   The departmental entry for a series comprises two parts — the geographic origin of the series (the name of the country, state, province, county, municipality, military or judicial district, etc.) and the legal name of the department.

24.   Typing. The departmental entry is begun on the first horizontal guide line of the card (one half inch from the top), at first identation (one inch from the left margin of the card.) If the entry requires more than one line, begin all lines after the first at second indentation (four typewriter spaces in). Capitalize the initial letter of each geographic name, the initial letter of the first word of each department and sub-department in the departmental entry, also proper nouns. Separate the geographic, departmental and sub-departmental entries by periods followed by two typewriter spaces, but avoiding double punctuation. Common abbreviations may be used, such as U.S., Ill., dept., div., etc.

Geographic Origin.

25.   Unless otherwise stated on the card it is assumed that all series were compiled by the governmental unit to which the archives department belongs. Therefore the geographic designation is omitted on the catalog card (being implied) except for series deposited by some other governing body, such as county or federal archives on deposit with the state archives.

>   EXAMPLES: Archives in the Illinois archives department
>   would be entered as follows:
>
>   Secretary of state. (meaning Illinois.
>   Secretary of state)
>
>   Cook county. County clerk (i.e., Illinois.
>   Cook county. County clerk)

Appendix 2

Data Sheet for *The National Union Catalog of Manuscript Collections*

THE LIBRARY OF CONGRESS
DESCRIPTIVE CATALOGING DIVISION—MANUSCRIPTS SECTION

DATA SHEET FOR THE NATIONAL UNION CATALOG OF MANUSCRIPT COLLECTIONS

Name of Repository:

Reported by: Date:

1. Name of collection and inclusive dates of material:

2. Principal name around which the collection is formed; i.e., person (full name, birth and death dates), family, business, society, governmental agency, or some other corporate body:

    Give relationship to the collection; i.e., writer____ , addressee____ , collector____ , other (specify) _____

3. Occupation or type of activity of the principal person, family, or corporate body; significant events and dates in the career or activity; and place of residence or location of activity:

4. Number of linear shelf feet (if 1 foot or more)_____ ; or number of items _____ (known ___ or estimated___).

5. If the collection contains copies of manuscripts, describe the form(s) of reproduction (handwritten or typewritten transcripts, positive or negative photocopies, positive or negative microfilm with no. of reels) and give the number (or fraction of total) of each kind. Give location of originals, and dates and circumstances under which the copies were made:

6. Full citation of any published or unpublished description, guide, index, calendar, etc.:

7. Research access restricted _____ , unrestricted _____ . State nature of restriction and when it will be terminated:

134

8.   Information on literary rights available in repository: Yes ___ , Do not know ___ .

9.   Nature of acquisition (gift, permanent deposit, etc.), date(s) and source(s) of acquisition and former owner(s):

10.   If this is, or was, part of another collection, state name and relationship:

11.   DESCRIPTION OF CONTENT AND SCOPE OF THE COLLECTION.

This description should cover: types of papers (e.g., correspondence, letters, diaries, documents, etc.); dates, subjects, and types of groups of materials that bulk largest; relationship of the material to specific phases of the career or activity of the principal named in item 2; full names, dates, and biographical identification of other persons and names of corporate bodies significant (by quality and quantity of material) to the collection, showing dates, types, and subject matter; geographical areas covered; specific events, topics, and historical periods with which the materials deal; and particular items of extraordinary interest.

Appendix 3

Hierarchical Controls, Record Group Level Control: Excerpts from the National Archives *Guide*, 1974

COMMENT: Illustrated is a brief administrative history followed by a general outline of series in the administrative office records. "Records of the Chairman" represents the beginning of a subgroup description. The second page of this appendix, "Basic Elements in Citation," illustrates the nature of hierarchical controls in general.

RECORDS. 1945-49. 20 lin. ft.

These consist chiefly of operating manuals, general and special orders, administrative letters, bulletins, circulars, and memorandums.

AUDIOVISUAL RECORDS. 1946-49. 2,800 items.

Photographs illustrating WAA activities, arranged alphabetically by subject, and of real estate assets, arranged by plant contract number.

RECORDS OF THE WAR MANPOWER COMMISSION (RECORD GROUP 211)

The War Manpower Commission (WMC) was established within the Office for Emergency Management by an Executive order of April 18, 1942, which transferred to the WMC the Civil Service Commission's National Roster of Scientific and Specialized Personnel, the Office of Procurement and Assignment of the Office of Defense Health and Welfare Services, and the labor supply functions of the Labor Division of the War Production Board. Within a short period the Committee on Fair Employment Practice, the U.S. Employment Service, the Apprentice Training Service, the Training Within Industry Service, the National Youth Administration, and the Selective Service System were all transferred to the WMC. On March 6, 1943, the Review Committee on Deferment of Government Employees was established within the WMC to pass on draft deferment requests; that same year the Committee on Fair Employment Practice was replaced by an independent committee, the National Youth Administration was transferred to the Federal Security Agency for liquidation, and the Selective Service System was made a separate agency.

The WMC recruited labor for war and essential civilian industries, trained labor for jobs essential to the war effort, analyzed manpower utilization practices to increase labor efficiency, and accumulated national labor market information. The WMC worked through a headquarters office, regional and State offices (which planned and supervised work), and area offices and local U.S. Employment Service offices (which handled operations). An Executive order of September 19, 1945, terminated the WMC and transferred its functions (except those of the Procurement and Assignment Service) to the U.S. Employment Service, reconstituted by a Labor Department order. The procurement and Assignment Service was attached to the Federal Security Agency.

There are 1,212 cubic feet of records dated between 1940 and 1947 in this record group.

GENERAL RECORDS OF THE COMMISSION. 1942-45. 3 lin. ft.

Representatives of the Departments of War, Navy, Agriculture, and Labor; the Federal Security Administration; War Production Board; Selective Service; and U.S. Civil Service Commission, with the Federal Security Administrator as Chairman, made up the Commission. The records consist of minutes, May 6 and 13, 1942; summary minutes, of, agenda for, and documents to be considered at meetings, 1942-45; and railroad labor contracts for transportation and employment of unskilled Mexican labor, 1943-45.

RECORDS OF THE CHAIRMAN. 1942-45. 18 lin. ft.

Included are correspondence with Government agencies, unions, and the

filed the record. The final two elements have been added by the archival depository for control and retrieval purposes.

An example of the method of identifying and indicating the hierarchical location of an originating office through subgroups would be, for example, "Metals Section, Mineral Deposits Branch, Geologic Division," which is part of Records of the Geological Survey, Record Group 57. Subsequent citations of items from the records of the Metals Section could omit the hierarchical location information; i.e., "Mineral Deposits Branch, Geologic Division." The first time records from another originating office are cited, however, the names of the successive administrative units in the hierarchy of which that office is a part should be given.

Basic Elements in Citation

Because of the great variety and complexity of some archival material, there are no convenient models that would be applicable to all records. The minimum initial citation, however, should consist of the item, file unit or subseries (i.e., volume, with title and page numbers, if applicable; or file or folder, with title or other designation), series title, subgroup(s) or originating office (including the hierarchy of administrative units of which that office is a part, if applicable), record group title and number, and name of depository. These are the elements necessary to identify adequately most archival material, and the above order of entry is that adopted by the National Archives and Records Service for its own publications. If in doubt regarding a particular citation, the researcher should confer with an archivist to determine what elements may be necessary to identify adequately specific records being cited. Because it is sometimes necessary to move records from one type of container to another and to rebox records, box or other container numbers should not be included in citations.

Unless the file unit or series is arranged chronologically, it is usually necessary to show exact file location of the document cited, as illustrated by the italicized symbols in the examples below, which also show some of the various orders in which the necessary elements of the citation may be entered, as determined by individual editors:

Commissioner of Indian Affairs to Chu-he-sa-da, January 12, 1883, *Letter Book 106, pp. 127–128,* Letters Sent, Land Division, Records of the Bureau of Indian Affairs, Record Group 75, National Archives Building.

Military Attache Report, National Archives Building, Records of the War Department General and Special Staffs, Record Group 165, *File 2657-I-281/120.*

Dispatch No. 1988, James G. Bailey to Philander C. Knox, December 25, 1909, *Case 13367/ 54, Vol. 941,* Numerical File, National Archives Building, General Records of the Department of State, Record Group 59.

Appendix 4

Hierarchical Controls, Accession Level Control, "Collection" Level Entry: Entries in NUCMC

COMMENT: "Accession" is preferred by the author over "collection" because it is more precise. Entry in the index is derived from the scope and contents note. A user of NUCMC can get in touch with the repository for more specific information—for example, dealing with correspondence between a particular person and Thomas Burke. If the repository has no better control than that noted in the NUCMC entry, the entire accession must be searched. If the repository has more precise controls, such as a collective entry for letters written by that person to Thomas Burke, the search is thereby narrowed. Each repository is capable of providing more specific retrieval information than the NUCMC entry; however, the information supplied by NUCMC is always valid as long as the letters to Burke remain with the Burke Papers. This statement also holds true for the same accession-level statement at the repository itself if the catalog or index entry simply refers the user to the inventory or register. The latter will complete the search process by indicating in its own index what subgroup(s), series, or file unit contains the desired files: that will depend on whether the repository has subgroup, series, or file unit control.

Wyneken, Friedrich Konrad Dietrich, 1810–1876.
Papers, 1838–1941.
ca. 130 items.
In Concordia Historical Institute collections (St. Louis)
In part, transcripts.
Lutheran clergyman and church official. Correspondence on pastoral and synodical affairs, comments on mission work in early settlements in Michigan and Indiana, biographical notes, sermons, programs of the Wyneken centennial, pamphlets appealing for more ministers for German immigrants, and photos. The material is related to the repository's Craemer, O. Fuerbringer, Loehe, W. Sihler, Walther, and Saginaw Valley collections.
Open to investigators under repository restrictions.
Information on literary rights available in the repository.
Gifts of L. Fuerbringer, H. Koenig, H. Steger, F. C. Wyneken, and others.

MS 62–1024

Funkhouser family.
Papers, 1786–1941.
1968 items and 13 v.
In Duke University Library.
Correspondence, diary, and other papers, chiefly 1836–1908, of the Funkhouser family of Virginia. Topics discussed include conditions in the West, opposition to slavery, and economic conditions in the U. S. after 1837; Civil War letters concern Northern opinion, camp life of Union and Confederate soldiers, and the state of the South. Post-war letters are mainly personal. Includes a diary (1863) kept by G. H. Snapp, a minister of the United Brethren in Christ Church, telling of religious life among soldiers and civilians.
Card index in the library.
Acquired, 1954–58

MS 62–1025

Freeman, Merrill Pingree, 1844–1915.
Papers, to 1920.
1 box.
In Arizona Pioneers' Historical Society collections (Tucson, Ariz.)
Banker. Articles or reprints of articles written by Freeman including Coronado's expedition in 1540, The dread Apache—that early day scourge of the Southwest, Early day experiences of an old-time telegrapher, The regeneration of Tucson, early day conditions contrasted with today, 1914, and When the Pope first heard of Tucson.

MS 62–1026

Bizzell, William Bennett, 1876–1944.
Papers, 1914–44.
14 ft.
In University of Oklahoma Library.
Author and educator. Correspondence (personal and business); speeches; MS. of Bizzell's work, The changing intellectual climate; scrapbooks; articles, newspaper clippings, and other printed matter on such subjects as China, India, defense, economics, education, political science, religion, and sociology; certificates; Bizzell genealogy; maps; and photos. Includes material relating to the University of Oklahoma.

MS 62–1027

Burke, Thomas, 1849–1925.
Papers, 1875–1925.
26 ft. (ca. 40,000 items)
In University of Washington Library.
Lawyer, businessman, and politician. Personal and business correspondence, and other papers. Concerns business promotions in the Pacific Northwest (especially railroads and real estate), Burke's legal business, the Great Northern Railway Co., the Carnegie Endowment for International Peace, the development of commerce with the Orient, and Washington State politics. Persons and groups mentioned include John Beard Allen, Erastus Brainerd, the China Club of Seattle, Harrington Emerson, Daniel Hunt Gilman, James Jerome Hill, Samuel Hill, William Ewart Humphrey, the Japan Society of Seattle, the Japanese Consulate of Seattle, Wesley Livsey Jones, John Harte McGraw, John Franklin Miller, Elihu Root and Root's law firms, James Dickinson Smith and Co., bankers of New York, Watson Carvosso Squire, Henry Lewis Stimson, William Howard Taft, and Ambrose Barkley Wyckoff. The material is related to the library's Caroline M. Burke, Gilman, and McGilvra collections.
Described in the library's Manuscript series, no. 3 (1960)
Open to investigators under library restrictions.
Information on literary rights available in the library.
Gift of Mr. Burke's estate, 1935.

MS 62–1028

West Virginia. University.
Personal papers and related materials, 1758–1957.
ca. 370 items, 4 v., 1 box and 26 folders.
In West Virginia University Library (25, 27, 28, 34, 39, 66, 80, 88, 104, 125, 128, 144, 148, 151, 189, 206, 208, 218, 229, 231, 246, 248, 250, 280, 284, 285, 286, 297, 331, 335, 337, 339, 341, 347, 353, 367, 369, 370, 381, 385, 390, 394, 423, 435, 439, 456, 466, 476, 488, 509, 510, 526, 530, 533, 547, 561, 562, 569, 606, 610, 626, 648, 664, 672, 687, 692, 730, 731, 737, 742, 748, 750, 760, 764, 787, 793, 804, 814, 827, 828, 868, 871, 889, 902, 905, 912, 917, 934, 938, 944, 945, 951, 971, 972, 976, 996, 1013, 1021, 1046, 1058, 1066, 1067, 1078, 1094, 1125)
In part, transcripts (typewritten) and photocopies.
Correspondence, certificates of various kinds, receipts, genealogical notes, family papers, business papers, household accounts, wills, deeds, commissions, school notebooks, military records of various kinds, legal papers, petitions, diplomas, land grants, invoices, bills, surveys, plats, tax lists, licenses, speeches, birth records, contracts, circulars, photos., and miscellaneous printed materials. Contains information on the Civil War, land, education, politics, genealogies, lawsuits, pensions, and literary matters as well as on trading, local history, commodities and prices, logging, crops, slaves, church activities and newspapers in West Virginia. Names associated with the more sizable collections in this group of approximately 100 are Daniel Boardman; Chapin family, William Cochran, Beatrice H. Cooper; John M. Daniel, Herbert Warder Dent, Thomas L. Dunn, Braxton B. Durrett; Charles James Faulkner; Thomas Gibson; Thomas M. Harris, Thomas W. Harrison, Noah Henderson, Henshaw family, John S. S. Herr, Rhett family; Johnson family; John R. Kenly; George Robert Latham; Z. T. McBee, McBee family, Henry O. Middleton; Neil family; George W. Orr, Jesse Parsons, Jacob Peirpont, Price family, William Price; Rector family, Powell Benton Reynolds; Sidney F. Shaw; Turner family; Van Meter family; and Anthony Ware.
Described separately in Guide to manuscripts and archives in the West Virginia collection, by Charles Shetler (1958)

MS 62–1029

Herzberger, Frederik William, 1859–1930.
Papers, 1892–1930.
ca. 140 items.
In Concordia Historical Institute collections (St. Louis)
In part, fragments (typewritten)
Lutheran clergyman and poet. Poems, songs, sermons, biographical sketches, obituaries, an oration on George Washington, and photos.
Open to investigators under repository restrictions.
Information on literary rights available in the repository.
Gift of L. W. Hake, 1953.

MS 62–1030

Rives, Alfred Landon, 1830–1903.
Papers, 1839–88.
1206 items and 5 v.
In Duke University Library.
Army engineer, Confederate officer, and architect, of Albemarle Co., Va. Primarily Rives' correspondence, relating to his attendance at the École nationale des ponts et chaussées, Paris; his military and civilian careers; family matters and social, political, and economic affairs in Virginia; and the Washington Peace Convention (1861). Includes a diary (1829–31) of Rives' mother, Judith Page Walker Rives, concerning life in the diplomatic community in Paris, travels on the continent, French social life and customs, the Revolution of 1830, U. S. political developments, and other matters; and three ledgers of Francis E. Rives, U. S. Representative. Correspondents include Francis R. Rives, Julia Page Rives, and Édouard Schwebelé.
Card index in the library.
Acquired, 1958–60.

MS 62–1031

McGilvra, John Jay, 1827–1903.
Papers, 1861–1903.
3 ft. (ca. 3500 items)
In University of Washington Library.
Lawyer, U. S. attorney, State legislator, and business promoter. Correspondence, 5 letter press copybooks (1873–90), legal briefs, and other papers. Concerns McGilvra's work as U. S. attorney for Washington Territory, 1861–66, his legislative work in 1866, his business promotions and legal business, and politics in Seattle and Washington. The material is related to the library's Caroline McGilvra Burke, Thomas Burke, and Gilman collections.
Unpublished guide in the library.
Open to investigators under library restrictions.
Information on literary rights available in the library.
Gift of the estate of Thomas Burke, 1935.

MS 62–1032

Appendix 5

Hierarchical Controls, Accession Level Control: Entry from Library of Congress for MR II Program

COMMENT: Besides seven subject entries, only the twenty-five proper names listed are indexed. These are a small fraction of major correspondents represented in the estimated 80,000 items that make up the Bonaparte Papers.

LIBRARY OF CONGRESS MANUSCRIPT DIVISION	DICTIONARY CATALOG OF COLLECTIONS ENTRY								
	Cataloged by: S. Hensen	Date Cataloged: 620 Cataloged 1960							
Master Record No. 001 78-13151	Record Type: 008 2.a#3.c	5.#	Date Revised: 620 Revised December 1978						
Main Entry: 100 Bonaparte, Charles Joseph, 1851-1921.									
Form of Material: 244 Papers, 1760-1921.		Bulk Dates: 560 1874-1921							
Items: 302#b 80,000 items.	Units: 303 262	Microfilm Locator: 091#b	Repository: 535						
Saves: 490									

General Note: 500

Scope and Content Note: 520

Lawyer, municipal and civil service reformer, and U.S. Cabinet member. Correspondence, articles, speeches, memoranda, notes, personal miscellany, legal papers, real estate papers, biographical material, clippings, and other printed matter. Correspondence, 1874-1921, comprises the bulk of the collection. Papers relate to his Progressive and Republican Party activities, his service as U.S. Secretary of the Navy, U.S. Attorney General, and his positions as member and chairman of council of the National Civil Service Reform League, overseer of Harvard, trustee of the Catholic University of America, president of the Enoch Pratt Free Library, member of the Maryland Board of State Aid and Charities, president of the National Municipal League, and member of the Executive Committee of the National Civic Federation. Legal papers of Bonaparte, his family, and clients cover the period 1760-1920. Correspondents include Louis D. Brandeis, Champ Clark, Richard H. Dana, Charles W. Eliot, James R. Garfield, Elbert H. Gary, James Cardinal Gibbons, Henry Cabot Lodge, Theodore Roosevelt, Carl Schurz, William Howard Taft, Benjamin R. Tillman, Richard M. Venable, Owen Wister, and Clinton Rogers Woodruff.

Finding Aid: 555
Finding aid published by the Library, 1958.

Provenance: 541
Gift of Mrs. Bonaparte, 1923.

Literary Rights: 540

Restrictions: 506

1) Head, Pr. Sec.	2) Editor	3) Head, R. Ser.	4) Specialist	5) Asst. Chief	6) Chief	7) Archivist	8) Cataloger
Specialist: 037			NUCMC No. 010 NUCMC MS60-2031		Languages: 046		
C N W Ⓟ R L S B H A F							

Profession/Occupation: 690 Lawyer; Reformer; Secretary of the Navy, U.S.; Attorney General, U.S.

References (600) Cross References (601) Added Entries (850) and other tags as necessary.

Progressive Party
Republican Party
National Civil Service Reform League
Harvard University
Massachusetts — Colleges and universities
Colleges and universities — Massachusetts
Catholic University of America
Washington, D.C. — Colleges and universities
Colleges and universities — Washington, D.C.
Enoch Pratt Free Library, Baltimore, Md.
Baltimore, Md. — Libraries
Maryland — Libraries
Libraries — Maryland
Maryland. Board of State Aid and Charities
National Municipal League
National Civic Federation
Bonaparte family
Brandeis, Louis Dembitz, 1856-1941
Clark, Champ, 1850-1921
Dana, Richard Henry, 1815-1882
Eliot, Charles William, 1834-1926
Garfield, James Rudolph, 1865-1950
Gary, Elbert Henry, 1846-1927
Gibbons, James, Cardinal, 1834-1921
Lodge, Henry Cabot, 1850-1924
Roosevelt, Theodore, Pres. U.S., 1858-1919
Schurz, Carl, 1829-1906
Taft, William Howard, Pres. U.S., 1857-1930
Tillman, Benjamin Ryan, 1847-1918
Venable, Richard Morton, 1839-
1910
Wister, Owen, 1860-1938
Woodruff, Clinton Rogers, b. 1868

Comments:

Appendix 6

Hierarchical Controls, Record Group Level Control: Entry from the Smithsonian Archives *Guide*, 1978

COMMENT: The Smithsonian Institution Archives have a single, integrated system with index entries referring to the inventories, and the inventories to the actual location (box/folder nos.). They have fairly comprehensive proper name control but have postponed dealing with topical terms.

(161)

Division of Reptiles and Amphibians, 1873-1968
Records (11.3 cubic feet).

The collection of reptiles and amphibians under the care of the Smithsonian Institution had its origins in the collection of Spencer F. Baird, which he presented to the Institution when he came to Washington to accept the position of Assistant Secretary in 1850. For the next three decades there was no curator officially in charge of the collection, and most of the early publications resulting from the collection were produced by Baird and Charles Frederic Girard, who from 1850 to 1860 was Baird's chief assistant.

In 1879 Henry Crecy Yarrow, an army surgeon who had served as naturalist on the United States Surveys West of the 100th Meridian led by Lieutenant George Wheeler, was appointed Honorary Curator of the Department of Herpetology, a position which he filled on a part-time basis until his resignation in 1889. During the early 1880's the Department was known variously as the Department of Herpetology, the Department of Reptiles, and the Department of Reptiles and Batrachians. By about 1885 the latter title had become standard. In 1947 the name was changed to the Division of Reptiles and Amphibians.

Curators since 1889 have included Leonhard Stejneger, Curator, 1889-1943, and Doris Mable Cochran, Assistant, Associate, and full Curator, 1927-1968. James A. Peters, Associate Curator, 1964-1966, became Curator in 1966.

The records contain general correspondence of the Division's curators; Leonhard Stejneger material pertaining to the international congresses he attended as a representative of the United States National Museum; and administrative memoranda regarding the National Museum operations for the Division of Reptiles and Amphibians and the Departments of Biology, Vertebrate Zoology, and Zoology, pertaining to requisitions, budgetary matters, publication policy, expeditions of curators, museum exhibitions, and personnel matters. For additional records of the Division of Reptiles and Amphibians, see the Leonhard Stejneger Papers, record unit 7074 and the James A. Peters Papers, record unit 7175.

ARRANGEMENT: (1) General correspondence, incoming and outgoing, 1873-1968; (2) outgoing correspondence, 1882-1883, 1889-1922; (3) correspondence related to scientific congresses, 1895-1911; (4) administrative memoranda, 1946-1966. FINDING AIDS: Description in control file.

Appendix 7

Hierarchical Controls, Subgroup Level Control: Entry from Preliminary Inventory to Department of State Records, Record Group 157

COMMENT: Bureau of Accounts is a subgroup. See Appendix 11 for series descriptions of this subgroup's records.

PART II: RECORDS NOT PART OF THE CENTRAL FILES

Part I of this inventory describes the central files of the Department of State. The records described in Part II are distinguished from records in Part I by their organization and arrangement and by the fact that most of them were never part of the central files. Such records in general are of three types: (1) records created and separately maintained within offices and bureaus of the Department of State, (2) records of and relating to certain special functions assigned to the Department, and (3) records that were initially part of the central files but were kept separate from the main chronological series of records in the central files because of their special relevance to particular subjects or events.

Many of the series of records described in this part of the inventory were created by administrative, housekeeping, and service offices of the Department, such as the Bureau of Accounts, Bureau of Indexes and Archives, Passport Division, and Visa Division. Other series relate to special duties that were assigned to the Department. Some of these duties were temporary, such as those of the Thomas Jefferson Statue Commission; others were expected to be permanent but have since been terminated, such as publishing the laws in current newspapers; and others were originally assigned to the Department but have been transferred to newer Government agencies. Still other series of records described in Part II relate to particular events or subjects, such as impressed seamen, the War of 1812, and the Civil War.

In this part of the inventory the several series of records relating to a particular office, bureau, function, event, or subject are referred to as a subgroup of records, and each subgroup has an appropriate title.

Because the Department of State has experienced so many reorganizations and because many of its original domestic duties have been terminated or transferred to other agencies it has been impossible to organize Part II of the inventory to reflect any organizational or functional pattern. Therefore this part has been arranged alphabetically by key word in the title of each subgroup. (The table of contents, pages vi to ix, serves as a guide to the alphabetized part of the inventory.) Under each subgroup the series of records are arranged to indicate the operation of the unit that created them or the subjects to which they relate.

RECORDS OF THE BUREAU OF ACCOUNTS

An appropriation act of 1797 (1 Stat. 494) made the first provision for a clerk to act as an accountant in the Department of State. This clerk and his successors apparently handled accounts and disbursements until 1833, when the Disbursing and Superintending Bureau was established. That Bureau was superseded by a Disbursing Agent in 1834, and the Agent was replaced in 1870 by the Bureau of Accounts. In 1938 the Bureau

Appendix 8

Hierarchical Controls, Subgroup Level Control: Entry from the National Archives *Guide*, 1974

COMMENT: Subgroups are those for Chief Signal Officer, Military Aeronautics Division, Aircraft Production Bureau.

Department of the Air Force

RECORDS OF THE ARMY AIR FORCES
(RECORD GROUP 18)

The Army Air Forces (AAF) originated August 1, 1907, as the Aeronautical Division in the Office of the Chief Signal Officer. In July 1914 the Aviation Section was created in the Signal Corps, and in July 1917 the Equipment Division was established in the Office of the Chief Signal Officer. In September 1917 the Aeronautical Division became the Air Division. An Executive order of May 20, 1918, divided the Aviation Section into two separate agencies: the Division of Military Aeronautics and the Bureau of Aircraft Production. A Presidential directive of May 29, 1918, created the Air Service of the Army and separated it from the Signal Corps. In August 1918 the Director of Aircraft Production was appointed Second Assistant Secretary of War and Director of Air Service, responsible for both the Bureau of Aircraft Production and the Division of Military Aeronautics, which were united by an Executive order of March 19, 1919.

The Army reorganization act of June 4, 1920, made the Air Service a combatant arm of the Army, and the Air Corps Act of July 2, 1926, changed the name of the Air Service to the Air Corps. In March 1935 the General Headquarters Air Force was created, and on June 20, 1941, a new position, the Chief of the Army Air Forces, was created. At the same time the General Headquarters Air Force was renamed the Air Force Combat Command. A general reorganization of the War Department united these two agencies as the Army Air Forces on March 9, 1942, placing them directly under the Secretary of War and the War Department General Staff. The National Security Act of 1947 redesignated the Army Air Forces

the U.S. Air Force under the newly created Department of the Air Force.

See *The Army Air Forces in World War II* (7 vols., 1948-58); and H. H. Arnold, *Global Mission* (New York, 1949).

There are 11,439 cubic feet of records dated between 1914 and 1952 in this record group.

GENERAL RECORDS OF THE OFFICE OF THE CHIEF SIGNAL OFFICER. 1914-18. 4 lin. ft.

These consist of compilations of extracts of letters, telegrams, and memorandums of War Department offices, relating to regulations and authorities for U.S. flying schools, including balloon instruction, training, airplane types, and performance. Included are charts, reports, and correspondence relating to the organization and duties of the Planning Section and to a program of airplane production. Other records reflecting the Chief Signal Officer's activities during 1918 are in the AAF central files.

RECORDS OF THE DIVISION OF MILITARY AERONAUTICS. 1914-19. 13 lin. ft.

These include correspondence, memorandums, orders, and other records relating to foreign and domestic air services, airplane construction and equipment, flight training, schools of military aeronautics, radio development, and training of radio officers.

RECORDS OF THE BUREAU OF AIRCRAFT PRODUCTION. 1916-21. 142 lin. ft.

These records consist of issuances, general correspondence, historical data, and other material relating to operation,

Appendix 9

Hierarchical Controls, Subgroup Level Control: Preliminary Inventory of the
Edward W. Allen Papers

144

Appendix 10

Hierarchical Controls, Series Level Control: Entry from the National Archives *Guide*, 1974

COMMENT: Series are: General Correspondence, Court-Martial Records, Records of Investigations.

RECORDS OF THE
OFFICE OF THE JUDGE ADVOCATE GENERAL (ARMY)
(RECORD GROUP 153)

A judge advocate of the Continental Army was appointed in 1775. Legal provision for a U.S. Army judge advocate was made in 1797, but the number and status of judge advocates varied during the following years. In 1849 provision was made for appointing a Judge Advocate of the Army. That officer was designated Judge Advocate General by an act of July 17, 1862, which also provided that he receive the records and proceedings of courts-martial and military commissions and keep the records of courts of inquiry. In 1864 the Judge Advocate General was designated to head the newly created Bureau of Military Justice, which by an act of July 5, 1884, was consolidated with the Corps of Judge Advocates of the Army to form the Judge Advocate General's Department. In 1942 the Judge Advocate General was placed under the Commanding General, Services of Supply (later the Army Service Forces). Since 1946 his Office has been an Army staff agency.

The Office of the Judge Advocate General (Army) supervises the system of military justice throughout the Army, performs appellate review of records of trials by court-martial as provided by the Uniform Code of Military Justice, and furnishes the Army's legal services. The Judge Advocate General serves as legal adviser to the Secretary of the Army and all Army offices and agencies, reports directly to the Secretary of the Army on court-martial cases, and gives legal advice concerning the administration, control, discipline, and civil relations of Army personnel.

There are 5,691 cubic feet of records dated between ca. 1800 and 1957 in this record group.

GENERAL CORRESPONDENCE.
1821-1942. 520 lin. ft.

Included are letters and reports sent by the Adjutant General, acting judge advocates, the Judge Advocate of the Army, and the Judge Advocate General to the Secretary of War, War Department officials, judge advocates, Members of Congress, and others, concerning military justice, 1842-89; letters sent by the Judge Advocate General, 1882-95; and selected letters sent by the Judge Advocate General as head of the system of military justice and legal adviser to the Secretary of War, 1889-95. There are indexes to the letters sent. Also letters received by the Judge Advocate of the Army and the Judge Advocate General, 1854-94, with registers and indexes. Further correspondence consists of letters sent, endorsements, a few letters received, and related records, 1894-1912; and correspondence relating to the Judge Advocate General's opinions and decisions and to administrative and operational matters, 1912-42 (in WNRC).

Other records include the Attorney General's opinions and decisions concerning administration of military justice and legal actions of the War Department, 1821-70, and records of Brig. Gen. Norman Lieber, 1867-98, Brig. Gen. George B. Davis as Judge Advocate General, 1901-10, Col. Blanton Winship of the Judge Advocate General's Department, 1903-19, and Col. Mark Guerin, Judge Advocate of the 6th Corps Area, 1918-24. Also included are office files relating to maritime affairs, 1918-23, and the Commission for Adjustment of British Claims, 1932-33 (in WNRC).

COURT-MARTIAL RECORDS. 1805-1939. 5,269 lin. ft.

Included are court-martial case files for general courts-martial, courts of inquiry, and military commissions, 1809-1939 (court-martial cases dated after 1891 are in WNRC), with a partial index, 1891-1917 (in WNRC), including documents that describe court organizations and personnel; charges and specifications; pleas and arraignments of defendants; papers and exhibits submitted to courts for consideration; court proceedings, findings, and sentences; reviewing authorities' reports; statements of action by the Secretary of War and the President; and related correspondence. Files dated before 1812 are fragmentary. Also included are copies of records of general courts-martial and courts of inquiry, 1805-15; registers of court-martial cases

listing cases represented in the case files and giving names of court presidents and judge advocates, locations and dates the courts were convened, and defendants' names, ranks, and organizations, 1809-90; and case files lost during the Civil War but later recovered by the Judge Advocate General, 1861-65.

There are also applications for and correspondence regarding clemency for prisoners sentenced by general courts-martial to the U.S. Military Prison at Fort Leavenworth, Kans., and clemency orders issued by the Assistant Secretary of War, 1894-97. Records relating to court-martial procedures and regulations include a card file used in revising the manual on courts-martial that shows changes made in Army regulations, 1904-13; reports, correspondence, and working papers relating to later revisions of the *Manual for Courts-Martial*, 1919-27 (in WNRC); a report (in WNRC) made to the Judge Advocate General, relating to criticisms of the system of military justice, February 13, 1919; and records (in WNRC) from a study of the European administration of military justice, 1918-20.

RECORDS OF INVESTIGATIONS. 1864-1927. 13 lin. ft.

These comprise records relating to the investigation of President Lincoln's assassination, including reports, testimony of persons connected with the assassination trial, and correspondence; a "Military Commission Record Book" containing abstracts of letters, testimony, and reports regarding suspects in the assassination; and abstracts of correspondence received by or referred to Judge Advocate Col. H. L. Burnett, who investigated the assassination. Other records relate to activities of the secret Order of American Knights, investigated by the Provost Marshal of the Department of the Missouri, 1864 (in WNRC), and records of the Paxton Hibben and William Mitchell cases and the

Appendix 11

Hierarchical Controls, Series Level Control: Entry from Department of State's Subgroup, the Bureau of Accounts

COMMENT: See Appendix 7 for beginning of subgroup description.

Correspondence

Letters Sent

MISCELLANEOUS LETTERS SENT. Jan. 1832-July 1916. 222 vols. 18 ft. 202
    Mostly press copies of letters sent by the Bureau of Accounts to
diplomatic and consular officers, foreign embassies and legations, the
Treasury Department, other departments, despatch agents, newspaper pub-
lishers, and private individuals and firms, regarding State Department
appropriations, salary payments, the purchase of supplies and equipment,
the publication of proposals and notices, the transmittal of checks and
accounts, exceptions to accounts, and other fiscal subjects. Volume 107
is missing from this series, which is arranged chronologically, with
each volume containing an alphabetical index to the names of addressees.

LETTERS SENT TO RUFUS KING. 1802-3. 1/4 in.   203
    Copies of letters sent by the Treasury Department to Rufus King,
U.S. Minister to Great Britain, regarding bills of exchange. Arranged
chronologically.

LETTERS TO THE PRESIDENT REQUESTING AUTHORIZATION OF DISBURSEMENTS.
    May 22, 1830-Mar. 28, 1861. 2 vols. 4 in.   204
    Letters to the President requesting him, under an act of January 31,
1823 (3 Stat. 723), to authorize advances from appropriated funds.
Some letters are copies; others are originals. Many of them bear endorsements signed by the President authorizing the advances. The requests relate to such matters as obtaining the Florida archives from
Spain; the payment of special commissioners, ministers, and consuls;
and the expenses of U.S. district courts and marshals. Some related
receipts for payments are included. Arranged chronologically.

REPORTS TO THE PRESIDENT REGARDING SEA RESCUES AND TESTIMONIALS.
    Aug. 29, 1849-Mar. 8, 1861. 1 vol. 2 in.   205
    Reports to the President on rescues of U.S. seamen and passengers by
foreign seamen; and recommendations for the presentation of medals or
other testimonials to the rescuers. Medals were authorized to be made
in accordance with provisions of a joint resolution of March 3, 1847
(9 Stat. 208), and of later legislation that appropriated to the President money for suitable acknowledgment of the rescue services of masters
and crews of foreign vessels. Some of these reports bear the President's
signed approval. Arranged chronologically.

LETTERS SENT REGARDING THE NORTH EAST EXECUTIVE BUILDING. Feb. 11, 1837-
    Nov. 1, 1854. 1 vol. 1/2 in.   206
    Press copies of letters sent to watchmen, express companies, the
First Auditor, and private individuals and firms regarding regulations,
supplies, equipment, services, and accounts for the North East Executive
Building. Arranged chronologically.

Appendix 12

Hierarchical Controls, Series Level Control: Register Pages from the Charles Joseph Bonaparte Papers, Library of Congress

COMMENT: Although two subgroups are identified—Attorney General and Secretary of the Navy—neither runs sequentially and no other subgroups are identified for "legal, political, and civic activities." This illustrates the scattering of subgroups among series. Among these subgroups we could expect to find those related to Bonaparte's presidency of the National Municipal League and his chairmanship of the National Civil Service Reform League, for example. It is uncertain how one can distinguish subgroups from "subject files" in the register, because the subject files include both subject material and subgroups. There should be no guesswork required to make this distinction, and none is required if subgrouping is done on the basis of separate corporate activities in the process of arrangement. The arrangement and its recording in the inventory will convey this information inferentially.

4

Description of Series

Container Nos.	Series
1-117	Letters Received, General Correspondence, 1882-1919. 117 containers. Correspondence received relating to legal, political, and civic activities. Chronologically arranged by years and alphabetically by names of correspondents therein.
118-121	Letters Received, Financial and Office Correspondence, 1912-14, 1919-21. 4 containers. Largely bills received and correspondence relating to real estate office activities. Chronologically arranged by years and alphabetically by names of correspondents therein.
122-126	Letters Received While Secretary of the Navy, 1905-6. 5 containers. Alphabetically arranged by correspondent. A special group of letters received from the White House during this period is in container 126.
127-131	Letters Received While Attorney General, 1906-9. 5 containers. Alphabetically arranged by names of correspondents.
132	Special Correspondence With Theodore Roosevelt, 1905-9, 1915, 1917. 1 container. Mainly letters received, chronologically arranged.

133-173	Outgoing Letters, General Correspondence, 1874-1921. 40 containers. Bound letterpress copy books, chronologically arranged. Numerous gaps appear after November 1916. Some letterpress books overlap chronologically.
174-181	Outgoing Letters While Secretary of the Navy, 1905-6. 8 containers. Bound letterpress copy books, chronologically arranged. Letterpress copies of correspondence relating to telephone cost rates and Navy Department salaries and expenses are in container 181.

5

Container Nos.	Series
182-185	Outgoing Letters While Attorney General, 1906-9. 4 containers. Bound letterpress copy books, chronologically arranged.
186-187	Personal Miscellany, ca. 1880-1920. 2 containers. Biographical material, notes, memoranda, charity appeals, real estate office miscellany, and some printed matter, largely clippings.
188-210	Subject File, ca. 1880-1920. 23 containers. Memoranda, reports, clippings, printed matter, and a small amount of correspondence. The folders are alphabetically arranged by subject. There is little arrangement within folders.
211-218	Speech, Article, and Book File, ca. 1890-1920. 8 containers. Mainly typewritten or printed copies of speeches and articles. Also clipped and mounted portions of speeches and articles for unpublished book. The speeches are arranged in a numbered, indexed series, except for a small unindexed file arranged chronologically and three files grouped by subject. The index is in container 211.
219-256	Legal Papers, 1760-1920. 38 containers. Early family and personal legal papers, but mainly cases in which Bonaparte was counsel or litigant. Arranged alphabetically as docketed. Also papers relating to estates held in trust and printed briefs.

Container Nos.   Contents

OUTGOING LETTERS, GENERAL CORRESPONDENCE, 1874-1921
(Continued)

169   Nov. 10, 1913-Dec. 31, 1914

170   Dec. 31, 1914-Dec. 27, 1915

171   Dec. 27, 1915-Nov. 4, 1916

172   Feb. 23-Oct. 30, 1917

173   Nov. 10, 1920-Oct. 1, 1921

OUTGOING LETTERS WHILE SECRETARY OF THE NAVY, 1905-6

174   June 26-Oct. 6, 1905

175   Oct. 6-Dec. 10, 1905

176   Dec. 11, 1905-Feb. 1, 1906

177   Feb. 8-Mar. 24, 1906

178   Mar. 24-June 5, 1906

179   June 5-Aug. 24, 1906

180   Aug. 24-Nov. 13, 1906

181   Telephone rate book, July 16-Dec. 4, 1906
                   Statement of Navy Department salaries and
                      expenses, 1900-1904

OUTGOING LETTERS WHILE ATTORNEY GENERAL, 1906-9

182   Dec. 17, 1906-Apr. 12, 1907

183   Apr. 14, 1907-Feb. 28, 1908

184   Feb. 28-Sept. 7, 1908

185   Sept. 7, 1908-Mar. 5, 1909

Container Nos.   Contents

PERSONAL MISCELLANY, CA. 1880-1920

186   Biographical material
                    "Private"
                    Notes, memoranda

187   Charity appeals
                    Real estate
                    Printed matter

SUBJECT FILE, CA. 1880-1920

188   Baltimore Bar Association
                    Baltimore Reform League
                    Bar Association of America; of Maryland
                    Belgian Red Cross
                    Burnt District Commission
                    Catholic Club

189   Catholic University

190   Charity Organization Society
                    Children's Aid Society
                    Civic Federation

191-193   Civil Service Reform League, 1902-17

194   Consumers' League
                    Contested elections, 1909

195   Election campaigns, 1895, 1904, 1911

196   Enoch Pratt Free Library
                    Federated Charities
                    Good Government Club

197   Harvard, special reports, printed matter

198   Harvard, printed matter

199   Income and expenses
                    Indian investigation, 1903
                    Indians, 1912-17

Container Nos.	Contents
	SUBJECT FILE, CA. 1880-1920 (Continued)

SPEECH, ARTICLE, AND BOOK FILE, CA. 1890-1920

Speeches

Appendix 13

Hierarchical Controls, Series Level Control: Container List from the Register of the Charles Joseph Bonaparte Papers, Library of Congress

COMMENT: In registers the series description section is followed by a container list which records the sequence of the files. In this example there is no attempt to list major correspondents, nor any other contents information.

Contrast this container list with that for the Carl W. Ackerman Papers in Appendix 14, in which the name of every correspondent who has an individual folder is listed.

Container Nos.	Series
	LETTERS RECEIVED, GENERAL CORRESPONDENCE, 1882-1919
1	1882, A-Z
2	1883, A-Z
3	1884, A-L
4	1884, M-Z
5	1885, A-J
6	1885, K-Z
7	1886, A-J
8	1886, K-Z
9	1887, A-K
10	1887, L-Z
11	1888, A-Z
12	1889, A-L
13	1889, M-Z
14	1890, A-K
15	1890, L-Z
16	1891, A-H
17	1891, I-Q
18	1891, R-Z

Appendix 14

Hierarchical Controls, Series Level Control: Container List from the Register
of the Carl W. Ackerman Papers, Library of Congress

COMMENT: On page 13 of the container list, note the abundance of potential
index or catalog terms in the form of proper names. The registers at the Library of Congress are not indexed, however; instead the abbreviated scope
and contents note that precedes the series outline is indexed. Pages 26, 27,
and 65 from the Ackerman Papers register illustrate the failure to distinguish
subgroups from topical subject files. "Columbia University" seems to be a
subgroup, but what is the nature of the other file units? Note also the dispersal
of the Columbia University subgroup; it reappears in container 190.

13

Container Nos.	Contents
	FAMILY PAPERS, 1860-1970 AND UNDATED (Continued)
18	Correspondence with VanderHoof family Emma F. VanderHoof, Oct. 1915-Dec. 1921

19	Correspondence with VanderHoof family
	    Emma F. VanderHoof, 1922-36 and undated
	    Nancy S. VanderHoof
	Emma F. VanderHoof miscellany
	Correspondence with son, Robert Vanderhoof
	    Ackerman, 1918-42

20	Correspondence with son, Robert Vanderhoof
	    Ackerman, 1943-58 and undated
	Robert V. Ackerman
	    Correspondence concerning education of
	    Miscellaneous correspondence

21	Miscellaneous personal papers Student papers
22-24	Student papers

25	Robert V. Ackerman
	    Condolences on death of
	    Estate of
	Sweets, Henry H., correspondence with, 1939-49
	Family history miscellany

	GENERAL CORRESPONDENCE, 1907-70 AND UNDATED
26	"A" miscellany Abbot, Willis J.

154

Container Nos.   Contents

Container Nos.   Contents

SPEECH, ARTICLE, AND BOOK FILE, 1909-64 AND UNDATED
(Continued)

Books

188 (cont.)   <u>Eisenhower in Wonderland</u> (unpublished book),
          1956-57
               Research notes and drafts, 1956-57
                    Freeman, Douglas Southall
                    future of Columbia University
                    "the lighter side" (humorous clippings)
                    "Shh! This Is Columbia" demonstration,
                         Oct. 1940
               Miscellaneous research notes

189   Miscellaneous research notes and drafts
               Miscellaneous printed matter and clippings
                    used in research

Reports, Columbia University

190   <u>Report</u> of the Dean of the School of Journalism
                    1932
                    1933
                    1934
                    1935
          <u>Public Opinion Around the World: A Report</u> by
               Dean Carl W. Ackerman of the Graduate School
               of Journalism, Dec. 19, 1936
          <u>Report</u> of the Dean of the Graduate School of
               Journalism
                    1936
                    1937
                    Supplement, 1937: <u>The Black Plague of the</u>
                         <u>Twentieth Century</u>
                              correspondence, 1937-38
                              miscellany, 1937-38

191   <u>Report</u> of the Dean of the Graduate School of
               Journalism, 1938
                    Supplement: <u>The Refuge of World Opinion</u>

Appendix 15

Hierarchical Controls, Series Level Control: Inventory Page from the Washington Gladden Collection, Ohio Historical Society (microfilm edition, 1972, p. 30)

Morris; T. T. Munger; Francis G. Peabody; Theodore Roosevelt; Charles Sprague Smith; Roswell Smith; Samuel J. Swartz; Andrew D. White; and Frank P. Woodbury. (Boxes 2-3).

Roll 3 (Series 1, boxes 3 to 5)

Correspondence, June, 1900 - April, 1903. Contains invitations, thank-you notes, encouragements received for future publications, requests for advice and clarification of Gladden's views, and financial records. Also information on Iowa College, Professor Henry C. King, labor, Gladden's publications, Charles M. Sheldon, the Federal Gas and Fuel Company of Columbus, strikes and boycotts, domestic and international arbitration, Dr. Richard Storrs, Dr. Lyman Abbott, Gladden's ministerial ability, Elbert Hubbard, Gladden and the Columbus City Council, missionary work, public ownership of utilities, the Columbus Street Railroad, the Ohio Home Missionary Society, Leo Tolstoy, newspapers, Cleveland [Ohio], Oberlin College, street lighting, church and denominational federation, Mr. Ament and the American Board, the National Conference of Charities [in Washington], the Pan-American Exposition, Tom L. Johnson, civic pride in Philadelphia, the University of Michigan Good Government Club, the Committee of Fifteen of the Home Missionary Society.

Also information on the proposed Columbus gas ordinance, the Yale Chapel, Antioch College, the referendum, "tainted money," the Rochester Economic Club, McKinley's assassination, the courts, Unity, Gladden's election to the presidency of the American Missionary Association, the Michigan Political Science Association, the church and rural life, Christian citizenship, the Broadway Tabernacle Church, the Columbus city charter, the American Federation of Catholic Societies, saloons, the Atlanta Theological Seminary, socialism, the proposed governmental code for the cities of Ohio, the anniversary of the First Church, the Charity Organization Society, trusts, the South, Sunday schools, the Municipal Lecture Association, the Atlanta Conferences, W. E. B. DuBois, the Saturn Club, the American Board of Commissioners for Foreign Missions, Christian sociology, Christendom, John D. Rockefeller, and Samuel M. Jones' re-election as mayor of Toledo.

Correspondents include Lyman Abbott; G. Glenn Atkins; Edward W. Bemis; George D. Black; Samuel Bowles; H. A. Bridgman; Asa S. Bushnell; C. S. Carr; Charles C. Creegan; W. E. B. DuBois; Charles W. Eliot; Richard T. Ely; R. W. Gilder; William Rainey Harper; Franklin W. Hooper; Robert H. Jeffrey; Samuel M. Jones; Henry C. King; J. C. Lincoln; S. S. McClure; Shailer Mathews; George P. Morris; T. T. Munger; George K. Nash; Charles L. Noyes; Francis G. Peabody; Jacob A. Riis; Charles Mulford Robinson; J. M. Sheets; F. Herbert Stead; W. T. Stead; Edward A. Steiner; Graham Taylor; W. P. Tyler; William Hayes Ward; and Frank P. Woodbury. (Boxes 3-5).

Roll 4 (Series 1, boxes 5 to 6)

Correspondence, May, 1903 - March, 1905. Contains invitations, encouragements for future publications, thank-you notes, and requests for advice and clarification of Gladden's views. Also information on the Gideons, Gladden's publications, "Jim Crow," George Adam Smith, the American Board of Commissioners for Foreign Missions, the Bethel Sunday School feud, the American

Appendix 16

Hierarchical Controls, Series Level Control: NUCMC Entry for the Lillian Spear Papers; Excerpt from Article in *Drexel Library Quarterly*

COMMENT: The Spear Papers entry is a collection level description on NUCMC catalog cards. It does not lend itself to adaptation for series entries, nor file unit entries. Following it is an excerpt from an article by the author in the *Drexel Library Quarterly* (11 [January 1975]: 44–46) illustrating how a series card can be prepared for the Spear Papers.

MS 65–1055

Spear, Lillian Sylten, 1897–1963.
Papers, 1936–63.   7 ft. (ca. 6000 items)
In University of Washington Library (Seattle)
Teacher and civic leader. Correspondence, minutes of meetings, campaign material, and other papers relating to the following organizations of which Mrs. Spear was an official or secretary: King County Public Utility District Association, Public Ownership League of Washington, Puget Sound Utility Commissioners' Association, Snoho-

mish County Legislative Council, Snohomish County Public Utility Association, Snohomish County Public Utility District, Washington Public Utility Commissioner's Association, and the Washington Public Utility Districts' Association. Correspondents include Homer T. Bone, Jack R. Cluck, John M. Coffee, Henry M. Jackson, Joseph E. McGoran, Warren G. Magnuson, Hugh B. Mitchell, Mal-

colm M. Moore, Gus A. Peters, Martin F. Smith, Monrad C. Wallgren, and Adolph Ziebell, and the Bonneville Power Administration, the Democratic Party, Patrons of Husbandry (Washington), Public Ownership League of America, Puget Sound Power and Light Company, and the Washington Water Power Company.
Unpublished inventory record in the library.
Information on literary rights available in the library.
Gift of Mrs. Spear, 1963.

<table>
<tr><td>Name added entry (for subgroup)</td><td>League of Women Voters. Seattle
Baker, Elizabeth, 1915 –
  Papers, 1860–72. 20 ft.
    Correspondence, reports, committee records, ephemera, clippings relating to Seattle Office of Equal Rights Amendment Campaign, 1971–72, and to her work in Seattle League of Women Voters, . . .</td></tr>
</table>

Subject added entries can be made in standard style.

Series Level Control Illustrated

To illustrate control at the series level, one subgroup will be expanded, that for *Seattle. City Council.* Preceding the task of description, the papers would have been arranged into records series according to type of record, unless there is a recognizable original order which can be wholly or partially restored. It is assumed also that no refinement beyond grouping into series has been attempted; however, some general characteristics of each series are noted. A further assumption is that the size of the containers used at this stage are the same as in the subgrouping stage (10 x 12 x 15 cartons). At the next stage (file folder level) smaller acid-free containers will be used, requiring renumbering.

Box		Approx. # Items	Incl. Dates
6, 7	**Seattle. City Council**		
	General Correspondence.(With city, state, federal agencies, general public. Some major correspondents: Mayor's Office, Seattle Engineering, Lighting and Transit Departments, U. S. Federal Power Commission, Federal Housing Authority, Corps of Engineers, Washington State Public Utilities Commission, Legislative Council, Warren G. Magnuson, Henry M. Jackson, Thomas M. Pelly, Brockman Adams.) *See also* subject series and committee records for other general correspondence. *Committee Records*	2.5′	1962-68
	Utilities Committee.	2.5′	1952-68
8, 9	*Skagit Project.* Correspondence with city, state, federal agencies, Canadian and British Columbia government agencies, International Joint Commission; hearings, reports.		
9	*California Intertie.* Correspondence with city, state, federal agencies; hearings, reports.	1′	1960-65

10, 11	*Transit Committee*		1960-68
	Rapid Transit. Correspondence with city, state, federal agencies, citizen groups; hearings, reports *re* development of a rapid transit system for Seattle.	1'	1960-68
	Interstate-90. Correspondence with city, state, federal agencies, citizen groups; hearings, reports *re* development of rapid transit for greater Seattle intertie with I-90, Lake Washington Bridge.	1'	1966-68

From this description in page format, entries can be made in the card catalog. Although there are almost as many variations for form of entries as there are repositories, the following may be used. Refer to the NUCMC example in note 5 and notice the awkwardness of establishing series level control for that at any more refined level if the informational format is followed literally. However, by omitting the scope and contents note it is possible to include series information on one card. In the NUCMC example, the correspondence series in the King County Public Utility District Association subgroup could be noted:

```
King County Public Utility District Association
Spear, Lillian Sylten, 1897-1963.
  'Papers, 1936-63.  7 ft. (ca. 6000 items)
  Correspondence, 1939-41, box 1, folders 1-15.'
```

In the case of the Seattle City Council subgroup of Elizabeth Baker's papers, the following series of card entries can be made for subgroup and series level control.

Subgroup Control
```
        Seattle.  City Council.  Utilities Committee.
        Baker, Elizabeth, 1915 –
          Papers, 1860-1972.  20· ft.
          Seattle.  City Council.  Utilities Committee
          subgroup.  1952-68, in boxes 8 and 9.
```

---

*Interpretation: In the KCPUDA subgroup of Lillian Spear's papers, the correspondence series is in box 1, folders 1-15, for the years 1939-41.

Series	International Joint Commission
Control	Baker, Elizabeth, 1915–
Within	Papers, 1860–1972. 20 ft.
Subgroup	Correspondence with IJC, 1952–68, box 8.*

If more detail is deemed necessary the last element can be:

Correspondence with IJC in Seattle City Council Utilities Committee subgroup *re* Skagit Dam Project, 1952-68, box 8.

As an alternative to the above form of card entry the same line of reference can be made more briefly by a simple index entry in page format.

International Joint Commission**

For manuscripts of the above, see Guides to the following collections:

Baker, Elizabeth papers 1860-1972		
Seattle. Lighting Department. Records 1905-63		
Puget Sound Power and Light Company. Records 1895-1960		

The decisions as to whether the card entry in its variant forms or a simple index entry is better depends upon how much information needs to be given at the initial point of reference. This is a policy decision, of course, but one which many, if not most, repositories do not realize can be made.

---

*Interpretation: In the Seattle City Council subgroup of Elizabeth Baker's papers, correspondence with IJC for 1952-68 will be found in box 8 of her papers.

**Interpretation: There will be items authored by the IJC not only in the papers of Elizabeth Baker which span the period 1860-1972, but also in the records of the Seattle Lighting Department and those of Puget Sound Power and Light Company. From these simple index entries the user would proceed to the container listing for each of these accessions for the more precise location and other information.

Appendix 17

Hierarchical Controls, File Unit Level Control: Register Page from the Styles Bridges Papers, New England College Library

COMMENT: The user is referred to the specific file folder by number.

	Year	Folder Number	Contents
File 13			NEW HAMPSHIRE GUBERNATORIAL PAPERS
			Official State of New Hampshire Files 1935 - 1936
	1935	1	Adjunct General
		2	Agriculture Department
		3	Agriculture Advisory Council
		4	American Legion
		5	Arts and Crafts
		6	Attorney General
		7	Banking Commission
		8	Bank Investment Board
		9	Bureau of Investigation
		10	Cancer Commission
		11	County Farm
		12	County Jail Cases
		13	Comptroller's Department
		14	Dental Board
		15	Educational Department
		16	Embalmers and Funeral Directors' Board
		17	Employment Service (State)
		18	Feeble Minded School (Laconia)
		19	Fish and Game Department
		20	Forestry Department
		21	Forest Policy Committee
		22	Forest Department: Reorganization
		23	Golden Rule Farm
		24	Health, Board of
		25	Highway Department
		26	Highway Program
		27	Highway Safety
		28	Industrial School
		29	Insurance Department
		30	Interstate Cooperation Commission
		31	Laboratory of Hygiene
		32	Labor Department
		33	Labor Law Administration
		34	Labor Legislation
		35	Land Use Board
		36	Library Commission
		37	Liquor Commission
		38	Mailing Department
		39	Milk Control Board
		40	Minimum Wage
		41	Motor Vehicle Department
		42	New Hampshire Foundation
		43	Planning Board

Appendix 18

Hierarchical Controls, File Unit Level Control: Page from the Indexed Register of the Carl Parcher Russell Papers, Washington State University Library

SERIES I: FUR TRADE AND FRONTIER

Container	Folder		Number of Items
		A. Correspondence	
1	1	Alcohol	2
	2	Axes	114
	3	Boats	38
	4	Containers (glass, metal, pottery)	22
	5-7	Firearms	300
2	8-12	Firearms	527
3	13-22	Firearms	677
4	23-26	Firearms	412
	27	Furs	13
	28	Hardware	130
	29	Horses	9
	30	Indians	9
	31	Knives	59
5	32	Ornaments	25
	33	Persons: Arthur H. Clark Co.	98
	34	Persons: Artists	26
	35	Persons: Jack Haynes	19
	36	Persons: General	91
	37	Places	68
	38	Pipes	3
	39	Textiles	12
	40	Tobacco	6
	41	Traps	46
	42	General: 1943-1949	85
	43	General: 1950-1966	103

Appendix 19

Hierarchical Controls, File Unit Level Control: Cumulative Name Index Sheet and Inventory Page, University of Washington Libraries

COMMENT: On the cumulative name index sheet the entry for Guy C. Myers refers the user to the inventory/guide. The i/g reference is for the Seattle Lighting Department records, box 74, folders 12 through 19, containing 234 items, 1932–38. Control is at the folder level.

SEATTLE. LIGHTING DEPARTMENT

Correspondence: Incoming (Cont.)

74-2	Moore (Josiah C.) Company, Inc. [engineers], Seattle	1918-1931	13
74-3	Morgan, Arthur Ernest, 1878-	1933	3
74-(4-5)	Morrison, Earl W. [architect], Seattle sa: City Light Building Company	1932-1938	20
74-6	Morrison-Knudsen Company [contractors]	1926-1927	5
74-7	Mount Vernon, Washington. [govt]	1927-1937	6
74-(8-9)	Municipal League of Seattle	1913-1936	23
74-10	Nunn (Charles A.) & Company [patent attnys]	1913-1918	8
74-11	Mutual Power & Light Association, Tanner, Washington	1935	17
74-(12-19)	Myers, Guy C., d. 1960	1932-1938	234
74-20	Mystic Shrine. Imperial Session, Seattle	1915	13
74-21	Mystic Shrine. Seattle Committee	1936	3
74-(22-28) 75-(1-12)	M Miscellaneous		
75-13	Nanoose Collieries, Ltd., B.C.	1918	5
75-14	National Carbon Company, Cleveland, Ohio	1905-1938	38
75-15	National Committee on Gas and Electric Service	1918	5
75-16	National Electric Light Association	1918-1932	16
75-17	National Electric Service Corporation	1933-1934	9
75-18	National Municipal Utilities Association	1935	4
75-(19-20)	National Popular Government League (Judson King)	1926-1937	31
	Nebraska. Central Supplemental Water Assn see: Central Nebraska...		
	Nebraska. Central Nebraska Public Power and Irrigation District see: Central Nebraska...		
	Nebraska. Platte Valley Public Power & Irrigation District see: Platte Valley Nebraska...		
76-1	Ne-Page McKenny Company [electrical engineers] Seattle	1922-1937	
76-2	Neuberger, Richard Lewis, 1912-1960	1936-1938	37
76-3	New School for Social Research	1936-1937	8
76-4	New York City. [govt]	1916,1935	7
76-5	New York Herald Tribune [newspaper]	1933,1936	2
76-6	New York Times [newspaper]	1927-1936	3
76-7	Newhall, Charles Abbot	1919-1935	12
76-8	Nibley, Joel	1934	1
76-9	Nichols, Ralph D., 1874-1949	1915-1934	17
76-10	Nitze, Paul Henry, 1907- sa: Myers, Guy C.	1934	1
76-11	Nixon (George)-Kimmel Company [wholesale]	1925-1928	2
76-12	Norris, George William, 1861-1944	1927-1937	21
76-13	North Coast Electric Company, Seattle	1914-1939	10
76-14	North End Federated Clubs, Seattle	1925-1937	5
76-15	Northern Bond & Mortgage Company, Seattle	1914-1936	14

Myers, Guy C., 1896-1960

For manuscripts of the above, see Guides to the following collections:

SEATTLE. LIGHTING DEPT. RECORDS UW LIB. MSS. COLL.	HUGH B. MITCHELL MSS UNIV. OF WASH. LIBRARY	N. W. PUBLIC PWR ASSN. MSS. UNIV. OF WASH. LIBRARY
ROBERT W. BECK PAPERS U. OF W. LIB. MSS. COLL.	Guy C. Myers Papers U. of W. Mss. Coll.	GUS NORWOOD PAPERS U OF W LIB. MSS. COLL.
JAMES I. METCALF PAPERS U OF W LIB. MSS. COLL.	LILLIAN S. SPEAR MSS UNIV. OF WASH. LIBRARY	PUGET SOUND POWER & LIGHT COMPANY U OF W LIB. MSS COLL
HOUGHTON, CLUCK, COUGHLIN & SCHUBAT ARCHIVE U OF WASH. LIB. MSS. COLL.		

Appendix 20

Hierarchical Controls, SPINDEX II, III: Portland, Oregon, City Archives

COMMENT: Portland, Oregon, City Archives NHPRC no.: OR 720-600. City Archives is a SPINDEX III user. In this example of series level control (Aviation Commission) the full control number for general correspondence would be: OR 720-600-3245-03. The "03" is the series control number, and the Commission record group number is 3245. OR = Oregon, 720 = Portland, "600" is fictional because the Archives was not established in time for publication of the *Directory* (National Historical Records and Publications Commission, *Directory of Archives and Manuscript Repositories*, Washington, D.C.: National Archives and Records Service, 1978), thus "600" is the repository number in this example.

The index entries for the general correspondence series are drawn from all the name entries of the series description. The "Cordon, Guy" entry has a control number, 3245-03. In the absence of file unit control the entire series must be searched for Cordon's correspondence. When the records are arranged for control at the file unit level, the file units will be represented by digits following "03" and the Cordon control will become more specific. For example: 3245-03-1256, in which 12 is the box number and 56 the number of the folder in which Cordon's correspondence is filed.

City of Portland   LEVEL ASSIGNMENTS
SPINDEX DATA BASE DESIGN   March 2, 1979

	Control Number Position	Definition
Level 1	1-2	State
Level 2	3-5	City
Level 3	6-8	Repository
Level 4	9-10	Record Group (Bureau of Office)
Level 5	11-12	Sub-Group (Subdivision of Bureau or Office)
Level 6	13-14	Series
Level 7	15-18	Archives Folder

City of Portland   CONTROL NUMBER ASSIGNMENT SCHEME
SPINDEX DATA BASE DESIGN   March 2, 1979

Level	Control Number Position	Definition
1-3	1-8	State, City, Repository: Established by the NHPRC.
4	9-10	Record Group: Numbers assigned to place bureaus or offices in alphabetical or near alphabetical order. Numbers assigned in the <u>Records Manual</u> are used for current agencies, other agencies are assigned the unused number between.
5	11-12	Sub-Group: Numbers assigned according to sequence in <u>Records Manual</u> where applicable. Mayors and Commissioners will be placed in alphabetical order; special committees and commissions will be placed in chronological order.
6	13-14	Series: Numbers assigned according to sequence in <u>Records Manual</u> or as appear in archives guide.
7	15-18	Folder: Usually the 15th and 16th digits will be box number and the 17th and 18th digits will be folder number within the box.

```
000    427201203245/5
110    OR720-120/3245
123    3245
140    Aviation Commission
200    1945
210    1956
240    !!!1.5 c.f.
250    3245
270    The creation of the Aviation Commission in December
       1947 amended the City Administrative Code by adding
       Article 31.  Members of the Commission represented
       scheduled air transport, fixed base operators,
       reserve activities, certified airmen, and the
       general public.  An eight member non-voting advisory
       committee to the Aviation Commission represented
       City government.  The Commission functioned essen-
       tially as an information gathering body "for the
       purpose of furthering aviation and aviation legisla-
       tion."
420    Transferred from Auditor's Office.
550    AR
950    OR
960    AE
961    TR
970    PR
980    NG
990    1979/02
=
```

```
000    42720120324501/6
110    OR720-120/3245-01
123    3245-01
126    Vault 1, Room 4
140    Minutes
200    1952
210    1954
250    3245-01
270    Arranged chronologically.
550    AR
600    78A-8
950    OR
970    PR
980    NG
990    1979/02
=      .
```

```
000    42720120324502/6
110    OR720-120/3245-02
123    3245-02
126    Vault 1, Room 4
140    Annual Reports
200    1949
210    1954
250    3245-02
270    Arranged chronologically.
```

```
550    AR
600    78A-8
950    OR
970    PR
980    NG
990    1979/02
=
```

```
000    42720120324503/6
110    OR720-120/3245-03
123    3245-03
126    Vault 1, Room 4
140    Correspondence
200    1948
210    1956
250    3245-03
270    Letters sent and received.  Arranged chronologically.
       Principal correspondents include the Civil
       Aeronautics Board; Civil Aeronautics Administration;
       Oregon State Board of Aeronautics; Port of Portland;
       Portland Chamber of Commerce; U.S. Senator Wayne
       Morse; and U.S. Representative Guy Cordon.
550    AR
600    78A-8
660    U.S. Civil Aeronautics Board
661    U.S. Civil Aeronautics Administration
662    Oregon.  Board of Aeronautics
663    Port of Portland
664    Portland Chamber of Commerce
670    Morse, Wayne
671    Cordon, Guy
950    OR
970    PR
980    NG
990    1979/02
=
```

```
000    42720120324504/6
110    OR720-120/3245-04
123    3245-04
126    Vault 1, Room 4
140    Subject File
200    1945
210    1963
250    3245-04
270    Arranged alphabetically by subject heading.
550    AR
600    78A-8
950    OR
970    PR
980    NG
990    1979/02
=
```

3245
Aviation Commission, 1945–1956. 1.2 c.f.

The creation of the Aviation Commission in December 1947 amended the
City Administrative Code by adding Article 31. Members of the
Commission represented scheduled air transport, fixed base operators,
reserve activities, certified airmen, and the general public. An
eight member non-voting advisory committee to the Aviation Commission
represented City government. The Commission functioned essentially
as an information gathering body "for the purpose of furthering
aviation and aviation legislation."
Source: Transferred from Auditor's Office.

Series:

   3245-01
   Minutes, 1952–1954. Arranged chronologically.

   3245-02
   Annual Reports, 1949–1954. Arranged chronologically.

   3245-03
   Correspondence, 1948–1956. Letters sent and received. Arranged
      chronologically. Principal correspondents include the Civil
      Aeronautics Board; Civil Aeronautics Administration; Oregon
      State Board of Aeronautics; Port of Portland; Portland Chamber
      of Commerce; U.S. Senator Wayne Morse; and U.S. Representative
      Guy Cordon.

   3245-04
   Subject File, 1945–1963. Arranged alphabetically by subject
      heading.

Air Mail Field Post Office	1948–1949	1/8
Air Port Master Plan	1945–1948	1/9
Air Service to Hawaii	1946–1948	1/10
Alternative Airport	1945–1951	1/11
Budget	1948–1950	1/12
Bus Service to Airport	1949–1953	1/12
Economic Survey	1947–1949	2/1
History	1947–1951	2/2
Naval Air Reserve Unit	1948	2/3

   3245-05
   Dockets, 1947–1953. Civil Aeronautics Board legislative dockets
      included in connection with the Aviation Commission's role in
      recommending aviation legislation. Those dockets having a
      particular bearing on Portland International Airport activities
      are foldered individually and arranged by docket number. Other
      dockets are filed chronologically.

INDEX TO AVIATION COMMISSION, 1945 - 1956

Subject	Title	Index Ref. No.
Air		
	Air Mail Field Post Office	3245-04
	Air Port Master Plan	3245-05
	Air Service to Hawaii	3245-04
	Naval Air Service Unit	3245-04
Airport		
	Alternative Airport	3245-04
	Bus Service to Airport	3245-04
	Portland International Airport	3245-05
Alternative		
	Alternative Airport	3245-04
Annual		
	Annual Reports	3245-02
Aviation		
	Aviation Commission	3245
Budget		
	Budget	3245-04
Bus		
	Bus Service to Airport	3245-04
Commission		
	Aviation Commission	3245
Cordon, Guy		
	Correspondence	3245-03
Dockets		
	Dockets	3245-05
Economic		
	Economic Survey	3245-04
Field		
	Air Mail Field Post Office	3245-04
Hawaii		
	Air Service to Hawaii	3245-04

Appendix 21

Hierarchical Controls, SPINDEX II, III: Series Level Control Illustrated in Midwest State Archives *Guide* (in progress); Index Entry

COMMENT: Refer to index entry (p. 50): Chicago, Milwaukee and St. Paul Railroad WI/J90A-43. Interpretation: Documents relating to the railroad will be found in Wisconsin State Archives series 43 of the subgroup JA90A (Administrative Division) of Record Group J90 (Public Service Commission).

WISCONSIN STATE ARCHIVES

Long before the State Historical Society of Wisconsin was officially designated the state's archival depository in 1947, the Society had been accepting and administering some of the permanently valuable records of the State of Wisconsin. Though the state for the first one hundred years of its existence had no official archival agency, other important state papers were carefully preserved in the offices of their origin or filed with the Secretary of State. Although some records were destroyed through carelessness and ignorance, the great nemesis of archives--statehouse fires--touched few of Wisconsin's records. As a result most of Wisconsin's important records have come to the archives intact.

To date the state archives has accessioned and processed over 2,000 record series from more than 85 state agencies totaling nearly 28,000 cubic feet. An additional 2,000 series of county and local government records are also held by the state archives. These records, dating back to the formation of the Wisconsin Territory in 1836, touch on practically every facet of Wisconsin life and history.

The archives, located in the Historical Society building at 816 State Street, Madison, Wisconsin 53706, is open to the public for research. Material may be used in the Archives Reading Room on the fourth floor and is also available at the thirteen Area Research Centers located on college and university campuses throughout Wisconsin.

GUIDES: The records of the Wisconsin State Archives have been described in a variety of guides and inventories. The *Guide to the Wisconsin State Archives,* compiled and edited by David J. Delgado, although more than thirteen years old, is still the most complete. Unpublished inventories of individual series and record groups are available in the Archives Reading Room.

RECORD GROUP J90

PUBLIC SERVICE COMMISSION

The Public Service Commission is responsible for regulating railroads, motor carriers, and public utilities.

Railroad regulation in Wisconsin began with the passage of Chapter 273, Laws of 1874, when the office of Railroad Commissioner was established to monitor rates and service of steam and electric railways. Chapter 362, Laws of 1905 named the Railroad Commission to succeed the office of Railroad Commissioner and gave it more regulatory powers. With the passage of Chapter 499, Laws of 1907, the regulatory jurisdiction of the Railroad Commission was extended to include public utilities, both privately and municipally owned. The name of the Railroad Commission was

changed to the Public Service Commission in 1931 (Laws 1931, Chapter 183), and at that time the powers of the Commission were greatly expanded.

Although the original function of the Commission was the regulation of railroads, the Transportation Act of 1920 decreased the Commission's regulatory power over interstate railroads. Both this act and U.S. Supreme Court decisions shifted regulatory power to the federal Interstate Commerce Commission. The Railroad Commission was allowed to cooperate with the Interstate Commerce Commission on interstate rate matters, and continued to regulate intrastate rates. In matters of railroad safety and service, the Transportation Act did not greatly curtail the Commission's powers.

The Motor Carrier Law of 1933 had an important effect on the Railroad Commission's function by giving it regulatory responsibility over common carriers and for the assessment of the ton-mile tax against contract carriers. The Commission's involvement with motor vehicle regulation and a corresponding de-emphasis on railroad matters began with the passage of this law. In the area of motor transportation, the Commission provides economic regulation, while matters involving law enforcement and safety are within the jurisdiction of the State Department of Transportation.

The Securities Law of 1919, also known as the 'Blue Sky Law', gave the Commission responsibility over the classification of and investigation of stocks, bonds and all other forms of securities to be sold in Wisconsin. The reorganization law enacted at the 1937 Special Session of the Legislature transferred the Securities Division

Originally, the Railroad Commission was organized into three basic divisions: Administration, Transportation, and Utilities. These basic divisions were in turn divided into departments. For example, during the 1930's the Utilities Division was organized into Utility Rates, Department of Accounts and Finance, and Engineering Utility branches.

In 1942 the Commission was reorganized into its present form of six major divisions: Administration, Accounts and Finance, Utility Rates, Transportation, Engineering and Examining. The Commission is currently composed of three full-time commissioners appointed by the governor and confirmed by the Senate for staggered six-year terms.

The Public Service Commission has several counterparts on the federal level performing regulatory functions in relation to interstate commerce. These include the Federal Power Commission, the Federal Communications Commission, the Interstate Commerce Commission and the Securities and Exchange Commission.

The records of the Public Service Commission consist of the records of the Administration Division, which include letterpress copies of correspondence, and minutes and records of early hearings; the Examining Division, which include records of later formal hearings; the Utility Rates Division, which include rates, rules and contracts; the Accounts and Finance Division, which include annual reports issued by all public utilities; the Transportation Division, which include formal case files and statistical summaries relating to motor transport and railroad companies; and the Engineering Division, which include valuations of railroad and public utilities property and engineering drawings.

SUBGROUP   J9A

Administration Division

The Administration Division operates as the administrative and co-ordinating office and the general information bureau for the Public Service Commission.

The division maintains work, personnel and finance files, and keeps 'full and correct records of all transactions and proceedings of the commission' (Wisc. stats. 195.01 (8)). The division also produces indexes to commission files.

The Administration Division is the oldest of the Public Service Commission's divisions. Organized originally to serve the office of Railroad Commissioner, it was thus responsible for some of the oldest records of the Railroad Commission. One of the early functions of the Administration Division was the holding of formal hearings, this function was later assumed by the Legal Department.

The records of the Administration Division include early letterpress copies of correspondence of the the the Railroad Commissioner, minutes of the Railroad Commission and Public Service Commission, correspondence and other documents related to all phases of utility regulation, records of complaints filed with the Railroad Commission, working papers of early investigations and hearings held by the Commission, speeches of the commissioners, and indexes to correspondence and case files.

J90A-10
Railroad Commissioner's Letterbooks,   1874 - 1907
2.5 c.f. (20 volumes)

Letterpress copies of outgoing correspondence of the Board of Railroad Commissioners and the Railroad cämmissioners.

The records include letters to complainants and railroads about rate changes, freight classifications, service, passes, railroad legislation, traffic hazards, land grants, opinions of the Attorney General, examination of railroad properties and books, railroad reports, and railroad maps and publications.
ARRANGEMENT: Chronological.

J90A-20
Minutes of the Commission,   1874 - 1964
5.0 c.f. (34 volumes)

Minutes of the Public Service Commission, formerly the Railroad Commission, containing opinions, resolutions, procedures, policy and action on cases.

Between 1878 and 1905 the duties were performed by a single Railroad Commissioner and no minutes were kept.
ARRANGEMENT: Chronological.

J90A-30
General Correspondence,   1874 - 1962
38.4 c.f. (740 archives boxes)

Correspondence and other documents relating to all phases of utility regulation and other functions assigned by law to the Commission.

The records include telegrams, memoranda, circulars, news clippings, articles, reports, statistical data, blueprints, maps, charts, photographs, orders, opinions, briefs, transcripts, exhibits, and pictures relating to such subjects as the improvement of navigable streams and lakes, rent control in Milwaukee, administration of the motor carrier ton-mile tax, and the regulation of the issue of securities in Wisconsin.
ARRANGEMENT: Chronological and alphabetical thereunder through 1906; after 1906 by name of correspondent in numerical file, and by subject and chronological thereunder.
FINDING AIDS: After 1906, alphabetical index showing number of each correspondent. Additional point sheets list subjects in all files relating to more than one subject, with a decimal suffix added to the file number indicating each subject. The decimal suffix is a finding aid, not a subject code. See also Indexes to Central Files; and Index to Numerical Case Files and General Correspondence.

J90A-40
Railroad Commissioner's Complaint Record,   1884 - 1894
0.1 c.f. (1 volume)

Railroad Commissioner's record of complaints filed with him, showing date, nature of complaint, summaries of correspondence, and disposition of each case.
ARRANGEMENT: Chronological.

J90A-43
Railroad Investigation Working Papers,   1894 - 1906
3.0 c.f. (7 archives boxes)

Working papers of the Railroad Commissioner's office relating to an investigation of railway companies concerning possible violations of Wisconsin laws through discriminatory rates, illegal deductions, and earnings not reported leading to understatement of income and consequent underpayment of taxes.

The companies were investigated by the Commissioner under the authority invested in him by the Laws of Wisconsin 1903, Chapter 431. The railway companies investigated were the Chicago, Milwaukee and St. Paul; Chicago, St. Paul, Minneapolis and Omaha; Chicago and Northwestern; and the Wisconsin Central. The papers consist entirely of

presentations of figures of deductions from freight and pas-
senger earnings, vouchers car switching, car milage, recapit-
ulations, demurrage, milage paid car companies, switching
collections and gross freight earnings. Also included is a
printed report of Commissioner John W. Thomas, July 6,
1906.
    ARRANGEMENT: By railway company.
    RELATED RECORDS: See also General Fund Receipts,
box 8; and General Correspondence, boxes 2-5; *Misc.
Railroad Documents,* 1874-1906; and 00453312th Biennial
Report of the Railroad Commissioner, 1906.

J90A-45
Minutes of Hearings, 1905 - 1907
    3.0 c.f. (22 volumes)

Transcripts of testimony and proceedings of hearings before the Railroad Commission.
    ARRANGEMENT: Chronological.
    RELATED RECORDS: Subsequent transcripts filed with
formal case files, see Formal Case Papers: Railroads; Formal
Case Papers: Public Utilities; and Formal Case Papers: Suits
Against the Commission.

J90A-50
Indexes to Central Files, 1905 - 1931
    10 reels microfilm (16 mm negative)

Index to general correspondence and informal case files
by name and subject giving reference to file number.

Index references Series 1254, 1257, 1258, 1259, 1263,
1264, 1265, 1266, 1269, 1273 and 1277.
    ARRANGEMENT: Alphabetical by name , subject, or
locality.
    FINDING AIDS: See list of reel contents.
    RELATED RECORDS: See also Index to Numerical Case
Files and General Correspondence.

J90A-60
Speeches of Railroad Commissioners, 1908 - 1911
    0.1 c.f. (1 volume)

Scrapbook containing printed speeches of the Railroad
Commissioners after the Commission was given the responsibility in 1907 of regulating public utilities.

The speeches explain the purpose of the Commission, the
advantages to the utilities and to the public, and the methods of regulation obtained through the use of uniform accounting systems and the control of utility rates and
securities issues.
    FINDING AIDS: List of topics by page number included
with the scrapbook.

J90A-70
**Index to Numerical Case Files and General
    Correspondence,** 1914 - 1967
    24.0 c.f. (271 drawers)

Alphabetical index to general correspondence and case
files of the Commission showing subjects, names of utilities
and other companies, individuals, government agencies and
municipalities, geographical locations and index file numbers.

Index references Series 1254, 1257, 1258, 1259, 1264,
1265, 1268, 1269, 1270, 1273, 1274, 1276, 1278, 1281, 1826
and 1827.
    ARRANGEMENT: By span of years, and alphabetical
thereunder.
    RELATED RECORDS: See also Indexes to Central Files.

J90A-80
Quarterly Budgets, 1931 - 1938
    2.0 c.f. (2 archives boxes and 1 records center carton)

Quarterly budgets of Public Service Commission by departments, showing estimated resources, divided salaries
and breakdown by departments, and including lists of personnel.

SUBGROUP   J90B

Accounts and Finance Division

The Accounts and Finance Division audits the accounting practices and financial records of gas, electric, telephone
and water public utilities and investigates and studies utility
applications for authority to issue stocks, bonds, and all
other forms of securities.

The division conducts research into accounting matters
and designs uniform systems of accounting for all Wisconsin public utilites. It also prepares depreciation studies and
analyses of cost of capital and rate of return as well as
maintains files of annual reports of utility companies.

The Accounts and Finance Department was originally a
branch of the Utilities Division. In 1942 the department
became one of the Commission's six major organizational
divisions, and in addition to retaining its previous functions
it assumed responsiblity for securities regulation from the
Administration Department.

The records of the Accounts and Finance Division include annual reports prepared by all classes of electric, gas,
electric railway, heating, water, telephone and joint public
utilities, and authorizations of issues of securities.

J90B-10
Annual Reports of Utility Companies, 1907 - 1949
    272.6 c.f. (654 archives boxes)

Annual reports prepared by all classes of electric, gas,
electric railway, heating, water and joint public utilities
detailing organizational, operating, financial and physical
data.
    ARRANGEMENT: By span of years and thereunder by
file number.
    FINDING AIDS: See Indexes to Files

J90B-20
Annual Reports of Telephone Companies, 1907 - 1949
    119.2 c.f. (268 archives boxes)

Annual Reports prepared by telephone companies detailing organizational, financial, and physical data.
    ARRANGEMENT: Chronological by year and by file
number thereunder.

Appendix 22

Provenance as an Inferential System

COMMENT: Note that by rearranging the file units under series and sub-group designations their character is implied, whereas the original order did not permit such inferences to be made. In other words, a measure for self-access has been provided the reader of the rearranged list.

The "W.U." prefixes mean *Washington. University.* As these names are interfiled in the CNI with all other proper names it is necessary to use the prefix to indicate the name of the parent body. Similarly for the "Works Projects Administration" which was a U.S. federal agency.

By these procedures full advantage is taken of the provenance method and content analysis of file units that make up series is minimized.

Adjusted filing order by series and subgroups:

General correspondence (external)

Coordinated Studies in Education	1940-54
Group Health Cooperative of Puget Sound	1948-49
U.S. WorkProjects Administration	1933-42

Interdepartmental correspondence

W.U. Accounting Department	1931-36
W.U. Adult Education	1946-58
W.U. Governmental Research Institute	1946-50
W.U. Home Economics Department	1939-45
W.U. Intercollegiate Athletics Department	1962-63
W.U. Public Opinion Laboratory	1947-55

Buildings and Construction (includes, specifications, bids, contracts, reports, plans, and correspondence filed by project name.)

Administration Building	1934-56
Library addition	1947-49
Nuclear Reactor Building	1959-61

Subject Series (includes correspondence and related items accumulated by the office under topical headings, which have been retained.)

- Accounting Policies
- Civil Defense
- Laundry
- Loyalty Oath
- Nepotism

Subgroups

W.U. Applied Physics Laboratory Advisory Board	1951-60
W.U. Metropolitan Center	
Metropolitan Building Company	1922-69
Olympic Hotel Metropolitan Theater	1922-38
Teaching Hospital Metropolitan Tract	
Revenue Bonds	1952-57
W.U. Surplus Property Committee	1945-47

Original file order (selected, but in original sequence)

- Accounting Department
- Accounting Policies
- Administrative Building
- Adult Education
- Applied Physics Laboratory Advisory Board
- Civil defense
- Coordinated Studies in Education
- Governmental Research Institute
- Group Health Cooperative of Puget Sound
- Home Economics Department
- Intercollegiate Athletics
- Laundry
- Library addition
- Loyalty oath
- Metropolitan Building Company
- Metropolitan Center
- Nepotism
- Nuclear Reactor Building
- Olympic Hotel Metropolitan Theater
- Public Opinion Laboratory
- Surplus Property Committee
- Teaching Hospital Metropolitan Tract
- WorkProjects Administration

Appendix 23

Archival – Records Management Relations

It is well to bear in mind that records management (RM) was invented by the National Archives to control the life cycle of records. Archival management is one end product of a comprehensive RM program. The degree to which archivists exercise full RM functions determines the quality of any institutional archives. To a large extent this holds true for manuscript collections in which the collection receives records from various organizations and individuals on a continuous basis as their records and personal papers become inactive. Any situation that impairs this control requires negotiation between different levels of administration that are responsible for archival and nonarchival RM functions respectively.

Usually archivists do not control nonarchival RM functions. In situations where archival functions of RM also are not controlled by the archivist, negotiation and compromise are necessary. In all archival – RM relations a better understanding needs to be cultivated about the goals of each. Essentially they are the same—responsible records use and administration leading to either authorized destruction or archival preservation and administration. Neither records managers nor archivists want to retain records that no longer serve a useful purpose. Archivists need to develop better appraisal standards, but they require active participation and cooperation of records managers if this is to be done.

With some justification, RM specialists have tended to dissociate themselves from archival specialists, because the latter have represented to them strictly a cost factor in the spectrum of RM functions—for archival management is one of those functions. All other RM functions can demonstrate cost effectiveness except archival ones, and that is regrettably unavoidable. An exception is the use of archives for some administrative purpose. In RM eyes archivists prefer to keep more records than need to be preserved. Records managers are correct to an undetermined degree, but they must bear part of the responsibility for the underdevelopment of the records appraisal function. Within the same operation they may both be concerned about appraisal of the same records. Although the archivist really does not want to retain any more records than necessary, he or she is inevitably more conservative than records managers about destroying unique records and often prefers to postpone a final decision. To keep records that ultimately are decided to be not of archival quality represents a waste, even if it is justifiable. Yet the matter cannot be resolved without the closest collaboration, the nature of which will vary from situation to situation. Some illustrations may help.

Ideally, from an archivist's point of view, the RM function should be under control of the archivist. Originally it was, and it remains essential to any institutional archival program. But the archivist's ideal is rarely the actuality. Instead, a RM program often already exists, and the problem for the archivist is to form an effective link with it. If there is no records center, the archivist can seek to establish one and use it as the linkage. In such cases the center would implement certain RM functions: intermediate storage and service of transient records, and archival retention. In such a situation the records manager is concerned with on-site management of records, and the archivist assumes responsibility when records are moved from the originating office. The center in this case serves as an archival staging area.

If the RM office controls the center as well as óther nonarchival functions, and if the archivist reports to a different authority, the archivist probably must deal with both the originating office and the center-held records through the RM office. Implementation of the archival program in such a situation is inevitably complicated and uncertain—too often dependent on nonobjective matters such as personality, administrative friction, competition, and the like.

The lack of a records center even for records of an ostensibly transient nature complicates the operation for both the RM and the archival offices. The best that can be hoped is that records schedules will be developed and that records destruction will be governed by them. There being no separate staging area to facilitate final appraisal, all operations must be done on site. Painstaking monitoring by both the RM and archives offices is required in the absence of a records center.

In each of the three situations outlined above in which the RM functions are not under archival jurisdiction, the archival control becomes more and more tenuous. Without a records center, all RM functions, including archival ones, are more complicated and less controllable. With a center that is limited to transient records, only the nonarchival functions are facilitated and are more cost effective. With a center that combines archival and other RM functions, all are better implemented. If the center is under authority of the RM office, however, the archivist must negotiate with that office for transfer of noncurrent records of archival quality that are in the center. If the center is under archival jurisdiction, however, such records can be transferred mainly on the strength of archival authority. It is clear from the outline of archival and RM relations that there must be a clear articulation of their respective programs for an archival program to succeed. Unfortunately for archivists, nonarchival RM programs can "succeed" independently of an archives. If the corporate body does not want its own archive—seeing it as representing an unjustifiable expense—the only archival option is to arrange for transfer of its records to a compliant or solicitous manuscript repository.

This last statement leads back to our increasing emphasis on the collecting of contemporary papers and records. What has been an "increasing tendency" should become more fully conscious if we are to attain the breadth of coverage and consecutiveness of documentation that is required for authoritativeness of whatever documents are collected. To achieve authoritativeness it is essential that curators of recent manuscripts become judicious records managers for the corporate bodies whose records they collect. To the degree that the curator receives unpurged files he can exercise full archival control of RM functions—an archival ideal that rarely happens. The curator, in exercising this function, does so at a stage when fresh additions of records are accessioned. He normally would not participate in those RM functions which are on-site in the originating agency. As a result, the curator is led back to exercising the appraisal functions. At its core RM is a system of records appraisal. Most RM techniques are intended to simplify the appraisal process, and RM owes its origins to this archival concern. Consequently, curators of contemporary records and papers need to master those RM functions relating to appraisal.

Notes

Chapter 1. Overview

1. This section relies mainly on U.S. National Archives, *Staff Information Circular*, no. 5, "European Archival Practices in Arranging Records," by Theodore R. Schellenberg (Washington, D.C.: GSA, 1939). See also Ernst Posner, *Archives and the Public Interest*, ed. Ken Munden (Washington, D.C.: Public Affairs Press, 1967), pp. 23–44, 87–97; S. Muller, J. A. Feith, and R. Fruin, *Manual for the Arrangement and Description of Archives*, trans. Arthur H. Leavitt, 1940 (New York: H. W. Wilson Co., 1968); and Hilary Jenkinson, *A Manual of Archive Administration* (London: P. Land, Humphries, 1937), for the British approach.

2. Reference is to Kenneth W. Duckett, *Modern Manuscripts* (Nashville, 1975).

3. See my review of Maynard J. Brichford, *Archives and Manuscripts: Appraisal and Accessioning* (SAA *Basic Manuals Series*), in *Midwestern Archivist* 4:2 (1979): 105–7.

4. A series of obituaries about Schellenberg appears in the *American Archivist* 33 (April 1970): 190–202. No other archivist has been comparably honored. Schellenberg became the most prolific and influential writer in the United States archival field after joining the National Archives staff in 1935. His career is traced through the course of chapters 2, 3, and 4.

5. In chronological order these are "The Arrangement and Description of Manuscripts," *AA* 23 (October 1960): 395–406; "Description of Private Papers and Archival Principles of Arrangement," *Symposium on Archival Administration*, May 1964, cosponsored by SAA, NARS, and the University of Washington School of Librarianship, transcript, pp. 17–23; "Archivists, Librarians, and the National Union Catalog of Manuscript Collections," *AA* 27 (July 1964): 401–9; "Manuscript Collections and Archives—A Unitary Approach," *Library Resources and Technical Services* 9 (Spring 1965): 213–20; with M. Gary Bettis, "Description of Manuscript Collections: A Single Network System," *College and Research Libraries* 30 (September 1969): 405–16; "Manuscript Catalogs and other Finding Aids: What Are Their Relationships?" *AA* 34 (October 1971): 367–72; chapter in *Drexel Library Quarterly* 11 (January 1975), "Arrangement and Description of Manuscripts," pp. 34–54 (the *DLQ* issue title is "Management of Archives and Manuscript Collections for Librarians," ed. Richard H. Lytle); "Perspectives on the Record Group Concept," *Georgia Archive* 4 (Winter 1976): 48–55; "Arrangement and Description: Some Historical Observations," *AA* 41 (April 1978): 169–81; and *Manual for Accessioning, Arrangement, and Description of Manu-*

scripts and Archives (Seattle: University of Washington Libraries, *Communications in Librarianship*, no. 1, 1979).

6. The first article to appear on this method was Robert E. Burke, "Modern Manuscript Collections and What to Do with Them," *Manuscripts* 7 (Summer 1955): 232–36.

Chapter 2. Public Archives and Historical Manuscripts, 1800–1936

1. Among the famous collectors are Jeremy Belknap, Jared Sparks, Peter Force, Lyman Draper, Thomas Prince, Ebenezer Hazard, and William B. Sprague. Each of their collections was subsequently acquired by an institution, becoming in many cases the cornerstone of that legatee's own collection. For general accounts see O. Lawrence Burnette, *Beneath the Footnote* (Madison: State Historical Society of Wisconsin, 1969); T. R. Schellenberg, *The Management of Archives* (New York: Columbia University Press, 1965), chapter 3; Kenneth W. Duckett, *Modern Manuscripts* (Nashville: American Association for State and Local History, 1975), chapter 1; Ernst Posner, *American State Archives* (Chicago: University of Chicago Press, 1964), pp. 1–36; Lucile M. Kane, "Manuscript Collecting," in William B. Hesseltine and Donald R. McNeil, eds., *In Support of Clio* (Madison: State Historical Society of Wisconsin, 1958), pp. 29–48; G. Philip Bauer, "Public Archives in the United States," in Hesseltine and McNeil, pp. 49–76. Detailed reports may be found in the annual reports of the American Historical Association's Historical Manuscripts Commission since 1896; and its Public Archives Commission, since 1900. See also the annual proceedings of the National Association of State Libraries, since 1911. Of special interest is Worthington C. Ford, "The Massachusetts Historical Society," in AHA, *Annual Report, 1912*, 1:217–23. See also Walter Rundell, Jr., *In Pursuit of American History* (Norman: University of Oklahoma Press, 1970), chapter 3.

2. For bibliographies of these publications see Adelaide R. Hasse, "Materials for a Bibliography of the Public Archives of the Thirteen Original States . . . to 1789," in AHA, *Annual Report, 1906*, vol. 2. Hasse's survey indicates that in most of the northern states, Maryland, North Carolina, and South Carolina, it was the state historical society that initiated concern for public records. See also Bauer, "Public Archives," pp. 57–63; [Edmund C. Burnett], "A List of Printed Guides to and Descriptions of Archives and Other Repositories of Historical Manuscripts," in AHA, Historical Manuscripts Commission, *Annual Report, 1896*, 1:481–512; Justin Winsor, "Manuscript Sources of American History: The Conspicuous Collections Extant," American Historical Association, *Papers* 3 (1889):9–27. Of special interest, although it is not a guide to publications, is Claude H. Van Tyne and Waldo G. Leland, *Guide to the Archives of the Government of the United States in Washington* (Washington, D.C.: Carnegie Institution, 1904). Subsequent editions were published. In the preface it was noted that "there could be no hard and fast line between historical collections and ordinary administrative records."

3. Cf. Schellenberg, *Management of Archives*, pp. 45–47, 53–54; Massachusetts Historical Society, *Collections*, 1:3 (quotation).

4. Massachusetts Historical Society, *Proceedings* 2 (1835): 16, 19; 2 (1849): 434; 14 (1875): 113–16; Schellenberg, *Management of Archives*, p. 36–37; AHA, *Annual Re-*

port, 1900, pp. 48, 51, "Report on the Public Archives of Massachusetts." See also Posner, *American State Archives*, p. 143; Massachusetts, Record Commission, *Report to the Legislature . . . on the Condition of the Records . . . in the Secretary's Department*, January 1885, for Felt's "enumeration" and for criticism of it, esp. pp. 14–15, 40–41.

5. Jared Sparks, *The Diplomatic Correspondence of the American Revolution* (Boston: N. Hale and Gray and Bowen, 1829), 1:ix.

6. Peter Force, *American Archives: A Documentary History*, (Washington, D.C., 1848). See his table of contents.

7. *Ibid.* Although only series 4 and 5 were published, Force's outline of six series is paralleled by Herbert Friedenwald's, and appears to have been the model for Friedenwald's. See also Fred Shelley, "Manuscripts in the Library of Congress: 1800–1900," *AA* 11 (January 1948): 15, and Schellenberg, *Management of Archives*, p. 39.

8. Schellenberg, *Management of Archives*, p. 43.

9. National Association of State Libraries, *Proceedings*, 1915, p. 24.

10. Theodore C. Blegen, *A Report on the Public Archives* (Madison: State Historical Society of Wisconsin, 1918), p. 51. Compare this treatment with Schellenberg, *Management of Archives*, p. 45. Mississippi, Department of Archives and History, *Annual Report*, 1902 (p. 18), 1903 (p. 12), 1904 (p. 25), 1906 (p. 55), 1907 (pp. 20–21). AHA, *Annual Report, 1912*, pp. 270–71; Paltsits in AHA, *Annual Report, 1922*, p. 156.

11. Benjamin F. Shambaugh, *A Report on Public Archives* (Des Moines, 1907); John C. Parish, *A Guide to the Administrative Departments, Offices, Boards, Commissions, and Public Institutions of Iowa*; AHA, *Annual Report, 1900*, 2:39–46. Ethel B. Virtue, "Principles of Classification for Archives," in AHA, *Annual Report, 1914*, 1:373–84; Cassius C. Stiles, "Lessons from Iowa," in AHA, *Annual Report, 1922*, 1:127–33; and Blegen, *Report on the Public Archives*, pp. 59–62, 75 (n. 9), 76–77.

12. Blegen, *Report on the Public Archives*, pp. 24–25, 31. Compare this treatment with Schellenberg's, *Management of Archives*, pp. 40–41, 208.

13. See Schellenberg, *Management of Archives*, pp. 43 and 55.

14. Ibid., and Waldo G. Leland, "American Archival Problems," in AHA, *Annual Report, 1909*, 1:346–47.

15. For the Library of Congress, John C. Fitzpatrick wrote a manual, *Notes on the Care, Cataloguing, Calendaring and Arranging of Manuscripts* (Washington, D.C.: 1913, 1921, 1928), discussed later in this chapter. For the most comprehensive chronicle of the Conference of Archivists, see William F. Birdsall, "The American Archivists' Search for Professional Identity, 1909–1936" (Ph.D. diss., University of Wisconsin, Madison, 1973). A useful summary is also given by Victor H. Paltsits, chair of the Public Archives Commission, "An Historical Resumé of the Public Archives Commission from 1899 to 1921," in AHA, *Annual Report, 1922*, 1:152–60. See also Donald R. McCoy, *The National Archives* (Chapel Hill: University of North Carolina Press, 1978), pp. 92–96, for the transition from the Conference of Archivists to formation of the SAA.

16. Dunbar Rowland, "The Concentration of State and National Archives," in AHA, *Annual Report, 1910*, 1:296–98. See also note 10 above for an elaboration of the Mississippi system. Muller, Feith, and Fruin, *Manual*, had been published before Rowland's European trip of 1905–6. They had insisted on the primacy of administrative service in their rule 19. He probably was made aware of this during his trip.

17. In this context see Schellenberg, *Management of Archives*, pp. 39, 45; and chapter 3 below.

18. Richard C. Berner, "Manuscript Catalogs and Other Finding Aids: What Are Their Relationships?" *AA* 34 (October 1971): 367–72.

19. On Paltsits see Margaret C. Norton, "Victor Hugo Paltsits, 1867–1952," *AA* 16 (April 1953): 137–40. See AHA, *Annual Report, 1922*, pp. 159–63, for Jameson's attitude. See also Paltsits, "Pioneering for a Science of Archives in the United States," in A. F. Kuhlman, ed., *Archives and Libraries* (Chicago: ALA, 1937), pp. 233–39. See also Posner, *American State Archives*, p. 26. Birdsall downplays Paltsits' effort, unjustifiably in my opinion.

20. W. G. Leland, "The National Archives: A Programme," *American Historical Review* 18 (1912): 1–28, esp. pp. 24–25. See also his "American Archival Problems" (1909), pp. 346–47. It was previously acknowledged at the sixth Conference of Historical Societies in 1909 that "a process of differentiation has developed by which questions relating to archives . . . should be considered in separate conferences of archivists," in AHA, *Annual Report, 1909*, 1:285.

21. Margaret Cross Norton, "The Archives as an Administrative Unit in Government," in National Association of State Libraries, *Proceedings, June 23–27, 1930*, pp. 44–48.

22. See also Thornton W. Mitchell, *Norton on Archives: The Writings of Margaret Cross Norton on Archival and Records Management* (Carbondale: Southern Illinois University Press, 1975), Posner, *American State Archives*, p. 25.

23. Blegen, *Report on the Public Archives*, pp. 37–62. Norton commented in her 1930 presentation that only in about a dozen states was there "sustained and systematic care to their official records" (p. 44).

24. Cf. Posner, *American State Archives*, pp. 26–31. Chapter 2 (pp. 37–307) describes each state archive agency. Pages 312–14 provide a useful summary to 1964.

25. AHA, *Annual Report, 1900*, 1: 588–89.

26. Cf. AHA annual reports for 1897–99.

27. Ibid., 1898, 1:572.

28. "Report of Committee on Methods of Organization and Work on the Past of State and Local Historical Societies," in AHA, *Annual Report, 1905*, 1:265. Reuben G. Thwaites of the Wisconsin State Historical Society was the chair, while Shambaugh of Iowa and Franklin Riley of the Mississippi Historical Society were members.

29. Cf. AHA, *Annual Report, 1909*, 1:287–88, and the annual reports through 1922.

30. Schellenberg, *Management of Archives*, pp. 38–40.

31. Quoted from the preface, p. iii, Fitzpatrick, *Notes* (citations are to the 1921 edition unless otherwise noted). The third edition was issued in 1928 and reprinted in 1934.

32. Schellenberg, *Management of Archives*, pp. 39–40.

33. See Force, *American Archives*, table of contents for comparison.

34. Fitzpatrick, *Notes*, pp. 12–13; see also Schellenberg, *Management of Archives*, p. 38.

35. Fitzpatrick, *Notes*, pp. 8–10, 17.

36. Ibid., pp. 10–12, 25, 29.

37. Ibid., pp. 9, 10.

38. Term used by Fitzpatrick, ibid., p. 8.

39. Collections at Duke University, University of North Carolina, Michigan Historical Collections, the Clements Library, the Baker Library, and the Houghton at Harvard are among them. Grace Lee Nute's *The Care and Cataloguing of Manuscripts as Practiced by the Minnesota Historical Society* (Saint Paul: Minnesota Historical Society, 1936) was clearly influenced by Fitzpatrick's *Notes*.

40. Reuben G. Thwaites, ed., *Descriptive List of Manuscript Collections of the State Historical Society of Wisconsin* (Madison, 1906). This was the first such guide published in the United States.

41. *Proceedings, 1916*, p. 48; Josephine L. Harper, "Lyman C. Draper and Early American Archives," *AA* 25 (July 1952): 211.

42. *Proceedings, 1906*, pp. 33–34.

43. H. C. Schulz, "The Care and Storage of Manuscripts in the Huntington Library," *LQ* 5 (January 1935): 80–81.

44. Nute, *Care and Cataloguing* (see note 39 above), and "Suggestions for a Code for Cataloging Historical Manuscript Collections," in A. F. Kuhlman, ed., *Archives and Libraries* (Chicago: ALA, 1939), pp. 54–63. Nute had been manuscripts curator at MHS since 1921.

45. Nute, *Care and Cataloguing*, pp. 11–12, 16–17, 37.

46. Nute, "Suggestions," p. 58.

47. Nute, *Care and Cataloguing*, p. 39.

48. Lydia Lucas supplied this additional information.

49. Nute, *Care and Cataloguing*, pp. 32, 11–12.

50. For an informative survey see Theodore C. Pease, "Historical Materials in the Depositories of the Middle West," AHA, *Annual Report, 1921*, pp. 114–16; and Kane, "Manuscript Collecting."

Chapter 3. Public Archives and Historical Manuscripts, 1936–55

1. Margaret C. Norton, "Organizing a New State Archives Department," *Illinois Libraries*, December 1946, pp. 499, 502. She applauded the HRS manual on inventory preparation; the manual had been prepared by T. R. Schellenberg and other National Archives staff members, cf. Schellenberg, *Management of Archives*, pp. 56, 265. There is a large body of literature on these subjects, including H. G. Jones, *The Records of a Nation* (New York: Atheneum, 1969), chaps. 1–3; McCoy, *National Archives*, pp. 64–66; Robert H. Bahmer, "The National Archives After 20 Years," *AA* 18 (July 1955): 195–205; Julian P. Boyd, "Recent Activities in Relation to Archives and Historical Manuscripts in the United States," *Proceedings of the Society of American Archivists* (December 1936 and June 1937); Sargent B. Child, "Status and Plans for Completion of the Inventories of the Historical Records Survey," in Augustus F. Kuhlman, ed., *Archives and Libraries* (Chicago: ALA, 1940), pp. 12–25, and "What Is Past Is Prologue," *AA* 5 (October 1942): 217–27.

2. Kuhlman, ed., *Archives and Libraries*. The 1937 and 1938 proceedings were combined with those of the Public Documents Committee. Those for 1939 and 1940 were published independently.

3. Ellen Jackson, "Manuscript Collections in the General Library," *LQ* 12 (April 1942): 275–83; Cappon's introductions to the annual reports of the University of Vir-

ginia's Historical Collections, 1940–45, are extraordinary for the period and deserve reprinting as a collection. That these writings appeared in relatively obscure places (for "practical" people) lessened their influence.

4. See the following: Bahmer, "The National Archives After 20 Years," pp. 195–205; Jones, *Records of a Nation*, pp. 95–103; McCoy, *National Archives*, pp. 77–85, 105–9; U.S. National Archives Bulletin no. 1, *The National Archives of the United States*, pp. 6–9; Bulletin no. 2 and its *Annual Report, 1940–41*, pp. 28–31, 65–68; Philip M. Hamer, "Finding Mediums in the National Archives: An Appraisal of Six Years' Experience," *AA* 5 (April 1942): 82–92; Paul Lewinson, "Problems of Archives Classification," *AA* 2 (July 1939): 179–90; Wayne C. Grover, "Federal Government Archives," *Library Trends* 5 (January 1957): 390–91.

5. Roscoe R. Hill, "Classification in the National Archives," in Kuhlman, ed., *Archives and Libraries* (1940), pp. 60–62. Lewinson, "Problems of Archives Classification," pp. 180–83, 190. See also Lewinson's review of *Archives and Libraries* (1940), in *AA* 4 (July 1941): 202–3. Compare with McCoy, *National Archives*, pp. 79–80. See Margaret C. Norton, "The Archives of Illinois," *Illinois Libraries*, March and May 1939. Her archival work under library administration enabled her to see clearly that the same terms had different meanings.

6. John R. Russell, "Cataloging at the National Archives," *AA* 2 (July 1939): 169–78; and "Some Problems in Cataloging Archives," in Kuhlman, ed., *Archives and Libraries* (1937), esp. pp. 286 and 291. Compare with McCoy, *National Archives*, pp. 80–81.

7. Russell, "Cataloging," p. 286.

8. Ibid., p. 169. See also Evangeline Thurber, "Suggestions for a Code for Cataloging Archival Material," in Kuhlman, ed., *Archives and Libraries* (1939), pp. 48–49. She was on the staff of the Catalog Division.

9. Russell, "Cataloging," p. 169.

10. Rundell, *In Pursuit of American History*, p. 241; and Jones, *Records of a Nation*, pp. 95–103.

11. Russell, "Cataloging," pp. 293–94.

12. This discussion is based on the following sources: U.S. National Archives, *Annual Report*, 1940–49 (see especially 1940–41, pp. 28–31, 65–68); *Staff Information Circular* nos. 11 and 13; *Staff Information Paper* nos. 15 and 17; Hamer, "Finding Mediums in the National Archives," *AA* 5 (April 1942); Jones, *Records of a Nation*, pp. 95–103.

13. This circular was probably written by Schellenberg. With no. 18, on arrangement, it became the basis of Oliver W. Holmes, "Archival Arrangement—Five Different Operations at Five Different Levels," *AA* 27 (January 1964): 21–41. Holmes participated with Schellenberg in the original, I am told. It was also the point of departure in the historical manuscripts field for reforms at the University of Washington Libraries beginning in 1962 and described below. For an excellent discussion of series arrangement see Kenneth Munden, "The Identification and Description of the Record Series," *AA* (July 1950); 213–27.

14. Jones, *Records of a Nation*, p. 97; U.S. National Archives, *Annual Report*, 1948–49, p. 19, and its *Guide to the Records of the National Archives* (Washington, D.C.: Government Printing Office, 1948).

15. See Mitchell, *Norton on Archives*.

16. On the work of this committee, reference is to Illinois State Library, *Catalog Rules: Series for Archival Material* (Springfield, 1938), and Revision no. 1, 1939. Spe-

cific page citations are not made. Robert Slover, regional director of HRS, identified the series as being "one of the most difficult things to deal with." See *AA* 2 (January 1939): 27.

17. Norton also presented the substance of this discussion, with more attention to classification, at the ALA's 1940 meeting. See "Classification in the Archives of Illinois," in Kuhlman, ed., *Archives and Libraries* (1940), pp. 78–92. In 1937 she had given a paper, "Scope and Function of a State Archives Department," in *Archives and Libraries* (1937), pp. 262–75.

18. Herbert A. Kellar, "Organization and Preservation of Manuscript Collections in the McCormick Historical Association Library," in Kuhlman, ed., *Archives and Libraries* (1938), pp. 363–64. See Schellenberg's comments on Kellar in *Management of Archives*, pp. 187–88. Kellar had induced the American Historical Association's Committee on Manuscripts in 1948 to recommend subgrouping within time frames and arranging alphabetically within these frames. Schellenberg recommended "scrupulous avoidance" of such a system.

19. Ruth Lapham Butler, *A Checklist of Manuscripts in the Edward E. Ayer Collection* (Chicago: Newberry Library, 1937), pp. v–vii. For a current description of Newberry practices see Amy Wood Nyholm, "Modern Manuscripts: A Functional Aproach," *LRTS* 14 (1970): 325–40. She recommends processing by stages, getting progressively more refined controls. But she does not relate controls to record levels. She emphasizes the need for proper-name control, a Newberry tradition, shared by the Bancroft Library and a few others.

20. Howard W. Peckham, "Arranging and Cataloguing Manuscripts in the William L. Clements Library," *AA* 1 (October 1938): 215–18, 225, 226.

21. Philip C. Brooks, *Research in Archives* (Chicago: University of Chicago Press, 1969), chap. 2, esp. pp. 19–20.

22. Ruth K. Nuermberger, "A Ten Year Experiment in Archival Practices," *AA* 4 (October 1940): 251–53, 256–57; Mattie Russell and Edward G. Roberts, "The Processing Procedures of the Manuscripts Department of Duke University Library," *AA* 12 (October 1949): 371–77.

23. William H. Bond, "The Cataloging of Manuscripts in the Houghton Library," *Harvard Library Bulletin* 4 (1950): 392–96.

24. See his part of Charles Cutter, *Rules for a Dictionary Catalogue*, 4th ed. (Washington, D.C., 1904), p. 136.

25. Schellenberg, *Management of Archives*, pp. 113, 275, and "Arrangement of Private Papers," pp. 12–13 of syllabus document used in his teaching, 1959, *GSA–Wash DC 59–9820*. A notable exception is Howard Peckham of the Clements Library, as described above. Ford and Schellenberg would have sanctioned the Clements practice, because users would want access because of the "personal" emphasis in its collection.

26. William P. Cutter, *Industries List*, 3d ed. (Boston, 1937).

27. Robert W. Lovett, "Some Changes in the Handling of Business Records at the Baker Library," *AA* 19 (January 1956): 40–41.

28. Arthur H. Cole, "Business Manuscripts," *LQ* 8 (January 1938): pp. 106–8, 112–13. Robert W. Lovett, in the preface to the 1979 edition of *Manuscripts in the Baker Library*, uses the term "series." The 1979 and 1969 editions update earlier editions; the system remained the same, essentially, after 1938.

29. Clifford L. Lord, "The Archival Program of Wisconsin," *AA* 12 (July 1949): 251.

30. University of Virginia, *Annual Report on Historical Collections, 1942–43*. Introductions were written by Cappon, 1940–41 to 1944–45.

31. Jackson, "Manuscript Collections," pp. 277–80.

32. Randolph W. Church, "The Relationship Between Archival Agencies and Libraries," *AA* 6 (July 1943): 145–50.

33. Philip C. Brooks, "Archives in the United States During World War II, 1939–45," *LQ* 17 (October 1947): 270.

34. Sherrod East, "Describable Item Cataloging," *AA* 16 (October 1953): 291–304. For an expansion of East's article see Ken Munden, "Cataloging Rules in the Departmental Records Branch," *AA* 19 (October 1956): 291–302.

35. Evelyn Hensel, "Treatment of Nonbook Material," *Library Trends* 2 (October 1953): 187–91. She gives a brief, knowledgeable historical survey.

36. Neal Harlow, "Managing Manuscript Collections," *Library Trends* 4 (October 1955): 203–10.

37. A. F. Kuhlman, ed., *Archives and Libraries: Papers Presented at the 1939 Conference of the American Library Association* (Chicago: ALA, 1939). Kuhlman headed the committee from 1936 to 1940. In this section no attempt is made to trace these concurrent developments, only to note their currency.

38. Buck to Librarian of Congress, November 8, 1949. By 1950 two-thirds of the Library of Congress's Manuscript Collection was composed of twentieth-century materials. By 1953 the proportion was estimated at 90 percent. Unpublished annual reports, 1940–47, of the Manuscripts Division indicate that these minor reforms had been undertaken by St. George Sioussat, Buck's predecessor. Sioussat had been a historian before becoming chief of the division. His predecessor, J. Franklin Jameson, was also a historian.

39. U.S. Library of Congress, *Manual 17: Manuscripts Division* (Washington, D.C., 1950), pp. 6, 22, 23. Dan Lacy of the Library of Congress reported that the old system had broken down. See his "The Library of Congress: A Sesquicentenary Review," *LQ* 20 (1950): 251. Indeed, the shelf list had not been completed until fiscal 1947 by Fred Shelley, and it omitted the large backlog of unprocessed collections stored in a variety of storerooms and vaults. See the unpublished annual report of the Manuscripts Division for 1946–47.

40. *Manual*, pp. 19–25.

41. Rundell, *In Pursuit of American History*, p. 241.

42. U.S. Library of Congress, *Annual Report*, 1951–52, pp. 34–35. The unpublished annual report of the Manuscripts Division for 1939–40 (p. 43) indicates an early preoccupation with a future national catalog, flowing from work of the HRS.

43. Katharine E. Brand, "Developments in the Handling of Recent Manuscripts in the Library of Congress," *AA* 16 (April 1953): 100–101, and "The Place of the Register in the Manuscripts Division of the Library of Congress," *AA* 18 (January 1955): 61.

44. Brand, "Register," pp. 59–61.

45. See Augustus F. Kuhlman, *Archives and Libraries*, papers presented at ALA conferences, 1937–40. Its proceedings for 1937 and 1938 were published together with those of ALA's Public Documents Committee, and independently for 1939 and 1940.

46. William F. Birdsall, "The American Archivists' Search for Professional Identity, 1909–1936," (Ph.D. diss., University of Wisconsin, Madison, 1973), pp. 199–204.

47. Solon Buck, Luther Evans, and Dan Lacy were only the most prominent and crucially placed of these leaders. Lacy had been on the National Archives staff before joining the Library of Congress.

48. See *AA* 12 (January 1949): 55. The SAA, AASLH, and LC were the institutional members.

49. See Report of SAA Secretary, 1948–49, in *AA* 13 (January 1950): 57–58, and Report of the Joint Committee, pp. 68–69.

50. See Joint Committee report in *AA* 14 (January 1951): 76.

51. U.S. Library of Congress, *Annual Report*, 1951–52, pp. 34–45. See Joint Committee report for 1951–52 in *AA* 15 (April 1952): 177–80.

52. See Joint Committee report for 1952–53 in *AA* 16 (January 1953): 94–95. Philip Hamer, executive director of the NHPC, was made chair of the Joint Committee in 1954. The reader should compare this presentation with that of Robert H. Land, "The National Union Catalog of Manuscript Collections," in *AA* 17 (July 1954): 195–207.

53. U.S. Library of Congress, Manuscripts Cataloging Committee, *Minutes of Meeting no. 11*, June 19 [1952].

54. Brand, "Developments," p. 103.

55. Land, "National Union Catalog," pp. 198–99.

56. Howard W. Peckham, "Manuscript Repositories and the National Register," *AA* 17 (October 1954): 321–23.

57. Mearns commented thusly on a paper by Francis L. Berkeley, Jr., "History and Problems of the Control of Manuscripts in the United States," in American Philosophical Society *Proceedings*, 98 (June 1954): 186.

58. U.S. Library of Congress, Committee on Manuscripts Cataloging, *Minutes of Meeting no. 44*, February 24, March 1, 1955; see also Library of Congress memorandum, Richard Angell, chair of Manuscripts Cataloging Committee, to John Cronin, director of the Processing Department, July 12, 1955 (from copies supplied by Harriet Ostroff, head of the NUCMC unit).

59. See Hamer, "Finding Mediums," pp. 82–92.

60. Rundell, *In Pursuit of American History*, p. 241.

61. Brooks to Morsch, November 6, 1952. From NHPC records, copies of which were provided by Frank G. Burke, executive director of the National Historical Publications and Records Commission.

62. Kahn to NAA, January 13, 1953, NHPC records. For a general discussion of this section on the NUCMC rules see Richard C. Berner, "Arrangement and Description: Some Historical Observations," *AA* 41 (April 1978): 172–74, 179. For the effect at the repository level see Terry Abraham, "NUCMC and the Local Repository," *AA* 40 (January 1977): 31–42.

63. Dorothy V. Martin, "Books on Cataloging of Manuscript Material," *AA* 11 (January 1948): 42–44.

64. Dorothy V. Martin, "Use of Cataloging Techniques in Work with Records and Manuscripts," *AA* 18 (October 1955): 317–36.

Chapter 4. Schellenberg and the Merging of the Public Archives and Historical Manuscripts Traditions, 1956–79

1. Lester J. Cappon, "Historical Manuscripts as Archives: Some Definitions and Their Application," *AA* 19 (April 1956): 104–5.

2. T. R. Schellenberg, *Modern Archives: Principles and Techniques* (Chicago: University of Chicago Press, 1956); *The Management of Archives* (New York and London: Columbia University Press, 1965). For Schellenberg's role see Robert L. Brubaker,

"Archival Principles and the Curator of Manuscripts," *AA* 29 (October 1966): 505–14. Waldo G. Leland in reviewing *Modern Archives* considered it "the most significant and useful statement yet produced on the administration of modern records and archives," *AA* 19 (October 1956): 325. On Schellenberg's wide influence see McCoy, *National Archives*, pp. 179–82; and for his role as educator/trainer when he served as head of the National Archives Division see chap. 14 and pp. 286–87 in McCoy.

3. Paul S. Dunkin, "Arrangement and Cataloging of Manuscripts," *Library Trends* 5 (January 1957): 355.

4. Robert W. Lovett, "Care and Handling of Non-Governmental Archives," *Library Trends* 5 (January 1957): 380, 384–85. In 1979 the Baker Library had published the fourth edition of its guide.

5. Lester J. Cappon, "Reference Works and Historical Texts," *Library Trends* 5 (January 1957): 373–74.

6. Cappon, "Historical Manuscripts," pp. 101–10.

7. Brooks, *Research in Archives*, pp. 6–7.

8. Posner, *American State Archives*, pp. 369–70.

9. *Modern Archives*, p. 18. Many of the expressions here are comparable to those expressed earlier by Curtis W. Garrison in "The Relation of Historical Manuscripts to Archival Materials," *AA* 2 (April 1939): 101–5. Garrison contrasts them: "archives are better organized, better concentrated, and more specific in nature. Manuscripts are unorganized, scattered, and general. Archives have continuity, and manuscripts are more or less sporadic." See also *Management of Archives*, pp. 113, 242, 251–52, 257, 274–76, and item 4 in his "Nationwide System of Controlling Historical Manuscripts," *AA* 28 (July 1965): 410.

10. T. R. Schellenberg, *Draft of a Manual on Archival Descriptive Techniques* (Austin, 1961). This was reproduced for use of the Institute on Archival Management, at the University of Texas Graduate School of Library Science, July 18–August 12, 1960.

11. This item is "GSA–Wash DC 59–9820" (19 pp.). In this paper he specifically acknowledges Cappon's inspiration, on pp. 2 and 9; he also cites the "excellent article" by Ellen Jackson, "Manuscript Collections in the General Library," *LQ* 12 (April 1942): 275–83.

12. Compare with his section "Factor of Relation to Activity," in *Management of Archives*, pp. 185–87, and with "Archival Principles of Management," *AA* 24 (January 1961): 17, where he advocates that on the basis of the different activities of a person the "collection falls into several natural series, *each relating to a particular activity*" (italics mine).

13. This practice of advocating the establishment of series before establising subgroups is found later, in David B. Gracy's *Archives and Manuscripts: Arrangement and Description* (Chicago: Society of American Archivists, 1977), pp. 7, 10, to be discussed, below. In *Management of Archives*, see pp. 98, 106–7, 185–88. See Appendix 12 for an example of submerging subgroups among series (Register to Bonaparte Papers).

14. "GSA–Wash DC 59–9818," p. 2. On p. 6 he wrote: "Private papers . . . fall into three kinds of physical units. These are (1) collections as such, (2) the series within collections and (3) the individual record items within series." Note also the absence of file folder/unit level. In *Management of Archives*, p. xvi, he limits subgroups by definition to public and institutional records: "An *archival subgroup* is comprised of records created by an organizational subdivision of the public agency that created an archival group."

15. "GSA–Wash DC 59–9818," pp. 2–3; and pp. 113–15 in *Management of Archives*.

16. On p. 270 of *Management of Archives*, Schellenberg evinces some sense of this role for the catalog: "A catalog is the only type of finding aid that facilitates a pooling of information about the documentary resources of the nation." This role is not, however, one that he sees for it in the local manuscript repository or public archive. Its role there is but one among many finding aids.

17. On p. 270 of *Management of Archives*, and only there, Schellenberg suggests a union function to the catalog: "Every manuscript repository should prepare a catalog of its manuscript collections for its own use and for use in cooperative cataloging projects." Since he neglected to integrate this perception into his discussion, it must be regarded as an aberration, although significant as an element beginning to percolate.

18. *AA* 28 (July 1965): 409–12.

19. Lucile M. Kane, "A Guide to the Care and Administration of Manuscripts," *Bulletin of the American Association for State and Local History* 2, no. 11 (1960): 333–88, rev. 1966. Page references are to the 1960 edition unless otherwise noted.

20. Cf. Robert E. Burke, "Modern Manuscript Collections and What To Do with Them," *Manuscripts* 7 (Summer 1955): 232–36. This article was cited in Kane's bibliography.

21. Ruth B. Bordin and Robert M. Warner, *The Modern Manuscript Library* (New York: Scarecrow Press, 1966).

22. Carolyn A. Wallace, "The Southern Historical Collection," *AA* 28 (July 1965): 427–36.

23. Brubaker, "Archival Principles," pp. 505–14, and "Manuscript Collections," *Library Trends* 13 (October 1964), especially pp. 240–43.

24. SAA, Finding Aids Committee, "Annual Report, 1978" (unpublished).

25. Oliver W. Holmes, "Archival Arrangement—Five Different Operations at Five Different Levels," *AA* 27 (January 1964): 21–42.

26. Mario D. Fenyo, "The Record Group Concept: A Critique," *AA* 29 (April 1966): 229–39.

27. Frank B. Evans, "Modern Methods of Arrangement of Archives in the United States," *AA* 29 (April 1966): 241–63.

28. See Fenyo, "The Record Group Concept," p. 235, for this and the preceding discussion.

29. Evans, "Modern Methods," p. 263.

30. Society of American Archivists, *Inventories and Registers: A Handbook of Techniques and Examples* (Chicago: Society of American Archivists, 1976). Frank G. Burke's purpose in having his committee focus on inventories and registers was to seek greater uniformity of practice.

31. These publications (1975–79) are listed in note 5 of chapter 1, and are those in the *Drexel Library Quarterly* and *Georgia Archive* and the University of Washington Libraries' division manual on accessioning, arrangement, and description.

32. Holmes, "Archival Arrangement," p. 23. The upper level relates to provenance, and the lower level to original or other filing order.

33. David B. Gracy II, *Archives and Manuscripts: Arrangement and Description* (Chicago: SAA, 1977).

34. Contrary to Gracy's contention that Holmes was the "first" to publicize this idea, Schellenberg had written in 1951 and the National Archives published *Staff Information Paper* no. 18, "Principles of Arrangement," in which these levels are identi-

fied. See the discussion on the National Archives in chapter 3. It was my familiarity with these publications that led me, in 1962, to integrate the concept of record levels with some elements from the library field. Both the subgroup and file unit levels were also identified as control levels at that time.

35. Holmes, "Archival Arrangement," p. 32.

36. Richard H. Lytle, "Intellectual Access to Archives: I. Provenance and Content Indexing Methods of Subject Retrieval," *AA* 43 (Winter 1980): 64–75 and "Intellectual Access to Archives: II. Report of an Experiment Comparing Provenance and Content Indexing Methods of Subject Retrieval," *AA* 43 (Spring 1980): 197–207.

37. H. Thomas Hickerson, et al., *SPINDEX II at Cornell University and a Review of Archival Automation in the United States* (Ithaca: Cornell University Libraries, 1976).

38. Phyllis Platnick, "Proposal for Automating a Manuscript Repository," in *Progress in Information Science and Technology, Proceedings, 1966* (American Documentation Institute, 1966), pp. 437–54.

Chapter 5. The Historical Manuscripts Tradition to 1979

1. Robert S. Gordon, "Suggestions for Organization and Description of Archival Holdings of Local Historical Societies," *AA* 26 (January 1963): 19–39; and Kenneth W. Duckett, *Modern Manuscripts: A Practical Manual for Their Management, Care, and Use* (Nashville: American Association for State and Local History, 1975).

2. At the time Gordon's article was accepted for publication, I was invited by the editor of the *American Archivist*, Ken Munden, to write a critique of it, which appeared under the unfortunate editorial title of "Endless Quagmire," in *AA* 26 (July 1963): 431–33. See Gordon's reply (pp. 433–34) in the same issue. My criticism would be more moderate now. Gordon, then and now a member of the Public Archives of Canada, addressed Canadian historical societies specifically; the article was equally applicable to the same audience in the United States. It is assumed that its acceptance by the *American Archivist* was for that reason. In any case, the article is much the fullest treatment available of a viewpoint that is only fragmentarily represented otherwise.

3. Tucked away is a particularly significant passing comment made by Duckett: "in a unit system [of cataloging], the inventory and secondary cards can be co-ordinated so that the dictionary card catalog is essentially *an index to the inventory*" (italics mine), p. 141. That he did not structure this observation into his writing is unfortunate.

4. There is a voluminous periodical literature on the *National Union Catalog of Manuscript Collections*. See Frank B. Evans's bibliography, articles cited above, and the Rules themselves, in the chapter on the Library of Congress. Particularly relevant to the discussion that follows are Terry Abraham, "NUCMC and the Local Repository," *AA* 40 (January 1977): 31–42; William C. Binkley, "A Historian Looks at the National Union Catalog of Manuscript Collections," *AA* 28 (July 1965): 399–407; Lester K. Born, "The National Union Catalog of Manuscript Collections," *AA* 23 (July 1960): 311–14; Richard C. Berner, "Archivists, Librarians, and the National Union Catalog of Manuscript Collections," *AA* 27 (July 1964): 401–9; and "Observations on Archivists, Librarians and the National Union Catalog of Manuscript Collections," *College and Research Libraries* 29 (1968): 276–80; Frank G. Burke, "Manuscripts and Archives," *Library Trends* 15 (January 1967): 430–35, and "Automation in

Bibliographical Control of Archives and Manuscript Collections," in Dagmar H. Perman, ed., *Bibliography and the Historian* (Santa Barbara: Clio Press, 1968), pp. 96–97; Arline Custer, "The National Union Catalog of Manuscript Collections," *Library Resources and Technical Services* 8 (Spring 1964): 188–90; Duckett, *Modern Manuscripts*, pp. 138–42; and Harriet C. Owsley, "The SAA Workshop on the National Union Catalog of Manuscript Collections," *AA* 28 (July 1965): 389–97.

5. Abraham, "NUCMC and the Local Repository" (see note 4 above).

6. From NUCMC *Information Circular* no. 5, "Guide for Filling Out NUCMC Data Sheets," August 1966, p. 5.

7. From *Rules for Descriptive Cataloging in the Library of Congress*, September 1954, p. 3. These are the rules originally used for NUCMC cataloging.

8. *Anglo-American Cataloging Rules* (Chicago: American Library Association, 1967); *Anglo-American Cataloguing Rules*, 2d ed. (Chicago: American Library Association, 1978). These will be referred to as AACR1 and AACR2, and were prepared cooperatively by the ALA, the British Library, the Canadian Committee on Cataloguing, the Library Association (Great Britain), and the Library of Congress.

9. Society of American Archivists, Finding Aids Committee, unpublished report of a user analysis survey, 1977.

10. The NUCMC office in August 1966 issued *Information Circular* no. 5, giving instructions for filling out the data sheets. These supplementary instructions were not incorporated by AACR1 or 2.

11. Other specific rules are 25.18A2, 25.13, and 25.22B, and they are of no help.

Chapter 6. Automated Archival Systems

1. There is a voluminous literature on SPINDEX. On the Library of Congress project the most readily available description is by Frank G. Burke, "The Application of Automated Techniques in the Management and Control of Source Materials," *AA* 30 (April 1967): 255–78. The most complete, but less accessible, is *SPINDEX II: Report and Systems Documentation* (NARS, 1975). See also Burke, "SPINDEX II and Applications to Large Record Holdings," unpublished paper given at a conference of Public Archives of Canada, October 17, 1979. An excellent, non-Burkean survey by a user of SPINDEX is H. Thomas Hickerson, Joan Winters, and Venetia Beale, *SPINDEX II at Cornell University and a Review of Archival Automation in the United States* (Ithaca: Cornell University Libraries, 1976). See also Burke, "SPINDEX II: An Aspect of Archival Information Retrieval," *Records Management Journal* 8 (April 1966): 298–302. For SPINDEX III see *Report on the Conference on Automated Guide Projects*; Nancy Sahli, "SPINDEX: A Computer Tool for Subject and Name Access," unpublished paper delivered at the annual meeting in 1979 of the ALA (Sahli is on the NHPRC staff); and *SPINDEX: An Introduction for New and Prospective Users* (SPINDEX Users Network, 1980). See also Duckett, *Modern Manuscripts*, especially pp. 151–66, for a good general discussion. An excellent review is by S. E. Hannestad, "SPINDEX II: A Computerized Approach to Preparing Guides to Archives and Manuscripts," in *Computing in the Humanities*, ed. Serge Lusignan and J. S. North, (Waterloo, Ont., 1977), 273–82.

2. Fred Shelley, "The Presidential Papers Program of the Library of Congress," *AA* 25 (October 1962): 429–33; Russell M. Smith, "Item Indexing by Automated Processes," *AA* 30 (April 1967): 295–302. Frank G. Burke has referred me to an earlier

one-time only project produced by Estelle Broadman for the Beaumont Collection at Washington University of St. Louis.

3. Marion M. Torchia, "Two Experiments in Automated Indexing: The Presidential Papers and the Papers of the Continental Congress," *AA* 39 (October 1976): 440–41.

4. Rita R. Campbell, "Machine Retrieval in the Herbert Hoover Archives," *AA* 29 (April 1966): 298–302, and "Automation and Information Retrieval in Archives—Broad Concepts," *AA* 30 (April 1967): 279–86. This method of organizing folders resembles the one recommended by Phyllis Platnick, also in 1966 (see chap. 4, note 38 above).

5. "Computer Applications for Archives at the Hoover Institution, 1965–1976." Supplied to the author by Charles G. Palm, deputy archivist of the Hoover Institution.

6. Frank G. Burke, "Automation in Bibliographic Control of Archives and Manuscript Collections," in Perman, ed., *Bibliography and the Historian*, p. 99. Burke acknowledged the prior work of Edwin Alan Thompson on the program's early development before Burke joined the Library of Congress staff, and of his subsequent tutoring by Thompson in the program.

7. Most of what is discussed here is to be found in Burke, "Application of Automated Techniques," pp. 264–78.

8. Letter to the author, May 15, 1979.

9. Letter to the author, April 23, 1980.

10. The four main sources for the following have been fully cited above in note 1. They are NARS, *SPINDEX II: Report and Systems Documentation*; Hickerson et al., *SPINDEX II at Cornell University*; Burke, "SPINDEX II: An Aspect of Archival Information Retrieval"; and Burke, "SPINDEX II and Applications to Large Record Holdings," unpublished paper given at a conference of the Public Archives of Canada, October 17, 1979.

11. South Carolina Archives and History Department, *The South Carolina Archives: A Temporary Summary Guide* (1976), pp. v–ix. The balance of information is from an unpublished paper by Sharon G. Avery of the archives staff, given at the 1977 annual meeting of the SAA, "Subject Access Through SPINDEX II at the South Carolina Archives."

12. Burke, "SPINDEX II and Applications," p. 12.

13. Information on SPINDEX III is derived from the *Report on the Conference on Automated Guide Projects*, July 19–20, 1977, Enclosure 13.

14. Burke, "SPINDEX II and Applications," pp. 9, 10. For a description of the Washington State survey and guide project see John F. Burns, "The NHPRC and the State of Washington's Historical Records," *Prologue* 11 (Spring 1979): 57–63.

15. The Portland, Oregon city archives, under an NHPRC grant, is describing records to the folder level (unpublished paper by Liisa Fagerlund and Loren Meyer for the 1979 meeting of Northwest Archivists).

16. Max Evans, director, Midwest State Archives Guide Project, unpublished, untitled talk given at a SUN meeting, fall, 1979, and letter to the author, September 1980, with enclosures illustrating the system. See Appendix 21 for illustrations.

17. Burke, "SPINDEX II and Applications," pp. 11–12.

18. Ronald G. Watt, "SPINDEX Application in the LDS Historical Department," unpublished paper [1979].

19. *Report on the Conference on Automated Guide Projects*, July 19–20, 1977, esp. Enclosure 13.

20. *SUN*, November 1979.

21. David Bearman, "Automated Access to Archival Information: Assessing Systems," *AA* 42 (April 1979): 187, and his review in *AA* 42 (July 1979): 350–51.

22. Richard M. Kesner, "The Computer's Future in Archival Management: An Evaluation," *Midwestern Archivist* 3, no. 2 (1978): 26–29. Lydia Lucas, "Efficient Finding Aids: Developing a System for Control of Archives and Manuscripts," *AA* 44 (Winter 1981): 21–26.

23. From an unpublished lecture, "Reflections on Archival Automation," given at University of Missouri, October 29, 1979.

24. Burke, "SPINDEX II and Applications," pp. 14–16.

25. Discussions of the NARS A–1 System is based on Alan Calmes, "Practical Realities of Computer-based Finding Aids: The NARS A–1 Experience," *AA* 42 (April 1979): 167–77; an internal NARS document by Leonard Rapport, October 19, 1976; "How to do 6710 A's—A Guide for NNFS Archivists (Preliminary Draft)"; and a critique of an earlier draft by Charles M. Dollar, director, Machine-readable Records Division, NARS, November 1980. Trudy H. Peterson and Charlotte Palmer of NARS also contributed information.

26. Information on PARADIGM is from a description issued in September 1978 by the University of Illinois Archives, supplemented by various annual reports, and letters from William J. Maher, assistant university archivist, March 19 and April 15, 1980.

27. Richard H. Lytle, "A National Information System for Archives and Manuscript Collections," *AA* 43 (Summer 1980): 423–26. Lytle is chair of the SAA's National Information Systems Task Force.

28. Richard H. Lytle, "Intellectual Access to Archives: II Report of an Experiment Comparing Provenance and Content Indexing Methods of Subject Retrieval," *AA* 43 (Spring 1980): 197–207.

Chapter 7. Archival Education and Training, 1937 to the Present

1. American Library Association, *Archives and Libraries*, 1937 (with *Public Documents*), pp. 298–305.

2. *Archives and Libraries*, 1937, p. 225. For Paltsits's outline see American Historical Association, *Annual Report, 1912*, pp. 253–63. See also the Paltsits résumé in the *Annual Report, 1922*, pp. 152–60, and his "Pioneering for a Science of Archives in the United States," *Archives and Libraries*, 1937, pp. 233–39.

3. Reference here is to the *Anglo-American Cataloging Rules* (1967 and 1978), and to their origin in the NUCMC's *Rules for Descriptive Cataloging* (1954). See discussion of these in chapters 1 and 4 above.

4. Kuhlman to Milam July 28 and January 11, 1937. Kuhlman appointed the following persons to his committee: Theodore Blegen, Margaret Norton, Herbert Kellar, Dorsey Hyde (National Archives), Thomas C. Martin (Library of Congress Manuscripts Division), and Leslie Bliss (Huntington Library). See ALA Archives, Archives and Libraries Committee Records (microfilm copies, from originals in the University of Illinois Archives).

5. ALA Archives, Archives and Libraries Committee Records, Kuhlman report, August 26, 1938.

6. Ibid., Kuhlman to Brown, June 4, 1940, Dooley (comptroller) to Kuhlman, October 16, 1940.

7. Ibid., unidentified clipping. The Archives-Libraries Committee continued until 1957 but accomplished little according to the committee records. When it was abolished in 1957, its chair, Jacqueline Bull, archivist of the University of Kentucky, wrote on August 22, 1957, to the deputy executive secretary of ALA, "There seems to be no place in the present organization of the A.L.A. to discuss liason [*sic*] between libraries and archival depositories. This is regrettable." She recommended forming a joint committee with SAA to continue the liaison. Not until 1970 was such a committee formed, and only then to counter a feared splintering of SAA.

8. Samuel Flagg Bemis, "The Training of Archivists in the United States," *AA* 2 (July 1939): 154–61. See also Robert M. Warner, "Archival Training in the United States and Canada," *AA* 35 (July/October 1972): 347–49; Frank B. Evans, "Postappointment Archival Training: A Proposed Solution for a Basic Problem," *AA* 40 (January 1977): 58–59, 68–69.

9. Houston G. Jones, "Archival Training in American Universities, 1938–68," *AA* 31 (April 1968): 144. Jones gives the best historical survey. This issue of the *American Archivist* was devoted to archival education, and is particularly valuable as a benchmark. On this early period see also Solon J. Buck, "The Training of American Archivists," *AA* 4 (April 1941): 84–90, and Frank B. Evans, "Postappointment Archival Training," pp. 59–61.

10. See also U.S. National Archives, *Annual Reports* through 1949, for the course of National Archives involvement. In 1945 the Maryland Hall of Records joined in the program, which for the first time included "custodians of institutional and business archives." Also inaugurated in 1945 was a four-week training program, to reach archivists, manuscript curators, and records administrators outside of Washington who were not able to take the full course in the university. The Library of Congress in 1948 joined in this presentation. This program continues down to the present. An excellent historical review of this program is provided by G. Philip Bauer, "Recruitment, Training, and Promotion in the National Archives," *AA* 18 (October 1955): 291–305; McCoy, *National Archives*, pp. 97–104.

11. Buck, "Training of American Archivists," pp. 85–86.

12. Jones, "Archival Training." See also Evans, "Postappointment Archival Training," pp. 60–64.

13. Schellenberg, "Archival Training in Library Schools," *AA* 31 (April 1968): 155–65.

14. Colson, "On the Education of Archivists and Librarians," *AA* 31 (April 1968): 167–74.

15. See Philip P. Mason, "Report of the Committee of the 1970s," *AA* 35 (April 1972): 206–10, on education and training.

16. See Robert L. Brubaker, "Professional Communication," in Robert L. Clark, Jr., ed., *Archive-Library Relations* (New York: Bowker, 1976), pp. 186–89. See also Mason, "Secretary's Annual Report, 1967–68," *AA* 32 (January 1969): 62–63. Custer and I opposed joining the Rare Books Section, but the audience favored a trial marriage.

17. Documentation is in my own Work Manual Committee records at the University of Washington Libraries, University Archives. These are also represented along with related files in the ACRL records in the ALA's archives at the University of Illinois

Archives, of which the author has microfilm copies; hereafter cited as ALA Archives, ACRL, RBMS Records.

18. ALA Archives, ACRL, RBMS Records, Minutes, June 21, 1969.

19. Ibid.; Custer to Richard Gray of Publications Department, December 30, 1969; Custer to Alderson, February 4, 1970.

20. RBMS Records, Clapp to D. Thomas, executive secretary of ACRL, January 6, 1971.

21. Philip Mason recalled these events in a telephone discussion, April 6, 1980.

22. See *SAA Newsletter*, March 1980, p. 1, regarding professional education, "Keeping Library Schools from Controlling Archival Education Programs." The author knows of no attempt on the part of library schools to "control" these programs.

23. Warner, "Archival Training," p. 356. More recently, however, history departments have enhanced their role in archival education. James W. Geary conducted a survey which shows an increase of their preappointment archival education courses from seven departments in 1973 to twenty-one by 1978, whereas offerings in library schools remained steady—twelve in 1973 and fourteen in 1978. See Geary, "A Fading Relationship: Library Schools and Preappointment Archival Education Since 1973," *Journal of Education for Librarianship* 20 (Summer 1979): 25–35.

24. Warner, "Archival Training," p. 353; and Evans, "Postappointment Archival Training," p. 68–69. Evans considers the Bemis theme to have been detrimental to the proper training of archivists in "basic arrangement and description, and reference service responsibilities."

25. See *AA* 41 (January 1978): 105–6.

26. Published in *SAA Newsletter*, July 1979, pp. 19–21, as "Proposed Program Standard for Archival Education: The Practicum."

27. On library schools see Lawrence J. McCrank, "Prospects for Integrating Historical and Information Studies in Archival Education," *AA* 42 (October 1979): 443–55. See Organization of American Historians *Newsletter* from January 1977 to the present for the "public" or "applied" historian field. The term "applied" is resented by many historians who regard their own research, writing, and teaching as being applied.

28. See Nancy E. Peace and Nancy F. Chudacoff, "Archivists and Librarians: A Common Mission, a Common Education," *AA* 42 (October 1979): 460.

Chapter 8. Hindsight, Foresight

1. See Lucile M. Kane, "Manuscript Collecting" (pp. 29–48), and Philip G. Bauer, "Public Archives in the United States" (pp. 49–76), in William B. Hesseltine and Donald R. McNeil, eds., *In Support of Clio* (Madison: State Historical Society of Wisconsin, 1958). Chapter 1 in Kenneth Duckett's *Modern Manuscripts* (Nashville: American Association for State and Local History, 1975) is also useful. Duckett's book is fully within the HMT.

2. Waldo G. Leland, "American Archival Problems," in American Historical Association, *Annual Report, 1909* 1:346–47.

3. See H. Thomas Hickerson, Joan Winters, and Venetia Beale, *SPINDEX II at Cornell University* (Ithaca: Cornell University Libraries, 1976), especially pages 35–49. For a critique of the relationships between manual and automated systems, see Lydia Lucas, "Efficient Finding Aids: Developing a System for Control of Archives and

Manuscripts," *AA* 44 (Winter 1981): 21–26; Richard H. Lytle, "Intellectual Access to Archives: I. Provenance and Content Indexing Methods of Subject Retrieval," *AA* 43 (Winter 1980): 64–75; and Lytle, "Intellectual Access to Archives: II. Report of an Experiment Comparing Provenance and Content Indexing Methods of Subject Retrieval," *AA* 43 (Spring 1980): 191–207.

4. Dagobert Soergel, *Indexing Languages and Thesauri: Construction and Maintenance* (Los Angeles: Melville Publishing Co., 1974).

5. Richard H. Lytle, "Intellectual Access to Archives: I," pp. 70–71.

6. Ibid., pp. 64–65.

7. See Sherrod East, "Describable Item Cataloging," *AA* (October 1953): 291–304; and Ken Munden, "Cataloging Rules in the Departmental Records Branch," *AA* 19 (October 1956): 291–302.

8. Mary Lynn McCree, "Good Sense and Good Judgment: Defining Collections and Collecting," *Drexel Library Quarterly* 11 (January 1975): 21–33.

9. See Charles M. Dollar, "Appraising Machine-Readable Records," *AA* 41 (October 1978): 423–30.

10. See Samuel F. Bemis, "The Training of Archivists in the United States," *AA* 2 (July 1939): 154–61, and Robert M. Warner, "Archival Training in the United States and Canada," *AA* 35 (July/October 1972): 347–49. The *AA* 31 (April 1968) is particularly useful for the historical information provided by the authors: Houston G. Jones, "Archival Training in American Universities"; Theodore R. Schellenberg, "Archival Training in Library Schools"; and John C. Colson, "On the Education of Archivists and Librarians." Two 1979 articles carry the debate to the present: Lawrence J. McCrank, "Prospects for Interpreting Historical and Information Studies in Archival Education," *AA* 42 (October 1979): 443–55; and Nancy Peace and Nancy Fisher Chudacoff "Archivists and Librarians: A Common Mission, a Common Education," *AA* 42 (October 1979): 456–62. McCrank would rely on instructors in librarianship to teach archival management, while Peace and Chudacoff would make cataloging the cornerstone of archival courses.

Bibliography

UNPUBLISHED SOURCES

American Library Association. *Records*. Association of College and Research Libraries. Rare Books and Manuscripts Section. Manuscripts Collection Committee. *Rec-
ords*, 1961–77. (Microfilm copies of originals at University of Illinois.)
———. *Records*. Archives and Libraries Committee. *Records*, 1935–47. (Microfilm
copies of originals at University of Illinois Libraries.)
Avery, Sharon G. "Subject Access Through SPINDEX II at the South Carolina Ar-
chives." Unpublished paper, 1977.
Burke, Frank G. "Reflections on Archival Automation." Paper given at University of
Missouri, October 29, 1979.
———. "SPINDEX II and Applications to Large Record Holdings." Paper given at a
conference of Public Archives of Canada, October 17, 1979.
Evans, Max. Untitled presentation at SPINDEX Users Network meeting, October
1979.
Fagerlund, Liisa, and Loren Meyer. "Finding Aids for City of Portland Records."
Portland, Oregon, 1979.
Hoover Institution on War, Revolution and Peace. "Computer Applications for Ar-
chives at the Hoover Institution." 1965–76.
Sahli, Nancy. "SPINDEX: A Computer Tool for Subject and Name Access." Paper
presented at annual meeting of ALA, 1979.
Society of American Archivists. Finding Aids Committee. "Annual Report, 1978."
U.S. Library of Congress. National Union Catalog of Manuscript Collections Office.
Records, 1952–55. (Copies supplied by Harriet Ostroff.)
U.S. National Historical Publications Commission. *Records, 1952–55*. (Copies fur-
nished by Frank G. Burke.)
Watt, Ronald G. "SPINDEX Application in the LDS Historical Department." Paper
presented at SUN meeting, October 1979.

BOOKS, BOOKLETS, MANUALS

American Library Association. *Catalog Rules: Author and Title Entries*. Chicago:
American Library Association, 1908, 1941, 1949, 1967, 1977.
Angle, Paul M. *The Library of Congress: An Account, Historical and Descriptive*.
Kingsport: Kingsport Press, 1958.

Anglo-American Cataloging Rules. Chicago: American Library Association, 1967.

Anglo-American Cataloguing Rules. 2d ed. Chicago: American Library Association, 1978.

Blegen, Theodore C. *A Report on the Public Archives*. Madison: State Historical Society of Wisconsin, [1918].

———. "Problems of American Archivists." U.S. National Archives *Bulletin No. 2*. Washington, D.C.: Government Printing Office, 1936.

Bordin, Ruth B., and Robert M. Warner. *The Modern Manuscript Library*. New York: Scarecrow Press, 1966.

Bourne, Charles P. *Methods of Information Handling*. New York: Wiley, 1969.

Brichford, Maynard J. *Scientific and Technological Documentation: Archival Evaluation and Processing of University Records Relating to Science and Technology*. Urbana: University of Illinois Press, 1969.

Brooks, Philip C. *Research in Archives: The Use of Unpublished Primary Sources*. Chicago: University of Chicago Press, 1969.

Burnette, O. Lawrence. *Beneath the Footnote: A Guide to the Use and Preservation of Historical Sources*. Madison: State Historical Society of Wisconsin, 1969.

Butler, Ruth Lapham. *A Checklist of Manuscripts in the Edward E. Ayer Collection* [of the Newberry Library]. Chicago: Newberry Library, 1937.

Clark, Robert L., Jr., ed. *Archive-Library Relations*. New York: Bowker, 1976.

Cole, John Y., ed. *The Library of Congress in Perspective*. New York: Bowker, 1976.

Cutter, Charles A. *Rules for a Dictionary Catalogue*, 4th ed. Washington, D.C.: Government Printing office, 1904.

Duckett, Kenneth W. *Modern Manuscripts: A Practical Manual for Their Management, Care and Use*. Nashville: American Association for State and Local History, 1975.

Dunlap, Leslie W. *American Historical Societies, 1790–1860*. Madison: State Historical Society of Wisconsin, 1944.

Dunlap, Leslie W., and Fred Shelley, eds. *The Publication of American Historical Manuscripts*. Iowa City: University of Iowa Press, 1976.

Ewing, William S. *Guide to the Manuscript Collections in the William S. Clements Library*. 2d ed. Ann Arbor: Clements Library, 1953.

Fitzpatrick, John C. *Notes on the Care, Cataloguing, Calendaring and Arranging of Manuscripts*. Washington, D.C.: Government Printing Office. [3 editions, 1913, 1921, 1928.]

Force, Peter. *American Archives: A Documentary History*. Washington, D.C.: M. St. Clair and Peter Force, 1848.

Goodrum, Charles A. *The Library of Congress*. New York: Praeger, 1974.

Gracy, David B., II. *Archives and Manuscripts: Arrangement and Description*. Chicago: Society of American Archivists, 1977.

Hesseltine, William B., and Donald R. McNeil, eds. *In Support of Clio: Essays in Memory of Herbert A. Kellar*. Madison: State Historical Society of Wisconsin, 1958.

Hickerson, H. Thomas, Joan Winters, and Venetia Beale. *SPINDEX II at Cornell and a Review of Archival Automation in the United States*. Ithaca: Cornell University Libraries, 1976.

Illinois State Library. *Catalog Rules: Series for Archival Material*. Springfield: Illinois State Library, 1938.

Jenkinson, Hilary. *A Manual of Archive Administration*. London: P. Land, Humphries, 1937.

Jones, Houston G. *The Records of a Nation: Their Management, Preservation, and Use*. New York: Atheneum, 1969.

Kane, Lucile M. "A Guide to the Care and Administration of Manuscripts." *Bulletin of the American Association for State and Local History* 2 (1960): 333–88.

———. *A Guide to the Care and Administration of Manuscripts*. 2d ed. Nashville: American Association for State and Local History, 1966.

Kuhlman, Augustus F., ed. *Archives and Libraries: Papers Presented at the 1937 Conference of the American Library Association*. Chicago: American Library Association, 1937.

———. *Archives and Libraries: Papers Presented at the 1938 Conference of the American Library Association*. Chicago: American Library Association, 1938.

———. *Archives and Libraries: Papers Presented at the 1939 Conference of the American Library Association*. Chicago: American Library Association, 1939.

———. *Archives and Libraries: Papers Presented at the 1940 Conference of the American Library Association*. Chicago: American Library Association, 1940.

Lord, Clifford L., ed. *Keepers of the Past*. Chapel Hill: University of North Carolina Press, 1965.

Lusignan, Serge, and J. S. North, eds., *Computing in the Humanities*. Waterloo, Ontario: University of Waterloo Press, 1977.

McCoy, Donald R. *The National Archives: America's Ministry of Documents, 1934–1968*. Chapel Hill: University of North Carolina Press, 1978.

Maryland Archives Division. *An Inventory of Maryland State Papers*, vol. 1. Annapolis: Archives Division, Hall of Records Commission, 1977.

Massachusettes Record Commission. *Report to the Legislature of Massachusetts Made by the Commissioners Appointed under Resolve Chap. 60, 1884, upon the Condition of the Records, Files, and Papers and Documents in the Secretary's Department*. January, 1885. Boston: Wright and Potter.

Mitchell, Thornton W. *Norton on Archives: The Writings of Margaret Cross Norton on Archival and Records Management*. Carbondale: Southern Illinois University Press, 1975.

Muller, Samuel, J. A. Feith, and R. Fruin. *Manual for the Arrangement and Description of Archives*. Translation of 2d ed. by Arthur H. Leavitt. New York: H. W. Wilson Company, 1968.

National Association of State Archives and Records Administrators. *Report on the Conference on Automated Guide Projects*. St. Louis, 1977.

Nute, Grace Lee. *The Care and Cataloguing of Manuscripts as Practiced by the Minnesota Historical Society*. Saint Paul: Minnesota Historical Society, 1936.

Perman, Dagmar H., ed. *Bibliography and the Historian: The Conference at Belmont*. Santa Barbara: Clio Press, 1968.

Posner, Ernst. *American State Archives*. Chicago: University of Chicago Press, 1964.

———. *Archives and the Public Interest: Selected Essays by Ernst Posner*. Edited by Ken Munden. Washington, D.C.: Public Affairs Press, 1967.

Rundell, Walter, Jr. *In Pursuit of American History: Research and Training in the United States*. Norman: University of Oklahoma Press, 1970.

Sahli, Nancy. *SPINDEX: An Introduction for New and Prospective Users*. Prepared for SPINDEX Users Network, 1980.

Schellenberg, Theodore R. "Arrangement of Private Papers" (GSA–Wash DC 59–9820).

———. "Description of Private Papers" (GSA–Wash DC 59–9818).

———. *Draft of a Manual on Archival Descriptive Techniques*. Austin: University of Texas Graduate School of Library Science, 1961.

———. "European Archival Practices in Arranging Records." U.S. National Archives, *Staff Information Circular*, no. 5, July 1939. Washington, D.C.: General Services Administration 51–4500.

———. *The Management of Archives*. New York and London: Columbia University Press, 1965.

———. *Modern Archives: Principles and Techniques*. Chicago: University of Chicago Press, 1956.

Shambaugh, Benjamin F. *A Report on Public Archives*. Des Moines: Historical Department of Iowa, 1907.

Society of American Archivists. *Inventories and Registers: A Handbook of Techniques and Examples*. Chicago: Society of American Archivists, 1976.

Sparks, Jared. *The Diplomatic Correspondence of the American Revolution*. 12 vols. Boston: N. Hale and Gray and Bowen, 1829.

SPINDEX: An Introduction for New and Prospective Users, prepared by Nancy Sahli for SPINDEX Users Network, 1980.

Stevens, Rolland E., ed. *University Archives*. Champaign: Distributed by Illini Union Bookstore, 1964.

Stiles, Cassius C. *Public Archives: A Manual for Their Administration in Iowa*. Des Moines: 1928.

Thwaites, Reuben G., ed. *Descriptive List of Manuscript Collections of the State Historical Society of Wisconsin*. Madison State Historical Society of Wisconsin, 1906.

Thomison, Dennis. *A History of the American Library Association, 1876–1972*. Chicago: American Library Association, 1978.

U.S. Library of Congress. *Manual No. 17: Manuscripts Division*. Washington, D.C.: Government Printing Office, 1950.

U.S. National Archives. *The Control of Records at the Record Group Level*. Washington, D.C.: Government Printing Office, 1950.

———. *Guide to the National Archives of the United States*. Washington, D.C.: National Archives and Records Service, 1974.

———. *Guide to the Records in the National Archives*. Washington, D.C.: Government Printing Office, 1948.

———. *The Preparation of Lists of Record Items*. Rev. ed. Washington, D.C.: Government Printing Office, 1960.

———. *The Preparation of Preliminary Inventories*. Washington, D.C.: Government Printing Office, 1950.

———. *Principles of Arrangement*. Washington, D.C.: Government Printing Office, 1951.

U.S. National Archives and Records Service. *SPINDEX II: Report and Systems Documentation*. Washington, D.C.: National Archives and Records Service, 1975.

Van Tyne, Claude H., and Waldo G. Leland. *Guide to the Archives of the Government of the United States in Washington*. Washington, D.C.: Carnegie Institution, 1904, 1907.

Wisconsin State Historical Society. *Guide to Manuscripts*. Madison: State Historical Society of Wisconsin, 1944.

Works, George Alan. *College and University Library Problems*. Chicago: American Library Association, 1927.

DISSERTATION

Birdsall, William F. "The American Archivists' Search for Professional Identity, 1909–1936." Ph.D. dissertation, University of Wisconsin, Madison, 1973.

PERIODICAL ARTICLES, ANNUAL AND OTHER REPORTS

Abraham, Terry. "NUCMC and the Local Repository." *AA* 40 (January 1977): 31–42.

American Historical Association, Historical Manuscripts Committee. "Report of the Committee on Methods of Organization and Work on the Part of State and Local Historical Societies." In American Historical Association, *Annual Report, 1905*, pp. 251–325.

American Historical Association. "Report of Ad Hoc Committee on Manuscripts, December 1948." Reprint ed. in *AA* 14 (July 1951): 229–40.

———. *Annual Report*, 1900–1936.

American Library Association. "Report of Committee on Archives and Libraries." In *Bulletin* 40 (October 15, 1946).

Ames, Herman V. "Resume of the Archives Situations in the Several States in 1907." In American Historical Association, *Annual Report, 1907* pp. 163–87.

Andreassen, John C. L. "Archives in the Library of Congress." *AA* 12 (January 1949): 20–26.

Bahmer, Robert H. "The National Archives After 20 Years." *AA* 18 (July 1955): 195–205.

Bauer, G. Philip. "Public Archives in the United States." In Hesseltine and McNeil, eds., *In Support of Clio*, pp. 49–76.

———. "Recruitment, Training, and Promotion in the National Archives." *AA* 18 (October 1955): 291–305.

Berkeley, Francis L., Jr. "History and Problems of the Control of Manuscripts in the U.S." In American Philosophical Society, *Proceedings* 98 (June 1954): 171–78.

Berner, Richard C. "Archivists, Librarians, and the National Union Catalog of Manuscript Collections." *AA* 27 (July 1964): 401–9.

———. "Arrangement and Description of Manuscripts." *Drexel Library Quarterly* 11 (January 1975): 34–54.

———. "Arrangement and Description: Some Historical Observations." *AA* 41 (April 1978): 169–81.

———. "Description of Private Papers and Archival Principles of Arrangement." In Symposium on Archival Administration, Seattle, May 23, 1964 (transcript, pp. 17–23).

———. "The Management of Manuscript Collections." *Library Journal* 88 (April 1963): 1615–16.

———. "Manuscript Catalogs and Other Finding Aids: What Are Their Relationships?" *AA* 34 (October 1971): 367–72.

———. "Manuscript Collections and Archives—A Unitary Approach." *LRTS* 9 (September 1965): 213–20.

————. "Manuscript Collections: Their Place in the Library." Washington State Library, *Library News Bulletin* 33: 161–72.

————. "Observations on Archivists, Librarians, and the National Union Catalog of Manuscript Collections." *CRL* 29 (1968): 276–80.

————. "Perspectives on the Record Group Concept." *Georgia Archive* 4 (Winter 1976): 48–55.

Billington, Ray A. "Guides to Depositories of Manuscript Collections in Libraries in the United States." *Mississippi Valley Historical Review* 38 (December 1951): 467–96.

Binkley, William C. "A Historian Looks at the National Union Catalog of Manuscript Collections." *AA* 28 (July 1965): 399–407.

Birdsall, William F. "Two Sides of the Desk: The Archivist and the Historian, 1909–1935." *AA* 38 (April 1975): 159–73.

Bishop, William W. "The Librarians of Congress, 1907–15: Fragments of Autobiography." *LQ* 18 (January 1948): 1–23.

Blouin, Francis X., Jr. "The Relevance of the Case Method to Archival Education and Training." *AA* 41 (January 1978): 37–44.

Boll, John J. "A Basis for Library Education." *LQ* 42 (April 1972): 195–211.

Bond, William H. "The Cataloging of Manuscripts in the Houghton Library." *Harvard Library Bulletin* 4 (1950): 392–96.

Boyd, Julian P. "Recent Activities in Relation to Archives and Historical Manuscripts in the United States." In *Proceedings of the Society of American Archivists*, December 1936, June 1937, pp. 13–20.

Brand, Katharine E. "Developments in the Handling of Recent Manuscripts in the Library of Congress." *AA* 16 (April 1953): 99–104.

————. "The Place of the Register in the Manuscripts Division of the Library of Congress." *AA* 18 (January 1955): 59–67.

Breck, Allen de Pont. "New Dimensions in the Education of American Archivists." *AA* 29 (April 1966): 173–86.

Brichford, Maynard. "Appraisal and Processing." In Stevens, ed., *University Archives*, pp. 46–61.

Brooks, Philip C. "Archivists and Their Colleagues: Common Denominators." *AA* 14 (January 1951): 33–45.

————. "Archives in the United States During World War II, 1939–45." *LQ* 17 (October 1947): 263–80.

————. "The First Decade of the Society of American Archivists." *AA* 10: 115–28.

Browne, Henry J. "An Appeal for Archives in Institutions of Higher Learning." *AA* 16 (July 1953): 213–26.

Brubaker, Robert L. "Archival Principles and the Curator of Manuscripts." *AA* 29 (October 1966): 505–14.

————. "Manuscript Collections." *LT* 13 (October 1964): 226–53.

————. "Professional Communication." Chapter 5 in Clark, ed., *Archive-Library Relations*.

Buck, Solon J. "Let's Look at the Record." *AA* 8 (April 1945): 109–14.

————. "The Training of American Archivists." *AA* 4 (April 1941): 84–90.

Burke, Frank G. "The Application of Automated Techniques in the Management and Control of Source Materials." *AA* 30 (April 1967): 255–78.

————. "Automation in Bibliographical Control of Archives and Manuscript Collections." In Perman, ed., *Bibliography and the Historian*, pp. 96–102.

————. "Computer Techniques for the National Archives." *Computers and the Humanities* 4 (September 1969): 11–18.

————. "The Impact of the Specialist on Archives." *CRL* 33 (July 1972): 312–17.

————. "Manuscripts and Archives." *LT* 15 (January 1967): 430–43.

————. "Similarities and Differences." Chapter 2 in Clark, ed., *Archive-Library Relations*.

————. "SPINDEX II: An Aspect of Archival Information Retrieval." *Records Management Journal* 8 (April 1966): 298–302.

Burke, Robert E. "Modern Manuscript Collections and What To Do with Them." *Manuscripts* 7 (Summer 1955): 232–36.

[Burnett, Edward C.] "A List of Printed Guides to and Descriptions of Archives and Other Repositories of Historical Manuscripts." American Historical Association, Historical Manuscripts Commission, *Annual Report, 1896*, 1:481–512.

Campbell, E. G. "Functional Classification of Archival Material." *LQ* 11 (October 1941): 431–441.

Cappon, Lester J. "The Archival Profession and the Society of American Archivists." *AA* 15 (July 1952): 195–204.

————. "Historical Manuscripts as Archives: Some Definitions and Their Application." *AA* 19 (April 1956): 101–10.

————. "Reference Works and Historical Texts." *LT* 5 (January 1957): 369–79.

————. "Report of the Joint Committee on Historical Manuscripts." *AA* 15:2 (April 1952): 176–80.

————. "Report of the Secretary, Society of American Archivists, Nov. 15, 1943." *AA* 7:1 (1944): 52–61.

————. See also University of Virginia, *Annual.Report on Historical Collections*, for Cappon's introductions.

————. et al. "Report of the Joint Committee on Historical Manuscripts." *AA* 16: 94–95.

Child, Sargent B. "Status and Plans for Completion of the Inventories of the Historical Records Survey." In Kuhlman, ed., *Archives and Libraries* (1940), pp. 12–25.

Church, Randolph W. "The Relationship Between Archival Agencies and Libraries." *AA* 6 (July 1943): 145–50.

Clapp, Verner W. "Archivists and Bibliographic Control: A Librarian's Viewpoint." *AA* 14 (October 1951): 305–11.

————. "Subject Controls—Nature and Level of Controls." *American Documentation* 3 (January 1952): 11–15.

Cole, Arthur H. "Business Manuscripts: Collection, Handling, and Cataloging." *LQ* 8:1 (January 1938): 93–114.

Colson, John C. "On the Education of Archivists and Librarians." *AA* 31 (April 1968): 167–74.

Custer, Arline. "The National Union Catalog of Manuscript Collections," *LRTS* 8 (Spring 1964): 188–90.

Dunkin, Paul S. "Arrangement and Cataloging of Manuscripts." *LT* 5:3 (January 1957): 352–60.

East, Sherrod. "Describable Item Cataloging." *AA* 16:4 (October 1953): 291–304.

Evans, Frank B. "Modern Methods of Arrangement of Archives in the United States." *AA* 29:2 (April 1966): 251–63.

————. "Postappointment Archival Training: A Proposed Solution for a Basic Problem." *AA* 40 (January 1977): 57–74.

Farley, A. E. "Cataloging of Special Collection Material." *Journal of Cataloging and Classification* 12 (January 1956): 11–14.

Fenyo, Mario D. "The Record Group Concept: A Critique." *AA* 29 (April 1966): 229–39.

Field, F. Bernice. "The New Catalog Code: The General Principles and the Major Changes." *LRTS* 10 (Fall 1966): 421–35.

Finch, Jean L. "Some Fundamentals in Arranging Archives and Manuscript Collections." *LRTS* 8 (Winter 1964): 28–34.

Fish, Carl Russell. "Report on the Public Archives of Wisconsin." In AHA, *Annual Report, 1905*, pp. 377–429.

Fisher, Barbara, and Frank G. Burke. "Automation, Information, and the Administration of Archives and Manuscript Collections: Bibliographic Review." *AA* 30 (April 1967): 333–48.

Ford, Worthington C. "Manuscripts." In Charles Cutter *Rules for a Dictionary Catalog* (Washington, D.C.: Government Printing Office, 1904), pp. 135–38.

———. "Manuscripts and Historical Archives." In AHA, *Annual Report, 1913*, 1:75–84.

———. "The Massachusetts Historical Society." In AHA, *Annual Report, 1912*, 1:217–23.

Fox, Edith M. "The Collection of Archival Materials at Cornell University." In Stevens, ed., *University Archives*, pp. 36–45.

———. "The Genesis of Cornell University's Collection of Regional History." *AA* 14:2 (April 1951): 105–16.

Friedenwald, Herbert. "Historical Manuscripts in the Library of Congress." In AHA, *Annual Report, 1898*, pp. 37–45.

Garrison, Curtis W. "The Relation of Historical Manuscripts to Archival Materials." *AA* 2:2 (April 1939): 97–105.

Gordon, Robert S. "Suggestions for Organization and Description of Archival Holdings of Local Historical Societies." *AA* 26:1 (January 1963): 19–36.

Gracy, David B., II. "Finding Aids Are Like Streakers." *Georgia Archive* 4 (Winter 1976): 39–47.

Grover, Wayne C. "Federal Government Archives." *LT* 5:3 (January 1957): 390–96.

Hamer, Philip M. "Finding Mediums in the National Archives: An Appraisal of Six Years' Experience." *AA* 5:2 (April 1942): 82–92.

Hannestad, S. E. "SPINDEX II: A Computerized Approach to Preparing Guides to Archives and Manuscripts." In *Computing in the Humanities*, edited by Serge Lusignan and John S. North, Waterloo, Ontario: University of Waterloo Press, 1977, pp. 273–82.

Harlow, Neal. "Managing Manuscript Collections." *LT* 4:2 (October 1955): 203–12.

Harper, Josephine L. "Lyman C. Draper and Early American Archives." *AA* 25 (July 1952): 205–12.

Hasse, Adelaide R. "Materials for a Bibliography of the Public Archives of the Thirteen Original States . . . to 1789." In AHA Public Archives Commission, *Annual Report, 1906*, pp. 239–572.

Hensel, Evelyn. "Treatment of Nonbook Materials." *LT* 2:2 (October 1953): 187–98.

Hill, Roscoe R. "Archival Terminology." *AA* 6 (October 1943): 206–11.

———. "Classification in the National Archives." In Kuhlman, ed., *Archives and Libraries* (1940), pp. 60–77.

———. [Round table discussion of Hill's paper on his work as chief of N. Archives Classification Div.] In SAA, *Proceedings*, December 1936, June 1937, pp. 52–60.

Holmes, Oliver W. "Archival Arrangement—Five Different Operations at Five Different Levels." *AA* 27 (January 1964): 21–41.

———. "History and Theory of Archival Practice." In Stevens, ed., *University Archives*, pp. 1–21.

Hoover Institution on War, Revolution and Peace. "Computer Applications for Archives at the Hoover Institution, 1965–1976" (n.d.).

Hyde, Dorsey W., Jr. "The Integration of Work with Archives and Historical Manuscripts." In Kuhlman, ed., *Archives and Libraries* (1939), pp. 28–33.

Jackson, Ellen. "Manuscript Collections in the General Library." *LQ* 12 (April 1942): 275–83.

Jacobsen, Edna L. "State and Local Government Archives." *LT* 5:3 (January 1957): 397–405.

Jennings, John Melville. "Archival Activity in American Universities and Colleges." *AA* 12 (April 1949): 155–63.

Jillson, Willard Rouse. "The Indexing of Historical Materials." *AA* 16:3 (July 1953): 251–57.

Jones, Houston G. "Archival Training in American Universities, 1938–68." *AA* 31 (April 1968): 135–54.

Josephson, Bertha E. "Indexing." *AA* 10 (April 1947): 133–50.

Kahn, Herman. "Librarians and Archivists—Some Aspects of Their Partnership." *AA* 7 (October 1944): 243–51.

———. "Some Comments on the Archival Vocation." *AA* 34 (January 1971): 3–12.

Kane, Lucile M. "Collecting Policies at the Minnesota Historical Society, 1849–1952." *AA* 16 (April 1953): 127–36.

———. "Manuscript Collecting." In Hesseltine and McNeil, eds., *In Support of Clio*, pp. 29–48.

Kellar, Herbert A. "A Preliminary Survey of the More Important Archives of the Territory and State of Minnesota." In AHA, *Annual Report, 1914*, pp. 385–504.

———. "Organization and Preservation of Manuscript Collections in the McCormick Historical Association Library." In Kuhlman, ed., *Archives and Libraries* (1938), pp. 357–64.

———. "Where Are the Historical Manuscripts? A Symposium." *American Association for State and Local History Bulletin* 2:4 (1950): 103–27.

Lacy, Dan. "The Library of Congress: A Sesquicentenary Review." *LQ* 20:3 (July 1950): 157–79; 20:4 (October 1950): 235–58.

Lamb, W. Kaye. "The Modern Archivist: Formally Trained or Self-Educated?" *AA* 31 (April 1968): 175–177.

Land, Robert H. "The National Union Catalog of Manuscript Collections." *AA* 17:3 (July 1954): 195–207.

Leland, Waldo G. "American Archival Problems." In AHA, *Annual Report, 1909*, 1:302–48.

———. "Cataloguing of Archives." In AHA, *Annual Report, 1914*, 1:41.

———. "The First Conference of Archivists, December 1909: The Beginnings of a Profession." *AA* 13 (April 1950): 109–20.

———. "The National Archives: A Programme." *American Historical Review* 18 (1912): 1–28.

————. [Review of Schellenberg's *Modern Archives*.] *AA* 19 (October 1956): 325.

Lewinson, Paul. "Problems of Archives Classification." [Classification in National Archives 1939.] *AA* 2 (July 1939): 179–90.

Lord, Clifford L. "The Archival Program of Wisconsin." *AA* 12 (July 1949): 243–52.

Lovett, Robert W. "Care and Handling of Non-Governmental Archives." *LT* 5:3 (January 1957): 380–89.

————. "Some Changes in the Handling of Business Records at Baker Library." *AA* 19:1 (January 1956): 39–44.

Lucas, Lydia. "Efficient Finding Aids: Developing a System for Controlling of Archives and Manuscripts." *AA* 44 (Winter 1981): 21–26.

————. "Massive Collections from Warehouse to Reading Room." *Georgia Archive* 4 (Winter 1976): 56–63.

Lytle, Richard H. "Intellectual Access to Archives: I. Provenance and Content Indexing Methods of Subject Retrieval." *AA* 43 (Winter 1980): 64–75.

————. "Intellectual Access to Archives: II. Report of an Experiment Comparing Provenance and Content Indexing Methods of Subject Retrieval." *AA* 43 (Spring 1980): 191–207.

Lytle, Richard H., issue ed. "Management of Archives and Manuscript Collections for Librarians." *Drexel Library Quarterly* 11 (January 1975).

McCarthy, Paul H., Jr. "Overview: Essentials of an Archives or Manuscript Program." *Drexel Library Quarterly* 11 (January 1975): 5–20.

McCree, Mary Lynn. "Good Sense and Good Judgment: Defining Collections and Collecting." *Drexel Library Quarterly* 11 (January 1975): 21–33.

Martin, Dorothy V. "Books on Cataloging of Manuscript Material." *AA* 11 (January 1948): 42–44.

————. "Use of Cataloging Techniques in Work with Records and Manuscripts." *AA* 18:4 (October 1955): 317–36.

Martin, Thomas P. "Organization and Preservation of Manuscript Collections in the Library of Congress." In Kuhlman, ed., *Archives and Libraries* (1938), pp. 387–89.

Maryland, Hall of Records. *First to Fourth Annual Reports of the Archivist* [for 1935–39].

Mason, Phillip P. "Report of the Committee for the 1970s." *AA* 35 (April 1972): 193–217.

————. "The Society of American Archivists at the Crossroads." *AA* 35 (January 1972): 5–11.

Massachusetts Historical Society. *Collections.* 1:2–4, 1792.

Mississippi, Department of Archives and History. *Annual Report*, 1902–7.

Morris, Richard B. "The Challenge of Historical Materials." *AA* 4:2 (April 1942): 91–116.

Mumford, L. Quincy. "Archivists and Librarians: Time for a New Look." *AA* 33 (July 1970): 269–74.

Munden, Ken[neth]. "Cataloging Rules in the Departmental Records Branch." *AA* 19 (October 1956): 291–302.

————. "The Identification and Description of the Record Series." *AA* (July 1950): 213–27.

National Association of State Libraries. "Report on Public Archives Committee." In *Proceedings and Addresses* (18th Conv., 1915), pp. 23–37; (1928), pp. 6–7.

Newsome, Albert R. "Uniform State Archival Legislation." *AA* 2:1 (January 1939): 1–16.

New York State Library. *Annual Report*, 1899–1910.

Norton, Margaret C. "The Archives as an Administrative Unit in Government." In National Association of State Libraries, *Proceedings, June 23–27, 1930*, pp. 44–48.

———. Article in *Illinois Libraries*, March 1939, May 1939, December 1943, December 1946, April 1952.

———. "Classification in the Archives of Illinois." In Kuhlman, ed., *Archives and Libraries* (1940), pp. 78–92.

———. "Scope and Function of a State Archives Department." In Kuhlman, ed., *Archives and Libraries* (1937), pp. 262–75.

———. "Victor Hugo Paltsits, 1867–1952." *AA* 16:2 (April 1953): 137–40.

Nuermberger, Ruth K. "A Ten Year Experiment in Archival Practices." *AA* IV:4 (October 1940): 250–61.

———. "Suggestions for a Code for Cataloging Historical Manuscript Collections." In Kuhlman, ed., *Archives and Libraries* (1939), pp. 54–63.

Nyholm, Amy Wood. "Modern Manuscripts: A Functional Approach." *Library Resources and Technical Services* 14 (1970): 325–40.

Owsley, Harriet C. "The SAA Workshop on the National Union Catalog of Manuscript Collections." *AA* 28 (July 1965): 389–97.

Paltsits, Victor H. "An Historical Resumé of the Public Archives Commission from 1899 to 1921." In AHA, *Annual Report, 1922*, 1:152–60.

———. "Pioneering for a Science of Archives in the United States." In Kuhlman, ed., *Archives and Libraries* (1937), pp. 233–39.

———. "Plan and Scope of a Manual of Archival Economy for the Use of American Archivists." In AHA, *Annual Report, 1912*, pp. 253–63.

Papenfuse, Edward C. "The Retreat from Standardization: A Comment on the Recent History of Finding Aids." *AA* 36 (October 1973): 537–42.

Parish, John C. *A Guide to the Administrative Departments, Offices, Boards, Commissions, and Public Institutions of Iowa.* Appendix to *Second Annual Report on the Public Archives*, pp. 13–358. Historical Department of Iowa, 1907.

Parker, Wyman W. "How Can the Archivist Aid the Researcher?" *AA* 16:3 (July 1953): 233–40.

Peace, Nancy E., and Nancy F. Chudacoff, "Archivists and Librarians: A Common Mission, a Common Education." *AA* 42 (October 1979): 456–62.

Pease, Theodore C. "Historical Materials in the Depositories of the Middle West." In AHA, *Annual Report, 1921*, pp. 114–16.

Peckham, Howard W. "Manuscript Repositories and the National Register." *AA* 17:4 (October 1954): 319–24.

———. "Arranging and Cataloguing Manuscripts in the William L. Clements Library." *AA* I:4 (October 1938): 215–29.

Platnick, Phyllis. "Proposal for Automating a Manuscript Repository." In American Documentation Institute, *Progress in Information Science and Technology, Proceedings, 1966*, pp. 437–54.

Posner, Ernst. "Archival Training in the U.S." In Munden, ed., pp. 58–77.

———. "The National Archives and the Archival Theorist." *AA* 18:3 (July 1955): 207–16.

Radoff, Morris L. "A Guide to Practical Calendaring." *AA* 11 (April 1948): 123–40, (July 1948): 203–22.

Reingold, Nathan. "Subject Analysis and Description of Manuscript Collections." *Isis* 53 (March 1962): 106–12.

Rowland, Dunbar. "The Concentration of State and National Archives." In AHA, *Annual Report, 1910*, 1:293–314.

Russell, John R. "Cataloging at the National Archives." *A* 2 (July 1939): 169–78.

———. "Some Problems in Cataloging Archives." In Kuhlman, ed., *Archives and Libraries* (1937), pp. 286–97.

Russell, Mattie, and Edward G. Roberts. "The Processing Procedures of the Manuscripts Department of Duke University Library." *AA* 12 (October 1949): 369–80.

Sahli, Nancy. "Finding Aids: A Multi-Media, Systems Perspective." *AA* 44 (Winter 1981): 15–20.

———. See *SPINDEX: An Introduction for New and Prospective Users.*

Scammell, Joseph M. "Librarians and Archives." *LQ* 9 (October 1939): 432–44.

Schellenberg, Theodore R. "Archival Principles of Arrangement." *AA* 24 (January 1961): 11–24.

———. "Archival Training in Library Schools." *AA* 31 (April 1968): 155–65.

———. "The Future of the Archival Profession." *AA* 22 (January 1959): 49–58.

———. "A Nationwide System of Controlling Historical Manuscripts in the United States." *AA* 28 (July 1965): 409–12.

———. "The Principle of Provenance and Modern Records in the United States." *AA* 28 (January 1965): 39–41.

Schiller, Irving P. "The Archival Profession in Eclipse." *AA* 11 (July 1948): 227–33.

Schulz, H. C. "The Care and Storage of Manuscripts in the Huntington Library." *LQ* 5:1 (January 1935): 78–86.

Scott, Peter J. "The Record Group Concept: A Case for Abandonment." *AA* 29 (October 1966): 493–504.

Shelley, Fred. "Manuscripts in the Library of Congress: 1800–1900." *AA* 11 (January 1948): 3–19.

Shipton, Clifford K. "The Harvard University Archives: Goal and Function." *Harvard Library Bulletin* 1:1 (Winter 1947): 101–8.

Slover, Robert. [Comment on difficulty of establishing series and classification problems generally.] *AA* 2 (January 1939): 27.

Smiley, David L. "The W.P.A. Historical Records Survey." In Hesseltine and McNeil, eds., *In Support of Clio*, pp. 3–28.

Smith, Russell M. "Item Indexing by Automated Processes." *AA* 30 (April 1967): 195–302.

[Society of American Archivists.] "The Proposed Uniform State Public Records Act." *AA* 3:2 (April 1940): 107–15.

Stiles, Cassius C. "Lessons from Iowa." In AHA, *Annual Report, 1922*, 1:127–33.

Swan, Robert T. "Summary of the Present State of Legislation of the States and Territories Relative to the Custody and Supervision of Public Records." AHA Public Archives Commission, *Annual Report, 1906*, pp. 13–21.

Taylor, Hugh A. "The Discipline of History and the Education of the Archivist." *AA* 40 (October 1977): 395–402.

Thurber, Evangeline. "Suggestions for a Code for Cataloging Archival Material." In Kuhlman, ed., *Archives and Libraries* (1939), pp. 42–53.

Turner, Justin G. "Archives, Manuscripts and Collectors: Some Reflections." *Manuscripts* 19 (Fall 1967): 12–20.

U.S. Library of Congress. *Annual Report*, 1939–55.

U.S. National Archives. *Annual Report*, 1935–49.

Vail, R. W. G., issue ed., "Manuscripts and Archives." *Library Trends* 5 : 3 (January 1957).

Van Laer, Arnold J. F. "The Work of the International Congress of Archivists and Librarians at Brussells, Aug. 28–31, 1910." In AHA, *Annual Report, 1910*, pp. 282–92.

Virginia, University of. *Annual Report on Historical Collections*, 1940-41–1944-45 [Reports 11-15].

Virtue, Ethel B. "Principles of Classification for Archives." In AHA, *Annual Report, 1914*, pp. 373–84.

Wallace, Carolyn A. "The Southern Historical Collection." *AA* 28 (July 1965): 427–36.

————. "The University of North Carolina's Southern Historical Collection." *Manuscripts* 9 (Summer 1957): 140–42.

Walton, Clyde C., issue ed. "State and Local History in Libraries." *LT* 13 : 2 (October 1964).

Warner, Robert M. "Archival Training in the United States and Canada." *AA* 35 (July/October 1972): 347–58.

Wisconsin State Historical Society. *Proceedings*, 1906, 1916.

Winsor, Justin. "Manuscript Sources of American History: The Conspicuous Collections Extant." In American Historical Association, *Papers* 3 (1889): 9–27.

Index of Proper Names

Topical Index

Accreditation: by Society of American Archivists, 109

Added entries dealt with, 26, 34, 37, 38, 41, 56–57, 59, 66–67, 71, 74, 76–77, 80–83, 88–89

Alphabetical arrangements: as option, 34

Amalgamation of public archives tradition and historical manuscripts tradition, 55–59

Appraisal theory: its importance stressed, 6–7, 117–19, Appendix 23

Archival automation. *See* Automation in archives

Archival manual. *See* Manuals, archival

Archival mode: ascendancy of, 59–72

Archival networks, 94, 97–98, 112–14. *See also* Automation in archives. *See also* SPINDEX *in Index of Proper Names*

Archival theory: European origins, 2–3

Arrangement: general principles, 13–15, 19, 29–36, 55–56, 60–65; by subject opposed, 20, 55; in relation to workflow sequence, 20, 22, 55–56, 66, 76

Arrangement and description, 5–9; their separation in practice, 6

Automation in archives, 85–99, 112–14. *See also in Index of Proper Names*: Hoover Institution; Library of Congress: MR II program; National Archives: A-1 program; PARADIGM; SPINDEX

Bifurcated system, 9, 41, 55–56, 78, 81, 88

Calendaring, 6, 72, 74, 122

Card catalog, 5, 8, 22, 26, 30, 34–35, 38, 40–41, 45, 52, 55–58, 68, 77, 79, 88–98, 112

Catalogable unit, 6, 19, 22, 26, 31–32, 37, 45, 47, 48, 54, 56, 74

Cataloging: traditional, 6, 20, 41, 43–44, 57, 76, 78–83, 88–90, 110, 112, 117, 121; of series, 6, 26, 31–32, 35, 46, 48, 52, 54, 91; integrative role of, 9, 26, 30, 34–35, 38, 51, 57, 59, 64, 78, 84; in workflow sequence, 20, 22, 35, 54–55, 57, 75–77;

"describable item," 37–38; as one step in establishing controls, 45–46, 55; directly from manuscripts recommended, 74–78, 82–83

Cataloging code: for historical manuscripts, 2, 25, 39, 42–43, 78–80, 101–3; for public archives, 25, 31–32, 39. *See also in Index of Proper Names*: National Union Catalog of Manuscript Collections: origins

Cataloging policies and procedures. *See names of specific institutions in Index of Proper Names*

Cataloging rules. *See* Cataloging code

Chronological arrangement, 11–13, 19–20, 29, 34, 36, 41, 56, 74, 76

"Chronologic-geographic" arrangement, 18–19

Classification: modification of, 2, 4, 13–15, 25–28, 36, 41, 48–49, 54, 60–64, 68; practice of, 11–15, 18–19, 22, 25–26, 33–36, 50, 55, 60–64, 74

Collecting and collection development: effect on theory and practices, 1–2, 7, 11, 15, 18, 41, 48–51, 54, 59, 73, 77, 100, 111–12, 117–18, 123

Collecting of contemporary papers and records, 111–12, 117–18, 123

Collective description, 26–28, 31–32, 45, 50, 54–56, 58–59, 69, 74, 78–83

Container lists. *See* Inventories

Content analysis/indexing/notes, 34, 37, 70–72, 74, 76–77, 98, 113–17, 122

Corporate entry: importance of proper form, 66–67

Description: its separation from arrangement, 6, 8n, 43–44, 63, 65, 78–83; its translation into levels of control, 65–67, 69, 83–84, 90–95. *See also* Arrangement and description; Bifurcated system

Education and training, 100–10, 119–21

Employment in archives, 24, 100–2, 104, 109–10

This book presents an account of the evolution of archival practice in the United States. Two traditions have dominated in the collecting and intellectual control of manuscripts—the public archives tradition and the historical manuscripts tradition. The latter, rooted in librarianship, was dominant until about 1960. By then the nature of collecting was changing from a concentration on papers of remote vintage to an emphasis on those of recent origin. As a result, many major manuscript repositories borrowed practices and concepts from the public archives tradition. The amalgamated systems that developed pose problems that remain unsolved.

Unless effective techniques are developed to deal fully with contemporary papers and records, archives and modern manuscript collections will lack authority as documentation because the papers and records that are preserved will represent merely accidental documentary remains. Comprehensive coverage itself requires interinstitutional cooperation involving public and private libraries, historical societies, public archives, college and university archives, and other institutional archives and private manuscript collections.

In a chapter entitled "Schellenberg and the Merging of the Public Archives and Historical Manuscripts Traditions, 1956–79," Berner offers an analysis of how leading archivists have evolved practices that have been adopted widely although they have generally failed to develop a coherent body of theory derived from those practices, and which could serve as guidelines for their future refinement. Automated archival systems are described and assesssed in a separate chapter, along with the related issue of archival–records management relations. Berner devotes another chapter to the important subject of archival education. The book also includes extensive appendixes giving examples and the author's evaluation of data sheets, register pages, inventories, and related materials used by the National Archives, the Library of Congress, and other collections, illustrating the various archival methods currently in use and their shortcomings and advantages.

Richard C. Berner is head of the University Archives and Manuscript Division of the University of Washington Libraries.